ROCKIN' IN THE NEW WORLD

ROCKIN'
IN THE
NEW WORLD

TAKING YOUR BAND FROM THE
BASEMENT TO THE BIG TIME

BY
BOB TULIPAN

STERLING
New York

STERLING
New York

An Imprint of Sterling Publishing
387 Park Avenue South
New York, NY 10016

ISBN 978-1-4027-7058-6 (paperback)
ISBN 978-1-4027-8910-6 (ebook)

Distributed in Canada by Sterling Publishing
ᶜ/o Canadian Manda Group, 165 Dufferin Street
Toronto, Ontario, Canada M6K 3H6
Distributed in the United Kingdom by GMC Distribution Services
Castle Place, 166 High Street, Lewes, East Sussex, England BN7 1XU
Distributed in Australia by Capricorn Link (Australia) Pty. Ltd.
P.O. Box 704, Windsor, NSW 2756, Australia

For information about custom editions, special sales, and premium and
corporate purchases, please contact Sterling Special Sales at 800-805-5489
or specialsales@sterlingpublishing.com.

Manufactured in the United States of America

2 4 6 8 10 9 7 5 3 1

www.sterlingpublishing.com

I'd like to dedicate this book to Maureen Baker for being the best partner a creative person could ever imagine having, and for all of her dedication, support, encouragement, research, and hard work in helping me make this book comprehensive and timely.

I'd also like to dedicate this book to the memory of Richard, Rick, Fred, and Freddie, who each taught me so much about what it is to be an artist.

CONTENTS

ACKNOWLEDGMENTS

I'd like to thank Vladimir Litvinov, Sergei Yastrzhembski, Glorianna Bartolo, Matt Kent, Steve Riggio, and the Kremlin for creating the momentum that brought me to Sterling. Michael Fragnito for championing the project and for his vision and love of music, Laura Swerdloff for making the process painless, and all those at PMA for representing my interests so expertly.

I'd also like to thank the following people for their support and contributions to the book: Dave Lory, Lee Heiman, Gerry Gerrard, Rob Berends, Martin Atkins, Emma Quigley, Maria Egan, Roslynn Cobarrubias, Lisette Rioux Paulson, Lou Plaia, Bob Miller, Isaac Moredock, Bob Berman, Terry McBride, C. T. Tamura, Joshua Simons, Henley Halem, Mark Kates, Ken Krongard, Mark Donenfeld, Brad Rubens, Thomas Reitz, Keith Cooper, John Telfer, Peter Wright, Andrew Zizik, Steve Ayre, Etery Ordzhonikidze, Joe Brooks, Sascha Konietzko, Jen Ahlstrom, Jamie Perrett, Peter Perrett, Peter Perrett Jr., Jenny Maxwell, Howard Rosen, Pam Workman, Greg Benedetti, Bill Tierney, Tim McGrath, Cindy Sivak, Alia Dann Swift, Steve Swift, Scott (Scotty Hard) Harding, Greg Rollett, Nick Launay, and all of the artists I've worked with around the world.

REALIZE YOUR DREAMS

Of all the aspects of personal lifestyle, none surpass the power of popular music as the means by which people define their persona— their memories, their social connections, their sense of fashion and style, their source of entertainment, their refuge, and how they choose to devote much of their leisure time. Music fans everywhere continually seek ways to express and enjoy their love of popular music, from recorded material to concerts, artist-branded merchandise, fan clubs, Internet sites, TV and radio programming, music-based films, and more.

—Joshua Simons and John Caputo, itsBANG

There are more than eight million artists and bands posted on MySpace, according to the site Web Strategy by Jeremiah Owyang, and obviously so many more when you count all of the other websites and social networks. In fact, it was highly publicized through multiple media outlets and confirmed by *Billboard* on October 25, 2010, that Lady Gaga's YouTube videos were the first to reach one billion views. According to Oliver Chaing's Forbes.com blog of November 9, 2010, Justin Bieber hit the one billion mark as well. What this book will do is show you how to make your band stand out and be the one that people want to see, hear, and buy among the millions of artists and bands already out there in the marketplace. You are all smart enough to understand that having a band is having a brand, and that it takes a lot more than just great music and playing a few club gigs to make a name for yourself. I have interviewed people like you, with bands, from around the world and asked them to provide me with questions that I then posed to experts in today's music industry. This book, like no other book published before, will place you on the path to achieving your dreams in today's constantly evolving music industry. I'm providing lists of resources and my accompanying interactive website (rockininthenewworld.com) to assist you along the way.

For more than three decades as a music industry insider, I've seen creative genius, epic failure, booze, drugs, human endurance, heroism, miracles, humiliation, people who've ruined their lives, and people who've rocketed to the top and stayed there. A majority of musicians plod along for a while, scoring little successes here and there, getting a gig, or signing with a small or even midrange label. Then time goes by and their career goes nowhere. Things start to get repetitive. Personalities clash, the hours are grueling, shit happens.

It's not enough to have the drive, charm, skill, talent, and intuition. What is most important is that you are committed to your art, understand the business, and persevere. For those of you who have made the decision to commit yourselves and endure whatever's necessary to reach the top, this book is for you.

Together we will cover rehearsals, writing songs, recording, and performing live. We'll discuss contracts and money management. You'll read expert opinions on everything from making the most out of music-related Internet services, developing and selling your merchandise, physical and digital distribution of your recorded music, publishing, building a fanbase, and creating the team that you will need to support you and enhance your efforts along the way.

What I will do is provide you with an inside track on how the business really operates, how to maximize your band's potential, and how to reap the benefits of creative and financial success.

Chapter

7

THE BAND DYNAMIC

Everyone seems to think that it's record labels, agents, and managers who have all the ideas but it's not true. It's the artist. All the other persons' jobs are to interpret what the artist wants, so if the artist doesn't have a plan, then everyone's in trouble. 🙶🙶

—GERRY GERRARD, PRESIDENT, CHAOTICA BOOKING AGENCY

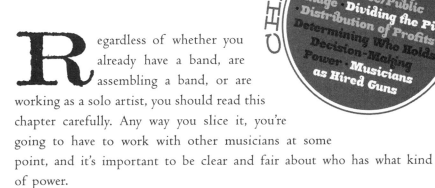

CHAPTER SPOTLIGHT

Start Me Up · Cut the Crap · Stage Presence/Public Image · Dividing the Pie · Distribution of Profits · Determining Who Holds Decision-Making Power · Musicians as Hired Guns

Regardless of whether you already have a band, are assembling a band, or are working as a solo artist, you should read this chapter carefully. Any way you slice it, you're going to have to work with other musicians at some point, and it's important to be clear and fair about who has what kind of power.

Your band is your core vehicle to success. If you're smart and a little lucky, you can put together your dream team right from the beginning and save yourself from a career dead end. Even if you're already up and running, you may find that you need to replace personalities that don't fit. Screwy issues between band members may seem small at first, but they'll grow out of control as time goes by. It's best to address issues head-on.

Which is better: figuring out roles, responsibilities, and money issues now, or waiting until later, after you've invested all your time and energy, only to have your band dissolve in a bonfire of vanities and lawsuits? It's important that you set goals. Start out with a list of what you'd like to accomplish in the first three months, then expand it to cover your first year and thereafter. Go back and look at this list often. Check off what you've done and add to it. So much will be coming your way as things begin to happen. But it is very important to be organized right from the start. By seeing that you've achieved your initial goals, your band will gain confidence and your commitment will be solidified.

Start Me Up

“Be original, follow your dreams, master your craft, and focus on going one step at a time rather than trying to get to the top of the mountain as fast as possible.”
—Henley Halem, president and founder, HRH Music Group

So how do you start a band? Start out by jamming in your bedroom or garage with friends from school or the neighborhood, playing interpretations of music you listen to. You'll also need to do some research. Go onto the Internet and search through music websites, blogs, and social networks and get involved. Check out local music magazines and fanzines, many have bulletin boards and useful classifieds. Go to gigs, and open up dialogue with others who have similar musical taste and attitude. That's where you will find people like yourself. Don't be afraid to get together to try to make music.

Superstar band Metallica formed when James Hetfield and Lars Ulrich found each other through an ad in a local music magazine, under the heading "Metal Musicians Wanted." Recent Grammy nominees MGMT started playing together at Wesleyan University, and Vampire Weekend met while attending Columbia.

I decided to speak with Sascha Konietzko, founder and leader of the hugely innovative and legendary German industrial band KMFDM. Sascha has never followed the pack, and KMFDM, who have sold millions of records around the world, are well known for their innovation. Their success is a result of hard work, dedication, and knowledge that's clearly apparent in the music they release, the concerts they perform, their fan interaction, and the offerings on their websites and social networks.

How and why did you start KMFDM? "My vision for KMFDM was really to create music that I liked. It was the early eighties and I was fed up with the post-punk and New Romantic stuff. I wanted to make music that was machine driven, and the juxtaposition had people playing their instruments very precisely. It was really just a self-serving kind of idea, and I never thought that it was going to go anywhere at all, and it was really just for fun.

"I always had an interest in technical stuff and always wanted to learn how to program sequencers and how to operate modular synths and that kind of stuff which, of course, was way too expensive for me to own back then. So I kind of started tagging along with some people who had equipment and when they didn't use it, I would borrow it and play with it at home. A simple little sampler back then was ten times the cost of my rent!"

Boston indie musician Andrew Zizik says, "I've always naturally been attracted to creative people who just happened to play music. I started my first band with some classmates while I was in freshman year of high school. We played the songs we heard on the radio. I recall playing a show in Boston with the French Kicks. They were pretty big at the time, they had a following, and it was the first time my band had opened for an international touring act. Their music (in my opinion) wasn't even that original or good, but they closed their set with a great version of John Lennon's "She Said She Said" and then they had me. I remember them simply because of that cover. So yeah, my band started playing mostly covers, and by playing them, much like learning a recipe or going to school, we figured out how to write originals that didn't sound half-bad. I could come up with cool parts, interesting chord progressions and sounds, but no lyrical contributions. Luckily my friends were into singing their own lyrics, so I learned through them. Eventually I realized how simple (in theory) the concept of marrying music and words and melody was. In practice, however, it is much more challenging. It takes a long time before you can be confident about songwriting, but it comes."

Steve Ayre from the Injured List, a pop-rock band from Lenawee County, Michigan, says he already had part of a band assembled but they were missing a strong lead singer. His drummer was very impressed with a singer/songwriter, Nathan Marks, whom he had seen playing with another band. A few months later, the singer's band broke up and he joined the Injured List. It couldn't have worked out any better. Besides being a terrific singer, Nathan is a prolific composer who writes all of the group's songs.

Jen Ahlstrom of the Brooklyn band Rabbi and the Popes said, "The drummer found me on Craigslist. Then, when I joined, it turned out that the bass player (who was not a member of the original band but met guitarist Dan Marks on a film shoot and had been jamming with them for a year) went to Wesleyan with me, so I already knew him. Instantly there were all kinds of other similarities. We all love music from the seventies and we all work in film. We later dropped the second guitarist/singer from the original band and we became a four-piece à la Queen. Dan writes most of the music. I brought in three songs of my own. I also took one of Dan's songs from the original band and rewrote the lyrics, and that's one of our strongest songs."

These stories are typical of what happens when you're starting out with a band. You may not have all the members, you may not have all the material, and you may not even have your direction totally set, but don't stress out. Everyone has to start somewhere and the pieces will come together. Your band is a work in progress, and throughout your career you will constantly be fine-tuning it.

Now it may be tempting to bring in your buddy because he's the one with the basement that you can rehearse in (or because he's funny, or because he's willing to throw money into the band), but you're going to have to make absolutely sure he can pull his weight on his own as a band member. Don't compromise your potential because of friendship or convenience.

Picking a Band Name

Today your band name is considered your brand name, and your brand is the perceived value and quality of you as an entertainer and its presenter. Be careful in choosing a name for your band. Make sure that it is something that stands out and relates to the image and message you wish to project. Think about your favorite bands and what it is about their names that interests you. Band names should reflect genre, attitude, or sensibility. Examples such as *Iron Maiden* and *Slayer* evoke images from mythology and power. *Barenaked Ladies* projects a humorous and satirical approach. *Vampire Weekend*, on the other hand, is mysterious and leaves you wondering. I'm not setting any guidelines, but you're going to be stuck with whatever name you pick, and you must remember that your name will identify you and become your brand. You'll also need to develop an eye-catching logo and artwork to represent your name of choice.

Some bands have chosen random words from a dictionary, lyrics from their favorite songs, characters from film, geographical locations, or pop culture references. Think of *R.E.M.*, *Fountains of Wayne*, *Linkin Park*, the *Decemberists*, *Veruca Salt*, and the *Sex Pistols*. Pick a name that stands out. Whether it is humorous, serious, or aggressive, it should be easy to remember and unique to you. You can also check out Band Name Maker (bandnamemaker.com) and other sites for help.

When you have come up with a name that you like, you'll need to see if the name has already been used and how you can immediately register the name you've chosen for your own use if it is available. Godaddy.com is a good choice to check on domain names, and Bandname.com can check on usage registrations, but it is suggested once you've decided on a name that you make an application at your state trademark office and later at the federal trademark office for complete protection. On more than one occasion, bands have had to change their name because of conflicts. MGMT was originally called the Management but had to change their name to MGMT when they found out another band had already been using that name. The British band the Beat had to change their name in the United States to the English Beat and on and on.

Cut the Crap

❝ *It's about teamwork. Everyone has to be committed to do everything they can to work together to get the result.* **❞**
—Peter Wright, owner and CEO, Virtual Label

There are many issues besides musical ability that can affect the longevity of a band. Personalities play a huge factor in band synergy. You're going to be spending a lot of time together in cramped quarters with your bandmates. Behavior regulates the equilibrium of the group dynamic. Band members need to be reasonable and reliable. It should come across in the level of commitment each member has in showing up not only for recordings and performances, but also for rehearsals and meetings.

I once worked with the Dead Boys, probably the best American punk band of their day. True to their roots—the grimy streets of Cleveland's inner city—

they were also hell-raisers. One night we pulled into Providence, Rhode Island, and played a gig at Lupo's Heartbreak Hotel. We'd gotten a lot of publicity and made the six o'clock news. The performance was powerful and aggressive and the crowd was amped up and frenzied. Afterward, a couple of band members tore apart the dressing room—breaking things and basically behaving like clichéd rock stars.

Later at the hotel, the group received, shall we say, a warm welcome from the local cheerleading squad. An hour later, the football team showed up looking for a fight. The band responded. The cops came, ran off the football players, and I had to go down to the police station and file a report. It was obvious to the cops my guys were innocent victims but it was still a mess. By the time I got back to the hotel room, the football players had returned and they'd had yet another full-blown brawl.

My point is that the people in your band can get you into trouble. Sometimes it's not even their fault, it can be collateral damage caused by groupies or people you party with after gigs. You can't make music if you're sitting in jail. General belligerence is hard on a group and being careful about whom you associate with is essential. So always err on the side of caution, be protective and supportive of one another, and kick back and enjoy the ride to the top—don't crash and burn along the way.

What can also impact the synergy of the group is personal relationships. Relationships within the band are tricky. It's natural for people to go through ups and downs, but it can be hairy when the downs are going down onstage.

As Etery Ordzhonikidze, a Russian alternative-rock singer/musician whom I met backstage at a Korn concert in Moscow's Gorky Park, told me, "I used to play in one band that I quit because I got sick and tired of doing the guys' jobs while they were fucking off and arguing about the authorship of our songs. Now I play bass and sing in a band called Commanche, where the environment is great. Everyone does their share and is committed to making the band a success."

When band members are in sync in both musical ability and common goals, it is a powerful thing. You'd better make damn sure that your definition of success is the same as theirs. What is the "ultimate" for you? Signing with a major record label and going platinum, or did you just hope to be able to play in that venue where you saw your favorite artist performing? When you and your band have a common goal, you know what you're trying to pull off. Who would have believed that among today's stadium-level concert artists, a majority of them are legacy rock bands like the Rolling Stones, the Eagles, Metallica, Aerosmith, the Who—all of whom have been together for over thirty years through thick and thin?

At the peak of their career, Rob Halford left Judas Priest to deal with personal issues and pursue a solo career. It was a huge setback for the band, which had to find a replacement singer, but after twelve years, Halford returned and the group had one of their best-selling records of all time. Success-oriented means you all have the same drive. Don't sweat the sacrifices. Be willing to travel the high roads and low roads to reach your destination: stardom.

Stage Presence/Public Image

Not every member of the band has to be a star. It's enough if you have one good front person who embodies the personality of the band. But that synergy leaps to a new level when all of you have a formidable stage presence. If you interact well and project excitement, the crowd is going to respond to and interact with you.

If you want a major record deal, you need to have obvious hit singles. This may sound clichéd to you, but record companies are in the business of generating maximum sales since they invest a large amount of time, money, and effort into every record they release. But to be successful, you also need to have a memorable and charismatic presence. Now more than ever, the first time people hear you perform, they also see you perform because of YouTube, MySpace, Facebook, Fearless Music, Big Live, and all of the other websites and social networks. So you had better think about what you look like onstage, what you wear onstage, and how you move onstage, because whether you like it or not, you are in competition with every other band that is out there. If you don't distinguish yourself visually, people may not take the time to listen to you.

I asked Lee Heiman, president of Track Entertainment, Fearless Music, and the Management Group, **What attracts you to a new band?** "I look at the lead singer. Does he or she have star appeal? Can they influence others? Can they influence the masses? Can they make a change? Does the band have a proprietary style? Do they have an attitude? Are they real? Are they different? Are they refreshing? That's what it's all about when signing and marketing bands."

Lee currently manages Hank & Cupcakes, a truly original and exciting group to watch. Check them out on MySpace and you'll see he means what he says.

Sony's Maria Egan says, "I look for singularity, accessibility, artistic vision, great songwriting, drive, and charisma."

What can you do that the big stars do to get noticed? Hire a publicist early. It's not as cost-prohibitive as you may have imagined. I spoke with Pam Workman, the well-respected New York City–based publicist/press agent who represents the Songwriters Hall of Fame, the New Music Seminar, BMI, and many major and indie recording artists. Pam offered some really useful tips that you can take advantage of now.

Does your publicist help create your public image and persona? "Yes. If you are lucky enough to have someone on board early on in your career, they can provide extremely helpful input in terms of the band's photos, bio, what their website looks like, their style. I think a big mistake that people make is that they bring in a PR person once everything is ready to go. I think that sometimes what happens is that publicists are handed materials that others have created, so the budget is gone. That would not be what I would do."

How can a band use a publicist on a cost-efficient basis early in their career, without having a record label? "I think the issue most people have is they think they can't afford that kind of quality care independently. One suggestion that might be interesting is to take a little bit of money to hire a publicist to consult on image as things are being put together, and if you are lucky enough to get a little bit more money, then you can actually hire them for a longer term. But at least you then have some kind of input from a professional on things like your band bio, what the best photos are, even a recommendation for a hot photographer who's affordable. These are tools that many publicists have already in their bag of tricks."

Even though many artists today believe that all the websites out there give them tools and provide them with help to promote themselves and get visibility on the Internet, do you believe they still need to have some professional guidance, and can it be done cost-effectively? "Yes. If I were an independent artist and couldn't afford a three-to-four-month PR campaign by a highly skilled professional with a great set of contacts and experiences, I would definitely consider hiring a publicist for a week for a small chunk of change and have them go through everything like bio, photos, and website styling to put the whole thing together, or at least give advice and feedback and even help with press and promotion angles so that I could put my best out there. Maybe you can't afford a publicist to work the story, but maybe you can hire them to give you feedback as to what your best story is."

What are key items people should think of in their development so that they are projecting something that is unique? "I would say, 'What else is interesting about your view besides your music?' If it is all going to be all about the music, then it has to be something really unique. I think that, unfortunately—and I do understand the reasoning—many artists believe in their heart and their soul that because 'I work with these five musicians and they're the best,' that's what makes them so special. That might very well be true, and I'm not going to say it's not a story, but it had better be unique. I think a lot of times artists overestimate the uniqueness of their music. Even though it's hard to say, what often is more unique is the story of how they got there, the process: the personal beliefs that influence their lyrics, a philanthropic cause, a tragedy that inspired them. These, to me, tend to add and speak volumes as to why someone should pay attention to you."

When you look at a band like the Black Eyed Peas, just think about what Pam said and imagine the stories they have about getting together and their influences. They are a great example of a group that has multiple focal points with unique personalities who work together constantly expanding their repertoire, exploring new musical genres while creating their own unique sound encompassing electronica, rap, funk, jazz, and rock. They are always taking chances with their music and their stage presentation, adding brilliant, exciting choreography and high-tech production. The group takes their fans on a journey, constantly testing musical boundaries, creating extraordinary anticipation and excitement from their fans, who wonder what the group will do next. Their efforts have paid off with the band winning multiple awards, selling millions of records, and selling out major venues.

Dividing the Pie

You and your band members may get along and play well together, but what happens if one member gets paid more than the rest, or if one of you has all the decision-making power? In some bands, the distribution of power is uneven. Key members of the band are those members who are particularly important to the band's success. Whom you recognize early as key members will affect future negotiations, contracts, and major decisions. Your band's key members may be defined as:

- Songwriter(s)
- Front man (singer, lead guitarist/lead focal point)
- Band leader/founding member

It's common for bands to recognize members who assume these kinds of roles, but there is no set formula as to how control is structured. If several of you are writing songs, competition is going to arise for who gets the most songs into the band's set list. But most bands work this out among themselves after they find out which songs get the best response from their fans and audiences. Songwriters are entitled to publishing income for the songs they compose that the band records, which is an entirely separate source of revenue from record and touring income. But is the lead singer or lead guitarist entitled to a bigger share just because they are the focal point and the media darling?

Distribution of Profits: It Ain't Always Even

There are several different approaches in determining shares. You need to find the one that works best for you. After all, it is most important that you can work together as a unit and have as little friction as possible.

One option is that everybody in the band is equal no matter what his or her role. For example, if you have five band members and each member gets an equal cut of profits and ownership (and responsibility for expenses), that means each member is in for 20 percent of the total cut. In this situation, obviously if one band member advances more money for operating expenses, the easy solution is that you reimburse their expenses and then you split everything equally.

In many cases even the songwriters contribute their publishing income since they believe that all of the other members were part of bringing the songs to life. In that case, *all* income is equally divided.

But there is another model: in many cases the founding members, who might also be the songwriters, establish that they would take all income derived from publishing as well as a majority interest in the band's revenue and ownership, and the rest of the members would split the remaining profits. So suppose Fred writes the songs and Chris is the founder, and they have established that they each get 30 percent. After that the remaining 40 percent of the shares would be divided equally among the other band members.

Determining Who Holds Decision-Making Power

Sometimes the band needs to make important decisions as to whether to bring in a professional advisor, invest in new equipment, hire a crew, or other business- and expense-related items. You may choose to make decisions by vote. However, like the profit and loss equity distribution, voting power may or may not be balanced. A common practice is to set the voting process at majority rule for most decisions, but unanimous vote when it comes to issues regarding membership, contracts, and finances. You must explicitly outline this before you are in a situation where a decision must be made. Additionally, since the band is a business, the band has certain assets and issues as a result, such as ownership of the name of the band, ownership of the master recordings and all of the ancillaries: equipment purchased together, merchandising, publishing, sponsorship, and so on.

The Band Partnership Agreement

Every band member needs to be absolutely clear on the breakdown of roles and responsibilities within the group. Once you've figured out the roles and boundaries, it's important to get everything down on paper and have everybody sign off. It makes sense to consult an attorney early because several major issues will come up and you will need to be prepared to deal with them quickly. For example, you are offered a substantial record deal, publishing deal, merchandise agreement, sponsorship, or even want to contract with a manager, booking agency, or business manager. In order to do so, your band will need a mechanism for making decisions. You should also know that if you can find a good music business lawyer, they may be able to use their industry connections to help you find these deals.

Like many bands I have interviewed, you are probably operating on an oral understanding among yourselves, and the thought of having to enter into contracts may be repulsive. I have never used a band partnership agreement either, but trust me: I wish I had! It would have saved a lot of aggro and even some band implosions that I witnessed. Setting guidelines as to how the ownership, equity, and operational policy are established addresses problems before they begin. This means fewer arguments down the line.

Here are issues that will need to be considered when putting a band partnership agreement together:

Creative Decisions

- Who owns the songs? For example, does the songwriter own his or her songs, or are they band property once they are added to the set list?
- Who owns the master recordings?
- Who decides which songs to perform/record?
- What factors are involved when determining who gets songwriting credit?
- Who decides which gigs to play?

Business Decisions

- What is the process for making decisions?
- If decisions are made by voting, does it have to be unanimous, or is it a majority vote? Do certain members make key decisions if a consensus cannot be made?
- Do any band members possess veto power?
- How will the band resolve disputes?
- What is the process for making amendments to this partnership agreement?

Band Name

- Who owns the band name and logo?
- If the band breaks up, who can still perform using the name?
- What happens to the band name if the band breaks up?
- What happens to the band name if the band name owner quits or is ousted?

Money

- How will band profits and debts be distributed?
- How are performance fees and royalties distributed among members?
- What will happen when one band member contributes more or less time or money than expected?
- Who keeps track of the money?
- What is the system for recordkeeping?
- Who can sign the band checkbook and use band credit cards?

Equipment

- How will the band purchase equipment?
- How and where will it be stored and transported?
- Which items will be insured?
- What happens to the instruments, assets, etc., if the band breaks up?
- If the band has purchased musical instruments, what happens when a member leaves or is fired?

Members

- What happens when a new member joins?
- What happens when a member quits?
- What is the process for firing a band member? For example, unanimous, majority, or management decision?
- What is each member's primary role?
- What are the secondary roles within the band?
- Can members take on music projects outside the band, such as guesting with other bands or cutting a solo record?

Business Entity

- What is the legal structure? For example, corporation, partnership, etc.
- What are the tax, personal liability, and start-up expenses associated with operating as a sole proprietor, partnership, limited liability company (LLC), or corporation?

Even with the best of intentions, your band can be torn apart by unforeseen circumstances. Let's take, for example, what's recently happened to Brooklyn-based Jen Ahlstrom and her band Rabbi and the Popes. After getting a buzz started, releasing MySpace tracks for which they have several thousand hits, and doing an impressive number of gigs at New York City–area clubs including the Mercury Lounge, the band was broadsided when its key writer and guitarist, Dan Marks, notified everyone that he was moving to California.

So, Jen, **What happened?** "Basically, as well as being musicians, all of us are film students. Dan is moving to California because he was accepted into the American Film Institute in LA, which is apparently the Harvard of cinematography. It's too good of an opportunity to pass up, but he is really upset about leaving the band. His girlfriend told me at a BBQ last night that Dan's more upset about leaving the band than he is about leaving her."

So what are you going to do now? "We're not sure yet. Dan had written a majority of the band's initial music. I wrote some of the songs, too, and the rest of us are writing together now. It's hard to find people to play and write with who have the same taste in music and whom you get along with. This is the third band I've played with in New York City. Sometimes the issue is ego, sometimes just divergent musical interests, sometimes it's talent. I'm still going to try to find another guitarist, if not another band. Got to keep playing!"

Luckily the band had an understanding with Dan, so they are keeping their name and are going to try to replace him and/or figure out a way to collaborate with him via the Internet for recording, and in person when his schedule permits. But this is a lesson for all of you to complete your band agreements as soon as possible. Let's say that Dan wasn't the nice guy that he is and that he wasn't going to let the band continue to use the name that they'd all worked so hard to establish. Rather than leave it up to chance, spend a little time and draft a simple agreement between yourselves. It would be even better if you went to a lawyer for a formal agreement that encompasses the items I've listed above. We'll discuss later how to find a good lawyer, and you can find several band partnership agreements online that are available to download at low cost or even for free. Here are just two resources:

- ▶ **StarPolish** (starpolish.com). *An online community that offers business advice for musicians.*
- ▶ **LawDepot** (lawdepot.com/contracts/bandpartner/) *This offers many basic legal agreements, including those of band partnerships.*

As mentioned, your band is a business that you might want to incorporate. All income you initially generate is gross income, and there will be no profit. Even as you gain success, your band will still be losing money quickly as production, touring, and marketing expenses mount up. You should consult an accountant or business manager who can structure the cash flow and minimize tax liability for the band entity and for individual members. I will explain exactly how they can help you, and will offer a few resources in the following chapters.

You may also structure the company so that each member is an independent contractor, self-employed and potentially available to work with other artists. Or if you're a solo artist, you may be a sole proprietor who hires other musicians and pays them on a job-by-job basis for performances and recording.

You need to anticipate the potential that you or your fellow band members may want to branch out. Often band members will launch their own solo careers on the side. Your agreement should provide for this possibility and develop a mechanism that establishes guidelines to prevent side projects from conflicting with the band's touring and recording schedules. Case in point, once again: the Black Eyed Peas. Even though she started as a back-up singer, Fergie quickly became a major focal point in the band and was offered a solo record deal. The group embraced her success and will.i.am produced her multiplatinum hit CD. Another great example is the group Genesis. Peter Gabriel, Mike Rutherford, and Phil Collins all have huge solo careers that do not compete with or diminish the strength of Genesis. In fact, Genesis continues to sell out stadiums worldwide. So be flexible and understand that your band is based on the cumulative success of all of the members. Don't get caught up in petty jealousy and internal competitions between yourselves; maximize all of your band's assets and talent. If you are lucky enough to have more than one member capable of singing lead, go for it. The Beatles, the Band, and Crosby, Stills, Nash & Young all had several lead singers and made great use of them.

Musicians as Hired Guns: The Made-for-TV-and-Radio Music Artist

There have been several international mega-groups specifically created by savvy managers and television producers who wanted to capture the youth market and believed that music would do the trick. "Star makers" worked together to create original ideas and concepts that resulted in global successes on multiple fronts.

The perfect example of the star makers phenomenon that created an original music experience that became a renowned success through TV, recordings, and eventually the live concert stage is the Monkees. The idea was very simple: create a television property that could grab screaming teen girls, generate a horde of artist merchandise, and put the TV show on the road. All told, the Monkees became a short-lived but highly profitable success selling over seventy million albums that generated close to $1 billion in sales from music, concerts, licensed merchandising, TV syndication, and other ancillary income that still generates substantial revenue.

Enter: Menudo

What goes around can certainly come around again. Menudo was the Puerto Rican boy band formed in the 1970s by producer Edgardo Díaz. Releasing their first album in 1977, the band achieved great success during the 1980s, becoming the most popular Latin American teen musical group of the era. Much like the Monkees, they were controlled and run by managers who saw the potential to create teen hysteria and the chance to build a music brand that could strongly generate record, merchandise, concert, and other retail sales. It is all about an exciting stage show that captures the passion of an impressionable audience. Later successful examples of the phenomenon have been the Backstreet Boys, 'N Sync, Take That, and the Spice Girls.

The power of television has also been a key driver of superstar careers spawned by Disney hits. Miley Cyrus (*Hannah Montana*) and the Jonas Brothers (*Camp Rock*) became popular with young audiences, leading to global superstardom in music.

American Idol: For Better Or Worse

The *Billboard* music charts present over twenty categories. Less than 1 percent of such charted music came about because the artist first appeared on TV. However, the success of *American Idol* has fueled the successes of several music artists who are now headline performers. Debuting on the American shores in 2002, *American Idol: The Search for a Superstar* was the follow-up to Simon Fuller's successful UK show *Pop Idol* and soon found a home on the Fox TV network.

For the most part, the members of the groups listed above had no participation in any revenues created by the shows or by their work other than the salaries they were paid. However, their work within the group and the stardom achieved as members helped launch the successful solo careers of Ricky Martin, Justin Timberlake, and Robbie Williams. With *Idol*, it's a very different story. The contestants are in a major competition and those who achieve top positions are offered lucrative recording contracts and have the potential for their own successful careers. Just look at Daughtry, Carrie Underwood, and Kelly Clarkson.

My point in bringing up these examples is very simple. Although the individual members of the groups I've mentioned have had their own personal journey in reaching the stars—and may be extraordinary musicians, performers, and composers—there is a huge difference between them and the bond created by members of bands who struggled and starved together on their way to the top. In his 2010 memoir, *Life*, Keith Richards does a great job in describing how it was for the Stones when they first started out. Sharing a small flat, scrounging for a few shillings to pay for food, rent, and their electric bill, and relishing the joys of success when someone offered them a gig, even if it was for no money. For bands, success is not just measured by the money you make, it's measured by simple things like fans who love your shows and go crazy each time they see you play, by gaining recognition from your peers and being offered gigs at places you want to play or with bands you want to play with. In your early days, don't worry about crashing on someone's sofa or sleeping in a van with your bandmates, it's all part of the process and will make your band's later success taste even sweeter.

MAKE IT REAL

It's really as simple as getting one fan, managing that fan, and getting that fan to be your voice to get out there and spread the word; which is how it's always been. It's about doing everything and keeping things going. Fresh. Every month your website should be treated like a magazine of the old days. New cover, new music, new content, etc. so you keep driving traffic back and people keep purchasing your material.

—DAVE LORY, CO-EXECUTIVE DIRECTOR
AND PRODUCER, NEW MUSIC SEMINAR

CHAPTER SPOTLIGHT
- Creative
- Technical
- Business
- Your First Gig
- Recording for Reference
- Evaluate Your Progress

When you are at the stage when you truly believe that you can call yourself a band because you're all committed, when you're all making an investment in time, effort, and resources, then you must get organized. Organization is not something that you will find restrictive; it's actually something that will empower you. Sit down and make a list of your immediate goals. In this list, include rehearsal schedules and basic areas of responsibility for each member. There are three important aspects that must be addressed: creative, technical, and business. Initially your band needs to take care of all of these issues itself, so it is best to divide responsibility among the members. As you progress, you will be hiring professional experts and support people to take over these roles.

The creative aspect is the songwriting and song selection process, as well as developing your image and web presence. Songwriting and song selection may be shared by everyone, but usually one or two members are really the key songwriters and assume the role of creative leadership or direction, and in doing so they will set the tone of the rehearsals. The technical aspect is the equipment and production logistics. The business aspect is managing the operations, finance, booking, recording, and marketing.

Creative

Rather than preach about your attitude and your dedication and all of the elements that you need to put into your persona, image, and songwriting, I asked Sascha Konietzko of KMFDM, **What creative advice can you offer young artists today?** "Well, that's a loaded question and there are so many answers to it! The quantity of music, and the ease with which music can be created today by just buying software synthesizer programs, just pirating the whole thing . . . Using the same presets as a thousand other people doesn't really make your music sound original. Not knowing, for instance, technicalities like how to use compression doesn't contribute to making your music sound great, but it would be pretty good for someone who feels creative to also learn a little more about operating the gear and using it to its maximum potential. But of course we're living in a time where nobody wants to read the manual anymore.

"I think that if you want to be a rock star, first realize how to be real. It's not done by jetting in and out of places like Hollywood celebrities do. You've got to build relationships with your audience. If you don't like your audience, don't let them know it! Don't ask, 'Why aren't there cute young girls, why are there only fat men?' Be appreciative of the fat men!"

Songwriting

❝❞*Without a successful song, nothing else matters.*❞❞

—Keith Cooper, manager/publisher, Express Entertainment, the
Fourmula Group

Ask any professional in the industry what they think is the most important
ingredient for success and, no surprise, the answer is great songs. From a lyrical
standpoint, you can write about anything and everything. There is no boundary
other than standards and practices if you want your song commercially broadcast! From a musical and technical standpoint, however, there are some very
definite structures that have proven to be key to success.

Popular music is typically sectional. Many people agree that they know
a song is a hit right from the intro. Hit records have great intros and catchy
hooks, usually a chorus or bridge. A proven structure that works is intro, verse,
chorus, verse, chorus, bridge, chorus, coda. The verse and chorus are the primary
elements and are usually repeated throughout the song, while the bridge, which
gives a little change of pace, is used less often. Experiment with this structure
and improvise when you do your arrangements, finding ways to fit in an instru-
mental solo and repeat choruses.

Songwriters need to make sure that they copyright their songs with the
Library of Congress in Washington, D.C., before they perform in public and
especially before anything is put out on the Internet if they don't want their
material to be stolen. It's cheap and the complete instructions provided on
their website (copyright.gov/forms) are easy to follow. You may do this online
via the Electronic Copyright Office (eCO) system, which replaces the paper
performing arts works form (PA). The instructions note that you will need to
make payment by credit card, debit card, or electronic check, and that a copy
of your music in a digital file format must accompany the application. You'll
be given a barcode immediately so you can track your application online. As
long as you file the application, your rights of ownership are protected. You
can also check out TuneCore (tunecore.com), which offers free information
about copyrights.

Song Selection

How do you pick the songs that are going to make up your repertoire? It's
easy, says Steve Ayre, with the Injured List: "One guy writes everything and the

band plays them!" Everyone has suggestions about what cover songs, if any, they may perform. But what is important is that you play songs that people want to hear and that you "own" them. So when first starting out, don't get too crazy about playing fifty different songs; play a few really well.

Once you can play well, you'll need to think about presentation. At that point, your arrangements will take a leading role. Spend time figuring out who takes the solos, where the solos are taken, and what will make the most impact. You must figure out what makes the song hot and exciting. Even though you may have the technical parts worked out in the arrangement, you need to decide how to maximize each member's talent to get the best result. Is it a power rock song that everyone's playing right from the beginning with a few huge solos interspersed, or a more dramatic piece where you start out sparsely but then build throughout? You must establish an emotional connection with your audience, and your music and performance must instill that.

Your songs will come alive in rehearsal and will give you the impetus to highlight the elements you will use for your live presentation; and remember, songs and arrangements that you prepare for recording can be modified for live concerts. Onstage/in concert, it's OK to have a long intro or outro and a lot of solos, and these are things that you work out in rehearsal. For recording, you'll have to work on being able to present and capture all of the excitement in a three-minute format if your goal is to get radio airplay. As I mentioned, it takes hard work to achieve success, but the effort that you make will result in tight, powerful performances that your audiences will respond to.

Rehearsals

So how often should the band rehearse? You should rehearse every chance you get. There's just no substitute for a band clocking in hours playing together. Rehearsal time results in tight, polished music. From a creative standpoint, remember that a lot of music is written during rehearsals. When you're not rehearsing with the band, continue to practice as much as you can on your own. Reach for your instrument every chance you get. Your skills will improve exponentially, and so will your creativity.

When I talk about rehearsals, I'm not talking about tedium; I'm talking about excitement, energy, and fun. You can all play to some extent, but you'll all get better through rehearsal. Everyone will learn about face-to-face communication (no texting!), working in unison, keeping time, and maintaining a balance so your instrumentation blends. You can have a great lead guitarist, but if you don't have a tight rhythm section, nothing is going to work, so all of you need to put in the effort.

Make sure that you record every rehearsal. Don't worry about quality; it will just be for reference. This way you can review what you have done and also keep track of any new riffs or even new songs that may come as a result of your session.

At first, you might be able to work in somebody's garage, basement, or bedroom. Steve Ayre says, "Play anywhere, everywhere, and anytime, from your parents' basement to your dorm rooms at three in the morning."

But the time will come when you'll need to make an investment of a couple of hundred dollars and rent space in a professional rehearsal studio so you can use a proper stage, backline equipment, and PA system to develop your stage presentation. When you do this, videotape it, and just as athletes review games, carefully look at what you're doing and discuss it among yourselves. Make this part of your routine, and remember that even stadium-level rock bands spend months rehearsing prior to a tour. Great shows come from the result of great effort.

In addition to playing your songs well, you'll have to figure out how to put them in an order and pace a set. To be successful, you'll need to capture your audience, engage them, and leave them wanting more; that includes your music, set list, and your stage show. Once you feel comfortable with what you've accomplished, invite a group of friends down to one of your sessions and see how they react to the performance. Does it pass the "butt test" or is everyone fidgeting in their seats? Have you kept everyone's attention and electrified the room? If so, you're ready to book some gigs.

Web Presence

As you work on your rehearsals and put together your stage show, you have to start developing your web persona. You need to build a following, a fanbase. You also want to attract the attention of record labels, agents, managers, and media. And guess what they do today? They all look to the Internet; that's where they discover bands.

There are many sites including MySpace, Facebook, GothamRocks, RethinkPopMusic, OurStage, CD Baby, Bandvista, Bandzoogle, WordPress, and ReverbNation that offer services that will help you nurture your career both online and onstage. So if one of your members is Internet savvy, embrace their skill, or find friends or family to help design your web presence and research what other groups like you around the world are doing. It is imperative that you immediately set up social network profiles and a band website.

Sascha from KMFDM reaffirmed this when he told me, "If you really want to stay up top, you have to do it all. You can find people over time that you can partner up with. I started a partnership years ago with someone I've known since he was sixteen years old because he came to all of our concerts. He became a business major and worked at a big company's central computer station; very web-savvy guy. I offered him a partnership to do all of my online design and updates, do the fulfillment, run the KMFDM store. He's been doing that for almost seven years and earns enough to support his family. He also recruited three other hard-core KMFDM fans to work with him. They do the MySpace KMFDM site, the Vampire Freaks site, all the viral marketing, the banner stuff, customer service (coddling the types that say they ordered a shirt yesterday and didn't get it). . . . They help me develop and realize product lines that are marketable."

You should take a look at KMFDM's site (kmfdm.net) to see what you can do yourself. (Plus you'll get a chance to see some of Aidan Hughes's great artwork. Keep in mind, just like KMFDM did, bands often collaborate with artists and photographers to develop iconic images.) Later I'll go into further detail about many Internet services that offer you the software, widgets, and resources that will assist you in creating, designing, and managing your own website, as well as designing and manufacturing your band's merchandise, CDs, vinyl, and download cards that you can sell online or at gigs.

Maria Egan, Sony Music A and R executive, says, "Internet research is now the normal first step in evaluating an artist's merit and progress. We can look at live clips on YouTube rather than wait for a show to come to town. For the most part we want to see that an artist has taken some initiative in setting up a web presence, and we look in detail to see what that presence says about the artist. Is it creative, vibrant, unique, highly trafficked, well maintained? In a new media world where so many tools are available to an artist to self-promote, we usually want to see some progress there before introducing them to a major system before they're ready. Artists like Colbie Callait, who had huge MySpace traffic prior to her major label deal, have also proved that the industry is not always right in picking the next big thing. The Internet allows the consumer to have a vote with no middleman. Then our job also becomes to pay attention to those signs and be able to know the difference between a fleeting buzz or when an artist's base is legitimately snowballing into something real." This is also true of Internet sensation Justin Bieber, whose homemade performances on YouTube were discovered accidentally by his now manager, Scooter Braun, who brought him to the attention of Usher.

Technical

What about equipment and instruments? Don't expect to have all of your dream gear from day one, but does everyone have adequate instruments, amps, and the basic gear they need for your rehearsals and first gigs? If not, don't go out and spend your savings on that double stack of Marshalls. See what you can borrow from other bands; look in the want ads and online for used gear; get equipment from places like Studio Instrument Rentals and use whatever starter equipment you are able to round up. But make sure that you have enough strings, drumheads, sticks, and all the basics in adequate supply. Everyone should be responsible for his or her own gear, but delegate one or two of you to keep track of it all.

You will need to put together a stage plot that includes positions of instruments, amps, and monitors, and you'll have to learn to use lighting. I'll supply you with some sample stage and lighting designs in the Appendix to help you with all of this, but there are plenty of them available online, so get a good look for yourself.

Another great thing about working in a professional rehearsal studio is they may have a lot of equipment available and may provide you with an opportunity to use it. When you book the studio, make sure you find out what is included in the rate and take the time to go down and see for yourself. Paying fifty dollars an hour to rehearse in a space that offers nothing more than your garage is not a good investment. Paying fifty dollars an hour for a room with a stage, PA, full drum kit, and an assortment of backline gear makes sense.

Business

You'll need to put together an operational budget and establish a ledger (spreadsheets work) to keep track of all business expenses and receipts. It will initially include day-to-day expenses like transportation; equipment purchase, rentals, and maintenance; Internet software; digital and print subscriptions to trade magazines like *Billboard* and *Pollstar*; printing costs for flyers and merchandise; and hired help. You should also put together a date-planner database for appointments, interviews, contacts, and the rest of your schedule so you can keep track of everything. There are tools available from BandCentral, Bandize, Nimbit, ReverbNation, Topspin, and others listed in the Appendix that can help you with all of this.

Dave Lory, the chairman/CEO of DJL Live Music Productions and co-executive director of the New Music Seminar, says, "Give each member a duty and run the band like a business. This includes booking and arranging the shows and itineraries; lodging; sound check and showtimes; the financial deals; collecting money; merchandise and collecting fans from the merchandise table; artwork; a website keeping information flowing to the fans; collecting names off social networks; accounting and keeping the books. This *is* a business. Take responsibility for your career. Blame nothing, blame no one, love your fans, and make your relationship with them your main goal."

Your First Gig

> **"** *I would suggest going and developing a great live show first. That, more than anything, can propel a career.* **"**
>
> —Terry McBride, CEO, Nettwerk Music Group/cofounder Polyphonic

Even though I mentioned that you should pick your bandmates wisely and that there is no room for deadweight, understand that I'm not saying that every member of your band now must be at a peak in their career and ability. The more you rehearse, the more you go out together and watch other bands, the more you learn, the better you will be. Be passionate about what you are doing, and if you can convey that to your audience, you'll capture them.

Having said that, your first gig is more likely to be in your school cafeteria, frat party, or your friend's backyard than on a concert stage. Another great new trend that has come as a result of the DIY movement is the house party. It should be easy to get booked, is a great way to start out, and will prepare you for playing in a professional environment. A great performance and a few people skills as you mingle after your show will serve you well in developing your fan base, and that's what you need to have if you're going to move up the ladder. Exposure is most important right now. In today's world, interacting with your fans is primary. That means getting to know them, online, via Twitter and especially at your shows. If you want to be successful these days, don't be like the dinosaur artists who isolated themselves and looked down on their audiences.

Look in your local papers and online and you will find that many clubs have an open mic night. Call up: it's easy to get booked on one of these shows. Be prepared to play only one or two songs, but have several songs fully worked up to choose from. Most of the time you won't need to bring anything but your instruments as the club will provide all of the backline gear. But you must check this in advance. Go to the venue one night to see for yourself what the procedure is; and more important, see what other bands are booked there and compare yourself to them. Is your music right for this particular club? Are you as good as the competition or better?

Go online, post flyers around town, and get as many of your friends and newly found fans from your website, and from the parties you've been playing, to come to your show to cheer you on. If you make a great impression on the club owners, this will lead to proper gigs. Don't worry about getting paid, as Martin Atkins of *Tour:Smart* will tell you: "Play for *nothing*. It makes your show immediately more attractive than many of the others that week—or makes you more attractive as an opener to another show."

Remember that onstage you must make eye contact with the audience, quickly move from one song to the next. Make sure to rehearse and have your moves choreographed so that the stage is never static. Choose your songs wisely so they work in the venue's environment. No matter how many people are in the audience, play as though thousands are there. Create moments that capture the audience and get them on their feet and you are well on your way to having a career. If you exude passion, your audience will pick up on it. Mannequins are for shop windows, not concert halls. As Simon Cowell says, your performance has to sell the song, so make sure that you're well rehearsed, that you know what you're doing, and that the one or two songs you are going to play are tight and will kick ass. Don't go in there with the attitude that you are great; take into account any comments or feedback you got from the casual gigs you may have done before, and improve on them because even though you are only going to play one or two songs, you're going to be in a professional venue and it counts. You never know who is going to turn up and you can't afford to suck . . . ever.

When interviewed by VH1 for *Behind the Music*, Metallica front man James Hetfield said that to distinguish themselves from all of the other bands in the LA club scene, Metallica played their music louder and faster. It worked. The audiences caught on to their vibe, making them the iconic band they still are decades later.

It's good to connect after a performance, but you have to try to keep your distance from the bar. As soon as your show is done, you want to make sure you strike your gear so the next band can play. Now it's time to do the meet and greet. Mingle with your audience and talk to the club owner and other musicians who might be there. This is how you network in the music business. Although there is honest competition among bands, there is also a real cooperative spirit, and you'll soon find out that a big part of the audience might be comprised of other bands just like you and their friends. Compare notes, get names and e-mail addresses, and start putting together a database that you can use to develop your following.

At your next rehearsal, discuss what went down, how well the songs were received, and whom you spoke with after the show. Then you have to concentrate on putting together an even stronger presentation because it's always about improving step-by-step. Maybe the two songs you did at the open mic night weren't your best, so the next opportunity you get, you had better do something better.

I asked Cary Tamura ("C. T."), owner of Tech-9 Music and Gotham Rocks and musician in the bands Shadows Lie and Grayzone, **How does a band know when they're ready?** "I find people, as frustrating and impatient as it makes us, move at the pace they are intended to. Whatever stage you're at is usually the stage that you're ready for, but it's important for you to get ready for the next stage before you get there, because you may not get another chance. Once you get that shot to play the big venue or the big showcase, you have to be prepared and at the top of your game because if you suck, people are going to write you off. You don't necessarily get the second chance in a lot of cases."

While you're spending time promoting yourselves, you should also be rehearsing at least three or four days a week because it is very different to be booked on a proper show than just to be doing an open mic night. People will be judging you. You are no longer an amateur trying to make good. Now you are a professional performing at a professional venue. Will you be able to hold your own against the headliner? Will you be able to keep the crowd's attention? Now the pressure is on you. In order to succeed, your performance onstage will need to be memorable.

The other night I went to a great event presented by RethinkPopMusic at Crash Mansion on the Bowery in New York City: five unsigned bands, five bucks, free drinks. It is a great concept: great for the bands, great for the audience (which, by the way, comprised a lot of musicians), and it's great for the promoters. Of the five bands, three that I saw far surpassed the others in presentation and crowd response. Those bands played to the crowd. The musicians were tightly rehearsed and worked as a unit.

It is so important when you are onstage that you turn and play to the audience, and that your group leader gives signals that you can follow much the same as a catcher gives a pitcher in a baseball game. It's OK in rehearsal for your lead guitarist to stand sideways and spend most of his time looking at your drummer, but when you're onstage, you had better kick ass and play to your fans. The three bands that I liked engaged their fans and invited them to meet after the show at their merchandise tables, where each was selling CDs, download cards, T-shirts, and posters. They were also collecting the e-mail addresses of their fans for their mailing lists.

The two other bands appeared to be self-indulgent, playing more for themselves than the audience. At that point, bored by the bands' lack of engagement, the audience headed to the bar in droves and started checking their iPhones and BlackBerrys. That's not what you want. I hope we can attribute their failures to connect with their lack of rehearsal and not lack of commitment.

So once you've done a few of these open mic or showcase nights—and you definitely should do several—use what you've gathered and post it on your website. Whether it's a three-minute video taken from somebody's phone or still photos at the venue of you and other musicians, get it out there and start promoting yourself. But let me remind you once again that any song you perform in public, on record, or on the web, had better have your copyright. Another thing you're doing now is providing content for your website and social networks and putting together your electronic press kit (EPK). This is what you will need to get more gigs and expand your fan base. Use Twitter, Facebook, MySpace, YouTube, Foursquare, and every other social network and method of communication known to man.

Henley Halem, Kid Cudi's manager, **confirms the value of social networks.** "All of my management clients or artists that are signed to my One Records imprint utilize social networks. As an artist I think it is important to have an up-to-date MySpace page and Facebook fan page; but, most important, I think Twitter is the most valuable. It allows people to listen and watch your every move and feel as though they actually know the artist rather than just being a fan of your music. For example, when we released the Kid Cudi *Man on the Moon* album, anyone who received a promo code from his Twitter page was able to go to Amazon and purchase the album for two dollars for the first week of release."

Henley's point about Twitter should be taken seriously, and you should also go to twitter.com/tweetforatrack where you can "easily trade fans an MP3 for a tweet and their e-mail. You can be creating viral Twitter promotions in seconds."

Ken Krongard, a former A and R executive at Mercury and Arista who discovered Avril Lavigne, and is currently president of Major Label Scout and K-squared Entertainment and manager of UK MySpace music phenomena Joe Brooks, says, "These days, everyone in a young band knows their way around the Internet and understands how to use the social networking sites. Not enough can be said about how these tools have changed *everything*. That said, the best thing an artist can do is make things happen for themselves. First and foremost, create some truly great music, and then use the modern resources available to get the word out. It's very hard to keep secrets in today's world, and special music will be found quickly—hopefully by my scouts first!"

Recording for Reference

While you're busy thinking of creative ways to generate interest in your band on the web, you must also start recording and releasing your music. The world of recording has changed. I'm glad I didn't invest a million dollars in a recording studio ten years ago because recording technology has grown as quickly as social networks.

The first innovation in home recording came from Tascam, the professional audio division of TEAC Corporation, who invented the Portastudio, the first cassette-based multitrack home studio recorder. Though the analog Portastudio had revolutionized the home recording process, adding the computer took it a step further. Initially, studio recording consoles from Neves and Studer used computer automation to aid in the mixing process, and computer-based instruments such as synthesizers (starting with the Moog) also took life. But today, with digital recording, a laptop is one of your most important tools for creating music, recording it, and performing it.

You can record, edit, and mix amazing music on your home computer. Most people prefer to use Macs. It is essential that you invest in and learn how to use equipment and software available from companies like Avid (Pro Tools, www.avid.com/US/products/family/Pro-Tools), Audacity (audacity.sourceforge.net), Cakewalk (cakewalk.com), Tascam (tascam.com), Digital Portastudios, and others. There are also abundant supplies of free tutorials and software online if you put some effort into research. See Valuable Music Web Resources on page 177 for more websites.

A good way to get started with all of this is to compare notes with the other bands you have met. Find out who is doing what and how other groups are recording. Do they have gear you can rent or share? Is there a geek with a portable studio who would come to your practice space? Make him your friend! You are going to have to record a lot of music and it will cost money no matter what. You'll need to decide whether it is worth investing a couple of thousand dollars in enough recording gear that you'll be able to use as needed in your own space; or whether it makes more sense for you to spend the same amount of money in a recording studio for just a few days at a time. It also makes sense to give the live sound engineer at that club you're doing your showcase in a few bucks to do a recording of your live performance. It won't necessarily have the quality of a studio recording, but it might be a great reference and something you can use for promotion and to post on your website.

At a certain point in your career, you may meet a producer who believes in you, has a great studio, and will work with you, providing services and studio time on spec (meaning you pay for it later). A producer can do a lot for you, but for now, you must start with your basic recording. So find that geek, talk to that band, and figure out a way to record two or three of your best songs as soon as you can. Beg, borrow, or steal to get it done.

Don't think these songs will get you a record deal, as they will not be master quality. But they could be good enough to post on the Internet. What these songs will do is (I hope) excite your fans. People will begin downloading and sharing your music; that's how you develop a following. In later chapters we will discuss recording and producers.

So let's be very clear here. The purposes of reference recordings are:

- To catalog the songs you write
- To help you improve the songs in regard to their arrangement, lyrical content, solos, or other musical aspects
- To give your fans a taste, and to entice and attract new fans by giving them a sample of what's in store
- To use as a tool to help you get gigs and promotion and to post online

Don't be worried or pressured about doing a demo for labels at this stage in your career. As a matter of fact, don't be worried or pressured about doing demos at all. As Sony A and R executive Maria Egan and label scout Ken Krongard confirm, today more bands are found online. Artist manager and former record executive Mark Kates says, "Don't torture yourself over the quality of songs you put on MySpace."

Evaluate Your Progress

You have played your first gigs in public and you've posted on the web.

- Did you accomplish your first set of goals?
- What did the fans say? What did other musicians and bands say?
- Have you had any comments on your social networks?
- Have you had any follow-up with the promoters or club bookers you met?
- Did any industry people see you play? Did you talk to them? Get any feedback?
- Most of all, how was your experience? Did the band work well as a unit?

By now you should have fans from the showcases you've done, the videos you've put on social networks, and the database you have started generating. Gather all of this information, evaluate it, and discuss it as a band. Be honest and address your weaknesses and strengths. Maybe there are songs or actions that need to be reworked. It's a normal part of the process. Maybe it was perfect. Any successful band I have ever worked with is convinced and dedicated to the fact that they are forces to be reckoned with. If you don't believe in yourselves, your fans won't become passionate about you. Take ownership in what you are doing and believe that your band is on the road to greatness. But remember, this is only the beginning, and one success is not a career. Now it's time to go out and book real gigs, use tools to improve your web presence, expand your fan database, and add songs to your repertoire.

In a recent television interview, musician, producer, and reality TV personality Bret Michaels offered the following formula for success: "Stay focused. You need to believe in what you are doing in order to have anyone else believe in what you are doing."

ROCK ON

CHAPTER SPOTLIGHT

The Real Work Begins · Improving Your Web Presence · Booking · Staff Up · Show Day: Load-In · Press On · Live Recording

The Real Work Begins

There are a few things that will get you booked in a local club: someone you know owns the venue, you can show you can draw a crowd, or the headlining act wants you to open for them. But what will make everybody happy is if your band has created a buzz.

Do you now have a hundred fans in your area that interact with you? Do they follow you on Twitter, Foursquare, and Facebook? Have you developed incentives for them, and can you count on them to come out to see you play?

Take the time to build relationships with each person who supports your music. If you show club bookers that you can draw one hundred fans as a result of your showcases and web offerings, you should be able to get a slot as an opening act, which incidentally will probably pay nothing or, at most, a small piece of the door. So before you go out and make any phone calls to club owners, kick ass on your social networks and show that you have a lot of traffic, because this way, if you can bring in three hundred fans, you're golden, and you'll be able to get nearly any club gig you want. Sites like Band Metrics (bandmetrics.com) and Sonicbids (sonicbids.com) will help you discover trends, identify your fans, measure their social engagement, and find hot markets and clubs to play in.

Improving Your Web Presence

Set your priorities. Do everything you can to build up your fan base. Go explore sites like MySpace (myspace.com), ReverbNation (reverbnation.com), Grooveshark (grooveshark.com), BandCentral (bandcentral.com), Nimbit (nimbit.com), and others listed in the Appendix. Invest in software and research and consider getting involved with one or more of these sites to maximize the effectiveness of your marketing and promotion efforts, help you increase sales of tickets and merchandise, engage your fans, and promote your live performances. You'll need to spend time to fully complete and maintain your profile on these sites and make sure to include songs, images, bios, and your contact and show information.

These companies can offer (some for a fee) help in designing your own website and electronic press kits; management and expansion of your fan base; help with gigs, promotion, and marketing of your band, music, and website; and manufacturing and distribution of your CDs, download cards, and merchandise. In addition, some offer software, widgets, and other tools for band management, fan management, touring, and accounting. They will keep you organized and put you in a professional format. I wish I had had these systems available to me when I was on the road as they are easy to use, instructional, and informative. They have totally revolutionized the landscape for new and developing bands. It is essential that you investigate their services and use them as soon as you can, based on your budget. My advice is to initially work with a service that can help you grow your fan base and promote your music on social networks.

There is one site that every professional I've interviewed says should be number one on your radar, and that's MySpace. Some of the sites I previously mentioned offer help in getting you well placed there, and as I said, their tools, widgets, and services are important to consider. In October 2010, MySpace redesigned their website and expanded their brand. They now offer products that redefine the company as a social entertainment destination for music, film, games, and celebrities. Among the offerings I think are valuable to bands is a mashup with Facebook that allows for customization of one's interests, allowing the subscriber to follow the artists or celebrities they like and letting them establish a personal entertainment stream on their profile. I contacted Lisette Rioux Paulson, a business acquaintance I knew who now works as director of partner relations, East Coast, at MySpace Music, and she put me in contact with Roslynn Cobarrubias, MySpace Music's senior director of marketing. I asked Roslynn, **What are the steps an artist must take to get their music on MySpace?** "Any artist can get their music on MySpace by visiting myspace. com/signup. Once recorded, the MP3s can be uploaded to a MySpace profile player. But make sure your music is 100 percent original so it is not flagged for copyright infringement when uploading."

Next I asked, **What should artists do to maximize their presence and reap the most benefit?** "Make sure the web link (URL) you've chosen is fairly simple and easy to remember, not something like BestBritishBandFromUK but something like myspace.com/britband. A band name should be easy to spell and find for search purposes on MySpace and on the Internet. Place the web link on everything that the band creates, e.g., album covers, stickers, flyers to distribute at every show and meet and greet, etc. When visiting a radio station, everyone on site should receive something with the band's MySpace URL on it for anyone who would like to follow the band or listen to more music from the band post-interview or appearance. Whenever a band is on the radio or television, a MySpace URL that is fairly easy to spell and remember should be given out. It is better than a band website because you have the social feature.

"Also make sure you utilize every tool we have to offer: the calendar is not only for concert performance dates but appearance dates, such as television, in-store, or press events. The blog can be utilized to show a different side of the band or members, e.g., you can be a reggae band blogging about your favorite rock band so it may connect to new fans based on rare similarities.

"Fans love videos and photos. Established artists like T.I. like to post pictures of every appearance from radio to television to award shows. New artists like Justin Bieber create Webisodes or videos of cover songs that are easily shared and spread over the Internet. Photos with fans should be uploaded to the MySpace page to give a fan a feel of closeness to the band, maybe in a 'fan album' or 'friend album.'

"Bulletins and status updates (which can be synced to your Twitter and Facebook accounts) allow for a real-time interaction with the band to create impromptu meet and greets, performances, etc.

"There is an artist dashboard in every profile that allows bands to see where their fans are geographically, what gender they are, and what songs they are listening to. Every artist should take advantage of this.

"Something as small as who is in your Top 8 can help new fans determine whether or not they will like your music, e.g., if a new fan loves Phoenix and they are in your Top 8, they can assume that your music is similar or that you have similar tastes, which can go a long way in creating credibility."

I asked her, **How can artists get MySpace Music interested in their work, and is MySpace Music like a traditional label?** "I think as all major labels take notice of artists, these days they have less and less to spend on artist marketing. They want to sign bands that have created a following for themselves organically or in a grassroots-mentality sort of a way to assure there is a fan base. Make sure you are big locally and the labels will come knocking, whether indie, major, or MySpace Records."

To confirm the power of MySpace, I interviewed British singer-songwriter Joe Brooks. Joe recently released an album with Lava Records (co-owned by Universal) in the United States. Prior to that, his self-released music and single "Superman" had accumulated almost twenty million hits on MySpace. It's obvious he had been honing his writing skills and musicianship for a good amount of time. So I asked him, **When did you know that you were ready to record and release your music?** "From my bedroom as a sixteen-year-old to working in some of the most insane studios with some of the world's biggest writers, it's all one big learning curve. I think it has been a real organic process. By collaborating with more experienced writers, I've discovered my strengths and weaknesses as a writer and learned how best to harness them in the creation of a new song. I think, as an artist, it's common never to be completely satisfied with where your music is at, it can always be better in one way or another. . . . You are continuously morphing into the next, I hope better, version of yourself. However, at sixteen, my family and friends gave me a lot of encouragement to start laying down some of my ideas. So I bought a little home recording setup and began to make demos, for my own pleasure. And then I discovered MySpace. It wouldn't be an overstatement to say that without MySpace I wouldn't be in the music industry following my dreams."

How did you do it, and did you spend a great deal doing demos before releasing your first songs on the Internet? Also, how did you finance your efforts? "I was fortunate enough to grow up listening to my dad talk business on the phone, all day every day, and my mum playing the piano and singing in choirs. So the two sides of my brain are in constant battle over whether I should be looking at my career from a business perspective or an artistic one. I've never had the money to spend on making demos and marketing myself. I strongly believe that if you have the talent, if you show promise and have your shizzle together at an early stage of your career, you can do so much for free. There is *always* a way of achieving something and always a way around problems; it just depends how creative and intelligent you are in negotiation. So lack of finance, I believe, is used all too easily as an excuse. Lack of capital demands greater investment of time and effort. I managed to make simple but sufficient recordings displaying my art well enough to move me to the next rung on the ladder."

How did you attract attention on MySpace and generate so much interest? Did you launch some type of self-made viral marketing campaign first, develop a website, and do a lot of research? Or did it self-generate, and if so why? "There was a mixture of initial self-made viral marketing, but essentially you need to have content to make it stick. I have the best dad in the world! We would spend hours posting a banner linking to my site on all new friend requests. I was getting up to a thousand friend requests a week. Each of their sites would then receive a banner posted on their comments, so that each of their friends would see it and enter my site and send a friend request. Genius, yet the most simple strategy in the world!

"However, this isn't nearly enough; I know many people doing that exact same thing. You need the content to back it up: the image to match the music to match the lyrics to match the blah, blah, blah, and thus the snowball is born.

Gradually it built enough momentum where I didn't have to touch the profile site. It kept steamrolling its way out of control, at one time hitting sixty thousand plays a day and for over a year I was the number one unsigned artist on MySpace in the UK."

Joe's story clearly illustrates the extraordinary reach and power that MySpace has in the industry today. All I can hope for is that everyone who reads this book can do as well as Joe in attracting huge numbers of fans.

Everybody I spoke with in the physical and digital world confirmed how important it is to get on MySpace, Facebook, and Twitter. Roslynn from MySpace gave us some great insight and tips that can help you there, and what I'll now also do is remind you about other very important websites which will provide you with the expertise, tools, widgets, and know-how to ensure your place on every major social network that you'll need. You should also know that the copyrighted music you put on the Internet can generate money for you if it's played, as long as you join SoundExchange, the nonprofit performance rights organization, and register your songs with them.

I decided to talk with Lou Plaia, the cofounder and VP of artist relations at ReverbNation. I knew Lou when he held a similar position at Atlantic Records. While there, Lou handled marketing for such artists as Kid Rock, Simple Plan, Uncle Kracker, the Trans-Siberian Orchestra, Unwritten Law, Skindred, Cold, the Click Five, Antigone Rising, O.A.R., Nonpoint, and many others.

What is the real credo of ReverbNation? "Artists use ReverbNation as their home base for approaching marketing and promotion across the Internet, and that can be anything from social networks to blogs to the artist's home page. We provide all the marketing tools that artists can use to do this. We have something called a tune pack, we have an e-mail management system, we have widgets, street team programs, a Facebook application which is the number one artist application on Facebook, digital distribution, and electronic press kits, which we call RPKs (ReverbNation Press Kits), which are really robust in their data and give the artist the power to spread their music and information pretty much anywhere. By doing that we also collect all the data on everything we do and provide real-time stats so we can show the artist, label, or manager how the music is spreading, who is listening, which fans are passing it on to their friends, and how long songs are played. We get your website visitor demographics and a whole bunch of things that are really important for you to know about your fans. The more you know about things that are going on, the easier it is to market to the fans and be more efficient and coordinated, to be honest."

So basically, by providing tools and services, ReverbNation has resolved the "oh my God, how are we going to cope, there's so much to do" problem that today's DIY artists have. Use them to help you manage and take charge of the millions of new responsibilities you have outside of performing!

Your fees seem to be fairly modest. "Most of the stuff is free, but we do have some premium services like digital distribution; or, if you reach a certain cap on your e-mail list, we have to start charging a little bit but very, very reasonably compared to other companies. In a nutshell, ReverbNation is basically the artist's marketing partner. That's what I keep telling people, not just artists but also the labels, the managers, the venues."

I mentioned how I felt the real key for bands is how to get their message out. They're learning how to get something on YouTube or MySpace, but what they need to know is, **how do they promote themselves so people want to seek them out rather than just be one of five million bands on a site?** "The thing that most artists don't seem to do is use social networks properly. I just came back from a conference where I kept stressing this. Artists think people are going to come to their MySpace page or their Facebook page and they're automatically going to become famous and sell a lot of music. But really, you have to use those places where there are eyeballs, like a billboard sign, where a fan may come to that page, or a band might come to that page, and you want to really take them to your own website and get value out of it. If you're going to give away a song, at least get an e-mail address in return."

Lou's interview gave some insight, but here is what ReverbNation has to offer in its own words. It's worth spending time reviewing their site (reverbnation.com) and considering how their tools, widgets, and services might be worthwhile for you:

- **Get more fans:** Reach more fans with a ReverbNation Profile and an arsenal of free viral marketing tools for MySpace, Facebook, Twitter, blogs, and your home page. Grow your mailing list and send them slick e-mail newsletters with FanReach, the industry-leading e-mail system trusted by more than 100,000 artists. Fan Collection Features: comprehensive artist profile, music players and widgets, apps for Facebook, FanReach e-mail system, exclusive downloads.

- **Book more gigs**: Locate venues that book artists similar to you with Gig Finder (it's free). Enter the city you want to play and you'll receive recommendations from our database of more than 100,000 venues worldwide. Use our customizable Reverb Press Kit (RPK) to send out professional booking requests and media packages. Gig tools: gig finder and Reverb Press Kits.

- **Track more stats**: The Stats Dashboard tracks who's playing your music, where they are, and which social networks they inhabit. Sync with your MySpace, Twitter, and Facebook pages and we'll track activity there as well. See what people are saying about you all over the Internet with our Buzz Tracker. Don't worry; we do all the math. Stats tools: stats and tracking, band equity score, Buzz Tracker.

- **Earn more money**: Sell your music on iTunes, Amazon, etc. and keep 100 percent of the royalties. Use the free Reverb Store to sell T-shirts, CDs, downloads, hats, and ringtones directly to fans on Facebook, MySpace, Twitter, and your home page or blog. Looking for brand deals and licensing? Yup, we do that, too, for qualified artists. Opportunities to earn money: digital distribution, the Reverb Store.

Another service that offers various support tools and widgets to help you promote your music, get airplay, and expand your fan base is Grooveshark (grooveshark.com). I spoke with Isaac Moredock, VP of communications, and he explained that they are an artist-friendly distribution platform. This is another site for you to spend some time looking through. These are some of their offerings:

- **Gain new fans**: Autoplay allows you to promote your music to the right ears. Pick one of your songs and Grooveshark will match it to music with similar fans, helping them find (and love) you.

- **Share your music**: There are a number of ways to spread your music. Grooveshark can help. Pick a song and Grooveshark will share your music on Twitter, MySpace, and other sites.

- **Show yourself off**: Create and post ads on Grooveshark that will be shown each time your music plays. It's now easier than ever to advertise your next scheduled event, an upcoming album release, or even just yourself! Make an ad that will be shown to the Grooveshark audience whenever your songs get played, for free. You deserve your own fans' attention.

- **Merchandise**: Create and manage apparel. Give your fans what they want, your merch! Design, distribute, and sell all of your custom merchandise on Grooveshark and around the web. Work with Junkytees to design and sell your merchandise and sign up for Tunipop to maximize your sales.

- **License your music**: Ensure that your music is protected. Creative Commons provides free tools that let artists easily mark their creative work with the freedoms they want it to carry. You can use Creative Commons to change your copyright terms from "All Rights Reserved" to "Some Rights Reserved."
- **Land a deal**: Offer your wares to record labels. Grooveshark's partners are hooked into ears that count: labels and licenses that turn your music up. As a Grooveshark artist, you've got direct access to YouLicense—connecting bands with producers, directors, and other suits to license your music. Don't dig? Try Pick the Band, where fans can vote for their favorite bands.

Grammy Award nominee MGMT is a band that can attribute a good deal of its initial success to a groundswell of support they garnered from social networking. I spoke with Mark Kates at Fenway Recordings who manages MGMT, the Cribs, and several other acts, and was previously at Geffen Records and Grand Royal. I know Mark from when he was a college student and was the concert rep for one of my Public Image Ltd shows. I asked him, **What is the effectiveness of Internet sites and social networks, and their importance in today's model?** "I go to MySpace. It's still an efficient destination. It's the place to go when you hear an artist's name and are curious to hear their music and find out where they are playing."

Other than having great songs, what's the next most important thing for a band? "To build their network. They should employ a Webmaster even if it's one of their friends or family, initially, to help spread the word virally and find more people who will help them deliver their message. And honestly, MGMT is really the proof of all this, I think, not forcing your way. MGMT reached people because there's a migration of kids from schools like Wesleyan to Brooklyn who got immersed in the blog world and made it possible for the information and the music to spread really quickly without anyone pushing a button. We walked into this church on the Lower East Side and there were like two hundred kids, and they knew the songs. We thought, *This is actually going to be alright.* There's nothing more meaningful than word of mouth—someone telling you that something is good. And for me, especially, there are certain people who if I hear about something, I'll ask them about it and their reaction will probably have an undue amount of influence on me, but what else do you have? You can check something out and judge it and decide how you feel about it; then, if you need more info, you've got to talk to someone who has more info than you."

Is it harder getting label support now? Does everyone need to be smarter in knowing what he or she can ask for? "It varies. You have to be prepared to do anything. Ideally the record company will spend money, but I find we really have a unique situation in every way. From my past experience, I know too much of what does and doesn't happen. Record companies get smaller every day, and they have to be able to do what makes sense for them financially. The physical business may be dying but there have been some great success stories in recent years. The labels have the same challenges and they have fewer resources to draw on. What indies and DIY may have over a major in some cases is community, and I think that could be a very good way to get results today. There are people at the majors who think that way, but many have not experienced this era as a consumer so they will need to adapt to this mind frame to appreciate what's going on."

Realizing the whole value that the Internet and social networks have in our lives today, I thought there was another topic I should address, so I asked my publicist friend Pam Workman.

Do you agree with me that you need to take advantage of the Internet and social networks, but that you should think before you tweet? "Do have a social media philosophy and do try to stick to it. I will add that some publicists are more specialized in social media than others. I am someone who believes in including social media as part of an overall PR plan, but I have seen it backfire. There have been incidents where artists tweeted about something going on in the audience when they were onstage, and unintentionally almost started a riot. So I would advise thinking before you tweet."

Booking

Now you've had several weeks to rehearse, you have a digital press kit (EPK), and you've done some great reference recordings. You have a few songs on MySpace, videos on YouTube, and can show that you have an amazing amount of traffic to your website, Twitter, and Facebook accounts. It is time to book real gigs.

You'll need to be prepared, so have all of the above materials together to forward to clubs. Review any contacts that you've made with other bands or the booking people you've met at clubs you've already played. Don't overestimate your value at this stage by thinking you're ready to play in a major venue before your model is truly tested and proven. It's not happening.

Clubs have many expenses and huge overheads. They generate money from admissions and at the bar. If you can convince them that you can bring in the crowds, they will give you a chance. Start out with small clubs. It is much better to draw seventy-five people to a club that holds fifty than to have seventy-five people come to a club that holds two hundred and fifty. Often promoters like the Bowery Presents in New York City have many venues of all sizes, and if they see you've done well in their small clubs, they will work with you and you'll be able to grow with them as your career grows.

I had a conversation with Tim McGrath, whom I met years ago when he was a booking agent at Premiere Talent and I was managing bands. Tim is the general manager of the two-thousand-seat Wellmont Theatre in Montclair, New Jersey, operated by Bowery Presents. Tim and I were reminiscing about New York City clubs in the late seventies and eighties and how bands used to have to pay to play, and labels or managers had to guarantee radio and ticket buys in order to get their acts booked. But it was also the days when the record companies had deep pockets and needed venues where they could showcase their artists. So there was a kind of understanding between the labels and venue operators, and the pay-to-play aspect was just another cost of doing business. CBGB and the punk movement broadsided the pay-to-play model. Artists and bands like Patti Smith, Talking Heads, the Ramones, and Blondie caused a sensation and drew huge crowds and for the first time, bands were able to keep the money that came in on the door.

Tim's theater is operated by the Bowery Presents, so I asked him a question that related not just to the Wellmont but also to the other Bowery facilities, like the Mercury Lounge: **I'm happy to see you guys go outside the box a little bit in your booking policy. Can you provide some perspective?** "If you were to look at the Bowery Presents websites I would bet that many of the artists playing our facilities are artists that you've never heard of. Many of them I have never heard of, either, and we've both been in the business a long time. For example, before they gained national attention, we had State Radio play here and they sold close to a thousand tickets. Also, before they broke big we had

Paramore. When we put them on sale the show sold out very quickly. There was not a lot of traditional marketing, but when you looked at the show that night, the audience was made up of four little girls and their mom here, four little girls and their mom there. Those kids have their own network. It was like putting a match on gasoline. Just boom! They're networking, they're texting, and it's a totally different world and we're lucky to be included. We see it. Do we totally get it? No, but do we know we need it? Absolutely.

"I remember when I was working at House of Blues I had a conversation with our talent buyer Jeff Trisler about how one day we would put on a show and sell it out just by using e-mail blasts and not have to do any other advertising. The fact is, with bands like Paramore and State Radio, that's exactly what's happened. These bands put together their own networks of thousands of people. Another fact that's interesting to think about is that a label probably isn't interested until an artist has taken their own project by themselves to a Twitter/Facebook page and has around five thousand friends; that's when a label and promoters are going to take notice of them. It's not like the old days, not at all. So State Radio and Paramore were perfect examples of what's happening today."

To get some additional booking tips from a promoter's perspective, I spoke with my old friend Greg Benedetti, a marketing expert who has served as a marketing director for Live Nation, the Electric Factory, BRE Presents, CBS Television Group, and other firms, working on hundreds of events that included U2's Zoo TV stadium tour and others. **What's the best way for a group to generate a promoter's attention today? Should they call, e-mail, invite you to gigs; send you CDs, downloads, and press kits, or do you solely rely on agents?** "First of all, the group has to be generating a buzz and show that they are happening in the marketplace. Then if they want to send us materials, CDs, downloads, press kits, or invitations to get my attention they have to do all of the above and do it better than anybody else. Do it as creatively as they can while utilizing all of the technology that's out there.

"If somebody sends me a flimsy color photo of themselves folded in half and tells me that's their bio, I'm not very impressed. Put some imagination behind it, a little creativity behind your presentation (your presentation is the name of the game for everything; it doesn't apply just to music). The music business is known as being a place for artists and creativity, so you have to shine and really express that kind of artistry and creativity when you're presenting yourself to people you want to promote you."

How important are previous relationships in regard to promoters taking a chance on new bands? "Very important. A big part of the game is the relationship that a promoter has with the agent or the manager of the artist. A lot of these big artists have agencies that are always trying to cultivate new talent, too, because they know that their marquee artists may be at the point in their career where they're not going to be working as much, or they're too old, or maybe not as interested in going out on tour and maybe not as viable as they used to be, so they're trying to cultivate more new talent."

As a marketing expert, give young bands some advice to maximize their tour development. "There are all kinds of opportunities, but the biggest advice is to make sure you have your house in order. You have your image, your branding, all in line and ready to go, so that when you hand the promoter your package they can efficiently maximize your press and promotion without having to spend hours of their own time developing materials on your behalf. You should also know who the players are in the game: remember, you're trying to be part of the team, so read the trades, check out who the movers and shakers are in your own backyard, and begin networking there. A lot of bands come into our venues with the attitude that they are the greatest band in the world, but they don't know the business. And you may be able to succeed on your own, but understand the industry: there are a lot of old-school and traditional people who still hold the cards, and it's best to have them as friends.

"Another point is to really take control of your own destiny. Bands need to understand that nobody else is going to do it for them anymore. In the old days they said, "Oh, we got a record deal," and the record company was in a position to cater to them, pamper them, hold their hands, and take them around. It isn't happening anymore! I mean the tail is wagging the dog because the record companies completely missed the boat on the whole digital revolution, and they're still trying to catch the boat before it's too late. Like it or not, many people get their music from iTunes or Rhapsody, file sharing, video games—whatever it is; that's how people find out. There are way too many options and outlets. It's kind of underground like when we were growing up. It's an underground out there, but it's the Internet and it's not limited anymore. People have become 'stars' just by posting videos on YouTube.

"It's a viral thing and I see more and more of it every day. You kind of have to get involved yourself and then you begin to see. It crosses all kinds of boundaries and all generations. Today you can appeal to a lot of different types of people through social networking, people you'd never imagine would be part of it."

Now that you've heard from the horses' mouths how it is up to you to get your name out there and develop your following, and you believe the time is right and you've taken all of the steps, go out there to try to get some gigs. Here are a few simple tips. Find the contact information for each club and the booker's name, then call, e-mail, do whatever you need to get hold of them. Arrange to meet with them or forward materials as they direct. Have a concise fifteen- to thirty-second pitch as to why they should book you, and at this stage, be willing to take any slot they offer as long as you feel you have enough time to properly put the word out so you can pack the house. You may need to be somewhat persistent, as there are probably a hundred other bands trying to get them at any given moment and they are also tied up with the shows they have in progress. If your presentation is convincing, you will get booked.

Go to sites like Indie on the Move (indieonthemove.com) for lists and ratings of clubs in your area. Also check out GigMasters (gigmasters.com), RethinkPopMusic (rethinkpopmusic.com), Gigleader (gigleader.com), and Owngig (owngig.com).

Obviously you'll begin booking gigs locally. My local venue for up-and-coming bands is New Jersey's Tierney's Tavern. Tierney's is the oldest bar in Montclair and it has a great one-hundred-plus-capacity venue upstairs. Over the years they have booked a huge assortment of bands, including rockabilly legend Robert Gordon and Black 47. Most recently they hosted the three-day Boro 6 Indie Music Fest, which featured twenty New York metropolitan area bands. I went to see Billy Tierney, who owns the establishment with his brothers, and asked him about his booking policy.

How do you go about booking the bands to play here? "There are a few different ways I would do it. A big one is word of mouth. Some of my customers who I believe have good musical taste tell me about bands that they like, so I find out where the bands are playing and go out and see them. I check the vibe and see what kind of business they are doing at their gigs, and see if they are the kind of people I would want in my place. If I like the group, I discreetly approach them and ask them if they would like to play at my place, and how much money they would need. Another way is for bands to contact us directly and drop off some press, a CD, their website info, or whatever other materials they have. But I always prefer to go see a band if I can, because you can get sold a bill of goods and they don't bring anybody in."

Do you pay the bands? "For bands that come to us, unless I know that they are established and have a strong audience, I don't give guarantees. But if they bring in a lot of people, I will give them 100 percent of the door. I know for a fact that a lot of other places don't pay bands or deal with them fairly, but it's my belief that if you can bring in a lot of people, you deserve your take. We also let the bands dictate, to a point, the admission charge. If their fans are only going to pay five dollars, then so be it, that's all they're going to make. If they want to charge fifteen dollars and they don't think their fans are going to be scared away, then I let them charge fifteen dollars."

Do you charge the bands anything for sound and lights or bar tab? "No, I don't charge them anything. I supply the sound and lights for them to operate themselves, so they need to bring in their own sound and lights people. We let the band drink for free because we don't provide catering, but there is food available for them to buy downstairs if they want it. We're pretty liberal about it, especially at the end of the night!"

So you're doing it right, then? "Exactly. But sometimes with other venues, bands have told me the whole money issue becomes confrontational, and it shouldn't be. I want them to bring their friends in and I want them as customers, so I'm happy that they're able to make money from admissions charged at the door."

On shows for which you've provided bands with guaranteed fees, do you do the promotion? "I do all the listings in the newspapers and any other free stuff, including our website and some blogs. If it's far enough in advance, I'll get one of my liquor companies to put up a banner, and sometimes, if it ties in with one of their campaigns, I'll get the show mentioned in radio spots that the liquor companies do. Other than that, we'll help the band put flyers and posters up anyplace they want. But it's really important that the band takes steps to actively promote their shows by alerting their fans. It's their career, after all."

Billy is a special guy, one of the good ones, and I hope you will meet people like him as you make contact with clubs in your region. But you'll also run into some people who aren't as nice. Don't take it personally. You need to persevere and just get your band out there, get as much work as you can and as much visibility.

That said, your first gigs will probably be on Monday or Tuesday nights when business is traditionally slow. But if you can get your fans out, you'll be able to get better gigs, and before long you'll be able to pick the shows that you play. As soon as you have confirmed this first show, alert your fans, call other venues, and try to book a second show a week or two later. It should be easier because you can tell them that you're already booked somewhere else.

C. T. of Tech-9 Music and Gotham Rocks says, "In every region, when you go from being a band in your garage to being a band that can draw a hundred-plus people, a lot of opportunities open up, because you get a chance to support national acts in your local venues. We're lucky being in New York City because there is a lot of music industry here. I remember one of the bands I was in played a shitty little show at a lounge that holds about fifty people, but the Evanescence guitar player and drummer and the manager of Crossfade saw us play and were like, "Oh, you guys are great." And you get those opportunities when you play live and can draw people to your shows; that's when people start taking notice of you."

C. T.'s independent Gotham Rocks promotes modern/hard rock bands and produces shows in New York City at Live Nation's Gramercy Theatre and other venues, with plans to produce tour packages that will include many unsigned bands. If your band fits within this genre, make sure you contact them at gothamrocks.net.

What is Gotham Rocks? "Gotham Rocks is a modern rock showcase series that we do in New York City. We work with local and regional venues as well as with Live Nation and AEG Live to put on shows, and our focus is on promoting up-and-coming artists, be they local artists who are looking to move to a regional level, regional artists who are looking to move to a national level, or national artists who are looking to get exposure to our market for the right demographic of fan. What we do is try to incentivize the bands by helping them out and putting them on in front of relevant industries, so we bring down industry judges and award prizes at each showcase. We give away endorsements with DR Strings and Spector basses; we work with Godin, Marshall, and Fryette amps. Every band that plays a Gotham Rocks show gets an endorsement from Fryette, which was formerly VHT Amplification. We have the artist reps from DR Strings who come down and they choose their favorite band in each showcase to award a DR Strings endorsement to. We also work with marketing companies like Music Submit and media companies like Fearless Music to get prizes or to get more exposure for the bands that play our shows."

You're not necessarily a promoter in the classic sense that you pay bands a guarantee to do these shows. "We rarely give guarantees because of the endorsements and prizes. It's not to say that we don't, but we expect bands to draw. So we're happy to pay the bands very well for their draw, but it's not enough to say, 'Yeah, we usually draw this and that, like one hundred to two hundred people.' They come play a show and we'll pay them based on what they draw, so the more people they draw, the more money they're going to make. They'll make more than their guarantee, assuming that the guarantee is reasonable, if they, as a band, promote the show and bring a lot of people."

And how do you work with bands to really maximize their exposure in your shows? "We work with them with web flyers, traditional flyers. We make sure we do radio promo and we coordinate that promo with the bands, and in a lot of cases we do Internet stuff on Facebook and MySpace and we make sure the band is listing the show as a Gotham Rocks showcase. We make sure we're one of their friends on MySpace. On Facebook we create the invitations, and we'll create the event and we'll make sure that members of the band are administrators so they can actually invite all their friends to the show on Facebook. We do e-mail lists; we ask the bands if they have any shows coming up or are going on radio or anything like that so we can promote that as well. Usually, because of the nature of these showcases and because we have all these prizes, the bands know coming in that it's not your average show, so they're usually promoting it on their own anyway."

How have these bands generated a following? "They're great at what they do, and you got to have that, and this comes from my own experience. I've seen a lot of bands that are really great, and all the best bands that I've played with or presented in the last couple of years all play live. They tour regionally, at least. All the bands that have the best live performances, and typically the only bands that have any kind of regional draw outside their friends, family, and fans in their local town or city, are bands that tour within driving distance on weekends and sometimes during the week; and there's this network of those bands that exists. Everybody knows each other. They're under the major label radar but they are on the regional radar. A lot of the regional venues know all the same bands, they book them and they know the quality of what they're getting. So I think the way to do it certainly is to maximize your presence on the Internet. Facebook gets better results for bands and Gotham Rocks as promoters than radio promo does. We've hired radio promoters, we've done hard flyers with street teams, and we never get as many people to a show as we do by inviting them on the Internet. Some bands create personal pages, or you just do it as an individual. Certainly on a local level, on your own home turf, the best way is to reach out in a personal way, and that's what I think Facebook really provides. There's also YouTube, Twitter and MySpace, but for us, it's more about Facebook."

Another Show Essential

Design and create one or two merchandise items with your logo to sell at your shows. They are great promotion tools, your fans will want them, and they generate money for you.

Merchandise is a major part of the revenue model for all artists today. ReverbNation and several of the web-based services I've already mentioned can help you design and manufacture T-shirts, hats, posters, and other merchandise items, as well as design the artwork and manufacture your CDs and download cards. All of this can be ordered in quantities to suit your demands.

Dave Lory says, "I was recently on tour with Semi Precious Weapons, who were opening up for Lady Gaga on her sold-out tour. During every show the band mentioned from the stage that after they performed, they would be at the merchandise table. They did merchandise that was smart. They created a T-shirt that quoted a line from one of their songs, saying 'I CAN'T PAY MY RENT, BUT I'M FUCKING GORGEOUS.' Everybody who worked on tour within the first week said, 'We got to get one of those T-shirts.' So you start getting people to wear these things, and it's like the old Metallica shirt: the shirt that just says METALLICA is still the best-selling shirt. It's simple; an iconic logo."

To sum up:

- You've booked a couple of shows and the first one is in three weeks
- You have a tight, well-rehearsed set of ten songs and you have five others that you can use for encores or however else if need be
- You've arranged to have a couple of brilliant merchandise items produced that you can sell at the gigs
- You've got a big buzz on the social networks
- You've enlisted friends and fans to post flyers all over town
- You even have two people to help you with production and equipment

To ensure it all goes well, if possible, get a contract or e-mail confirmation for the performance that lists date, time, and location of the show; set length; your payment (if any) and potential fees that may be required for sound, lights, and equipment. Get all contact phone numbers and e-mails, and it is always good to get the bar phone number in case you have any emergencies. Also make sure that you've discussed hospitality, dressing rooms, and guest lists, and if possible, get a written confirmation from the club that specifically spells this out, or you may find yourself using a basement staircase for a dressing room and stuck with a bar tab for simple things like bottled water that's more than you earned for the evening. Later in your career, you will have full contracts and riders that will cover all of your specific needs (including having the brown M&M's removed), but at this stage, be happy if you get a few drink tickets and any guest list at all.

Staff Up

" A friend of the band could possibly take on the role of tour manager, but they need to understand that the bottom line is that the tour manager represents the band's business—they are not there just to mix drinks."

—Alia Dann-Swift, tour and production manager

Make sure you designate one person in the band to act as a tour manager. They'll need to contact the club's sound and lighting engineers and stage manager to confirm load-in times, sound check, gear storage, and any other technical and logistical procedures you will have to follow on the day of show. Provide everyone with a copy of your stage plot/setup that shows how many people are in the band, how many microphones and monitors you require, and how the gear is laid out. But be prepared for them to laugh and tell you there is a basic house setup for sound and lights and that's what you get to work with! Also find out if you can sell your merchandise yourself or does the club sell it for you (and do they take a percentage of sales?) If they sell for you, be prepared for them to charge 20 to 35 percent or more of your gross sales, and understand you may have no choice. Jeff Beck's manager, Harvey Goldsmith, led a revolt in the summer of 2010 against the exorbitant fees venues were charging for selling Jeff's merchandise but for now you'll have to bite the bullet. If you are lucky enough to play a club or venue which lets you sell on your own you may still have to pay a fee. Make sure to enlist a couple of friends, bring a small folding table so you can set up a place to sell from, and keep an inventory and accurate sales records. Also make sure you start a sign-up sheet so you can get e-mail addresses from the people you sell to. Remember, it's important to get members of your band to come to the table and meet and greet the fans after the show. This works wonders; it helps instill fan loyalty and gets them to buy your products.

Have any of your friends or fans asked if they could be your roadie? Have you met any roadies at the gigs you've gone to? It's important that you have one or two people who can be at the side of the stage to help you with any tech or equipment situations that could arise during your performance, and mark my word, they do. Use your best recruiting skills and add these people to your team ASAP. Have them come to your rehearsals so they can see you in action, learn about your gear and your needs; and you can also test their abilities. At this stage, teaching a novice to do a few simple things is better than nothing.

If you have two helpers, designate one to concentrate on the drummer and backline gear and the other to deal with your front men, mic cords, guitar leads, and if need be, crowd control. Teach them how to set up and break down your gear and move it on and off the stage so you don't have to do it yourself in front of an audience. It makes your band seem much more professional to the crowd. Set up a practice day in the rehearsal studio where you intentionally make things go wrong and see if your crew can deal with any crisis that may occur while the band continues to play. Remember, even if you break a string, a mic goes dead, or a cymbal falls down, the show must go on without interruption.

In the days leading up to the gig, make sure you contact the club to confirm times and to discuss promotion. Decide how you're going to get your band and gear to the club. Take delivery of your merchandise from the manufacturer. Make sure all of your equipment is working and you have plenty of spare drumheads, strings, picks, and other essentials. Alert fans and the media; get out an e-mail blast, post on Facebook and Twitter, and figure out what you're going to wear onstage.

Show Day: Load-In

Make sure you arrive at the venue a few minutes before your scheduled load-in time. Have your designated tour manager go in first to see if the club is ready for you. He should find the house manager, stage manager, soundman, and lighting director and let them know the band has arrived and ask if you can load in. (Please note, in a small club there may only be a house manager and you may have to run the sound and lights yourself. So remember, do your homework, call the club in advance, and make sure you're prepared.) Your tour manager should also find out if the band can use the dressing room if there is one.

Don't get upset if you have to sit around waiting because the headliner's sound check is running a half hour late. When instructed to do so, begin loading-in your gear and follow the stage manager's instruction as to setting up onstage. Have your crew work with him in arranging your gear according to your stage plot. Take into account that the lighting may be preset for the headliner.

Soundcheck

While you are loading in and setting up, your tour manager should discuss your mic plot with the soundman. But remember, in small clubs you may be doing the sound yourself, so it's best that during the rehearsals, either one of you knows how to do presets on a small board or that you have a friend who can learn to set up your mics and run the PA. Generally, PAs in small clubs are very simple, with only 8 × 2. Take your positions onstage once your tour manager gives you the go-ahead, and have your crew available to move or adjust any gear if necessary. Since your tour manager for now is also one of your bandmates, he or she should take their position onstage as well. Be patient, keep calm, and follow the soundman's instructions.

The soundman will test each mic's volume and EQ one at a time. Speak up if you need any adjustment, but the most important thing is that you concentrate on the monitor mix (the sound you hear onstage). Once the monitor sound is acceptable, your tour manager should get off the stage and listen to the house mix and politely ask for adjustments as needed. At this time you should also ask the lighting director if he or she could set a few of the lights for you (keeping in mind that most are already preset by the headliner). Bring your own color gels if you have some special color preferences. When you are finished with your technical checks, thank everyone for helping you and give them a T-shirt or some other piece of swag to show your appreciation. Having the club's crew on your side goes a long way in making your presentation better. Making friends prior to your performance works wonders.

Show Time

If for some reason you're not able to get a sound check, make sure you have tuned your instruments before you take the stage. Introduce yourself and be friendly to the stage crew and venue staff regardless of their attitudes. Make sure everyone has a written set list and something to drink and a few towels onstage. Remember to be tight, be concise, and don't waffle around. If you want to grab your audience from the get-go, come out with two guitars blazing rather than standing around for fifteen minutes tuning up and fidgeting with cables. Now it's time. Do it!

Open up your set with an up-tempo song. It will light a fire in the fans you already have which will spread through the rest of the audience. Follow up right away with a second one just as strong. Now you should have won everyone over. At this point, go ahead and introduce yourself, tell them about your merchandise for sale, and go into your next song. Your last song should be a killer. Don't hold back. Rock the house and leave your fans wanting more. Sweep them off their feet with your music and your presentation. If you're passionate, practiced, and organized, you will quickly get into the groove, your fans will catch on, and it will happen. Remember the tips I've given you about your stage show and, with a little luck, it should all go well.

After the show, make sure the gear gets broken down and packed up. If you're on a bill with other bands, go listen to them. Show your support. A few of the band members should go into the house and start interacting with the fans. Walk over to the merchandise table, sign autographs, get people's e-mail addresses for all of your contact lists, and mingle. You never know who is out in the crowd, and it's important that you do the meet and greet for both your fan base and the career opportunities that will arise.

Press On

Now that you've got the hang of it, concentrate on doing a string of gigs, because you will get better every time. Keep up daily communication with your core fans on Twitter, Facebook, your own website, other social networks, and blogs. By gig ten, your world should change. All kinds of offers and all types of people have come out of the woodwork—some good, some not so good. You are starting to make real noise in your region. By this time you might actually be getting paid for your shows, usually a percentage of the door. If so, it is smart to assign someone to count people as they come into the club. Remember, you should also still be selling your merchandise and actively interacting with your fans.

Things are starting to happen. Collective data from your website and reports from the suppliers and services that you use, like Sonicbids and Nimbit, now show you have a fan base of more than one thousand and you're getting offered good gigs within a fifty-mile radius of home. You must continue to rehearse on a steady basis and most of all explore new gig options. Book your band in colleges, enter competitions offered by radio stations and Battles of the Bands, and try your damnedest to get onto second stages at festivals.

Have a look at ArtistForce (artistforce.com), GigNation (gignation. com), GigMasters (gigmasters.com), and Band Promote (bandpromote.com). These services will help you book your band in clubs and venues across the United States, help coordinate your tours, and maximize your exposure via showcases and appearances at music industry conferences and events. Details regarding payment structures, advice on terms and conditions of engagements, as well as sample appearance contracts and contract riders are included in later chapters and the Appendix. You should also pick up Martin Atkin's *Tour:Smart* (available at Barnes and Noble) for detailed touring tips.

Right now you should do some research and invest in local Internet marketing. Facebook, Google, MySpace, and Grooveshark all offer concise demographic marketing plans that allow you to pinpoint your fan base by musical taste, age, and gender. Grooveshark is especially geared toward artists, according to Isaac Moredock. "With Grooveshark's model, you can target a location where you are going to be playing in the next few months, take out a display ad that will promote your band, and offer your music to fans of bands you believe sound similar or have the same demographic that you want, and then link them to your event page." As mentioned before, Grooveshark offers widgets, streaming music, and other support systems that will help you maximize your visibility and track your sales, fan base, and progress along the way.

You might also want to check out Greg Rollett's Gen-Y Rock Stars

(GenYrockstars.com) blog, which offers free resource guides that will help you with all of this. I asked Greg, because he has an extraordinary understanding of available Internet tools and is an avid proponent of the DIY movement, **What are the most important tools for management of your DIY efforts?** "For me the two biggest resources are an e-mail management system and a content management system. The two I recommend are AWeber for e-mail and WordPress for content management. There are tons of other choices for e-mail management, from FanBridge to ReverbNation to iContact, that will do the job as well. What you need to do is develop a list of people who are interested in your music, people who you can communicate with regularly, and send them offers for products. The next level is to segment this list into geographic regions, spending habits, and other criteria so that you can really grow your business.

"Having a content management system allows you to get content online quickly. WordPress is currently leagues ahead of the pack in terms of value and compatibility. They have plug-ins and extensions that can help you score better on search engine optimization, which maximizes your volume and quality of web traffic; add photos from Flickr; energize your website; turn your site into a fan club or membership platform; post blogs; showcase events; bring in video; and more. The best part is that WordPress and many of the plug-ins are open source and freely available. Every artist we work with is now using the Word-Press platform and posting content on a regular basis."

Consistently, throughout this entire process, you should be capitalizing on the contacts that you make; distributing flyers and putting up posters in shops, schools, and wherever you can throughout your community; contacting local press and media to make sure that the club lists your shows in their daily or weekly calendars and, if need be, doing it yourself. You should also make sure to call the assignment editors at your local radio and TV stations, as well as all of the local newspaper and print media, and invite them to your performances. At this stage it's best to offer the press free admission even if you have to buy tickets for them.

Don't be in a rush to sign contracts with any would-be managers or agents whom you meet in a club after one of your shows. Be polite, thank them for coming, seem excited by meeting them, and listen to what they say and may offer you. Take their cards and information and tell them you will be in contact. As soon as you can, Google them or ask around and find out who they are.

The worst thing you can do at this point in your career is sign a contract with someone to manage you, produce you, or book you unless that person has a proven track record, is known to the other bands you work with, and is not pushing you to sign any agreement without you first taking it to a lawyer. Too many bands have signed bad deals with unscrupulous record labels, agents, producers, and managers in bars, and they have lived to regret it. Patience is a virtue. Remember, your career is your life. Unfortunately, overnight success sometimes takes five years, but if everything is starting to happen, do it the right way, not the wrong way. And today more than ever, you are in the driver's seat when it comes to selecting the right way. By being prepared; by referring to the checklist we discussed earlier; and by using web tools, research, and conversations with other bands, you can take the time to plot a course and reserve your decisions on selecting the right people and the right companies to work with.

I understand how, at this stage in your career, there are so many overwhelming things going on outside of playing, so many issues you have to tend to, that the idea of having a support team of professionals sounds wonderful. Henley Halem, president and founder of HRH Music Group and manager of Kid Cudi, DJ Green Lantern, and others, says, "Be original, follow your dreams, master your craft, and focus on going one step at a time rather than trying to get to the top of the mountain as fast as possible." I totally agree with Henley. Don't rush it! I will explain in the following chapters how your support team members fit in, what they do, and how to choose them.

Live Recording

You may still be thinking about doing a demo recording, but first consider doing a live recording. Investing in a demo recording, which we have discussed, is not as important as it used to be, especially if your band has been getting an extraordinary reaction to its live gigs.

What do you want from a demo? Do you want it as a tool to get a record deal? Do you want something to offer to your fans? Do you want it for promotion to help you get gigs and press? To many of you, a studio is an unknown and sterile environment, so at this stage in your career, I believe you will get a much better result by doing a professional live recording. You should hire a company like Bob Miller Recording and Production Services (bobdigital.com) who provide on-location audio production via mobile trucks and various portable packages. Keep in mind that you should still be building your home studio, as it will be your laboratory for developing your music, recording song demos or references, and who knows, at some point in the future, maybe even some master-quality tracks. But for now, let's look at what a live recording with a professional studio engineer can do for your career, and how to go about it.

I interviewed Bob Miller to get his take on the subject. When I first met Bob, I was managing Public Image Ltd and had just set up a spec deal with the owners of Park South Studios in New York City for PiL to record a new album. Bob was the assistant engineer at the time and after a few sessions, the band asked me to get the studio to let Bob take over as the primary engineer. They liked working with him so much that we took him on the road with us and had him take care of all of our sound needs. He has never been afraid to push the envelope. The kind of shows we were doing in arenas and large ballrooms necessitated that we had sound that was as progressive as the music that the band was playing. Bob came up with an idea that really worked. He called it B-EFX, a strong bass reinforcement that rumbled the venue and really amped up the crowd. The band's relationship with Bob developed very well, and later he even coproduced as well as engineered some of PiL's music. Since then, Bob has set up his own company, built a beautiful remote truck, and has kept up with the times, working with all types of artists both in studio and on location as an engineer and a producer.

How difficult is it to arrange a location recording? "If it's planned correctly, location recording can be relatively simple. The top priority is to arrange a meeting with the artist or group to discuss the recording project and find out what their end-product concept is and what their expectations are. From there, you'll decide what equipment will be required. If you're using a remote truck, in most cases you'll have everything you need on board including mics, cables, direct boxes, splitters, snakes, outboard gear, mixers, monitors, tape machines, or hard drives, depending on individual needs and crew. You can also use a portable system that goes straight to computer. This method is used widely and can be very cost-effective. Portable systems may not offer as many bells and whistles as a remote truck, but in the hands of an experienced engineer, the end product can be remarkable."

Since we are discussing performances in smaller venues, I asked, **Is it easy to record in a club?** "Absolutely! Keep in mind that the venue itself plays a critical role. The club scene has its own set of problems from the size of the stage, the overall acoustics, and available equipment. It's not that different from studio recording once you've sorted out the venue's technical idiosyncrasies, like monitors that are too loud and cause isolation problems with vocals and instruments. In-ear monitoring can help a lot to reduce this bleed-through and make it easier for overdubbing later. Instruments and even drum kits must be tuned precisely. The amount of experience the artist or group has with doing live recordings can also be a huge factor. Having a good rapport with the artists and their crew also helps. You don't have to be like an army drill sergeant, but it's important for you to establish the ground rules to get the best recordings and save money by doing everything right the first time."

Is recording disruptive to the audience, for the venue, and for the band? "That depends on what you mean by disruptive. Generally, a well-planned live recording session is seamless. The audience is mostly unaware that anything is being recorded, unless you've told them you were doing a live recording or shooting a video at the same time. On the other hand, the artists themselves can feel the pressure to deliver that perfect performance. It keeps them on their toes!"

Is it expensive? "Live recording sessions, compared to professional studio recordings, are usually less expensive. A lot depends on the specifics of the venue. For the most part, when you're going live, the artist or group has one shot to perform—you're not going to retake any tracks or do anything over again, so you're not tying up a studio for hours or days on end, spending tons of money. The other costs, like mixing, mastering, and editing, are basically the same. If you plan ahead for a live recording session on location, you can get a lot accomplished at a lower cost. Basically, it costs anywhere from three thousand dollars and up, depending on what is involved after the recording—mixing, editing, mastering. But please keep in mind that you'll end up with a finished master ready for CD. The only extra expense would be for replication, packaging, and artwork."

What quality recording can a band expect? "It's exactly the same audio quality you'd get from a studio, with more energy. The key is that live recordings get the band's adrenaline going, so you'll often capture that extra little kick from playing live."

Can I overdub and mix later? "In many cases, yes. But preproduction planning with the group before the actual session is crucial for best results. It's up to the recording team to ensure that the equipment is set up correctly and that everybody is on the same page—the band, management, and technicians.

"Working within the limits of the venue itself is another factor. If the stage is large enough, setup will be much easier for balancing sound levels, setting mics, monitors, etc. In the hands of a skilled engineer, mixing and post-editing can bring out the magic in nearly any recording. Overdubbing should be possible if you've planned ahead. The idea, of course, is to get everything right from the beginning, so you won't need to add much in the mixing suite."

Can I film, too, and use a sound feed? "Of course. With nonlinear video postproduction, it's pretty simple. You just have to make sure that one camera gets the audio feed and the other cameras use their onboard mics. It's even better if all cameras get direct audio feed. Once your video is in the post stage, all footage can be synchronized with the direct audio feed. So you've got great audio and video unless—here's the kicker—if you've done any overdubs in the audio post stage that are not exactly in sync with original video, some compensating will be necessary."

Should a band consider doing a live recording instead of a traditional demo? "In my opinion, record companies aren't really listening to demos anymore, and are more interested in hearing finished recordings. Personally, I think a band would be much better off with a live recording for three reasons. First, a live recording says you're a real band that can perform before an audience. This separates you from other bands that must rely on the studio to get their special sound. Second, the relative economy of a live recording, compared to spending the extra money for a recording studio, can save the band a bundle. Third, you've got the added value of an actual live recording instead of just a demo."

I also posed the demo-versus-live-recording question to managers, labels, and record distributors. Peter Wright, president and founder of Virtual Label and a key force for the last three decades in independent record distribution, is a man whose opinion I value tremendously. **I asked if he agreed.** "Yes, live recording is a good way to go, and I also believe that there is no reason for anybody to be spending a lot of money recording a record anymore."

Another advantage to recording live is you can turn the show into something special. I suggest, when you decide the time is right, that you carefully choose where you want to perform and record, then work with the venue to make the whole show into a one-time special event. The event itself has many benefits. You can turn it into a huge marketing tool that will attract and instill passion in your fans, who would want to be there to be part of your history. The recording will capture the excitement of your performance and the roar of the crowd, who might also share it on their Facebook and MySpace pages and report it to other sites like Big Live (biglive.com), a social networking platform that broadcasts filmed concerts of emerging and unsigned bands on the web. Live recording is not a huge investment, and using your keen ability and the contacts you've now acquired, you might even find some corporate sponsors to help underwrite the costs. Disc Makers, TuneCore, ReverbNation and other services can manufacture and package the CDs, DVDs, vinyl, and download cards for you. You could then release the recordings and even filmed segments and sell them or give them away as a premium to your fans at gigs, via your website, or through online distributors like Virtual Label, CD Baby, Amazon, and iTunes.

Remember one thing: you can't take advantage of your fans and sell them crap. So if you are going to offer your music for sale, make sure you take the time to do it right. If your fans feel you're ripping them off, they'll leave you quickly for the next pretty face.

The MODEL HAS CHANGED

The most important thing an artist must do is have great music, an individual look, and a vision, so that branding can happen organically.

—Emma Quigley, senior marketing executive, EMI

CHAPTER SPOTLIGHT

Band as Brand • The 360 Deal • Proposal for a 360 Deal

Band as Brand

Today's revenue streams greatly differ from those of the past. Traditionally, publishing and recording were at the top of the income list, with touring, merchandise, and sponsorships/endorsements completing the model. The only exceptions were mega-acts. The Rolling Stones, U2, Bruce Springsteen, Madonna, and a few others consistently had tour grosses in excess of $100 million, with additional millions generated from concert merchandise sales.

Some of the groups have also earned substantial funds for themselves and/or their favorite charities by teaming up with major companies, like when the Rolling Stones endorsed the Mercedes-Benz R-Class, and Sting endorsed Jaguar. Other artists have launched successful fashion lines. Diddy's Sean John, Madonna's H&M collection, and Miley Cyrus's Disney-branded products each generate millions of dollars in ancillary income. It is conceivable some of these revenues might, in the near future, exceed income the artists receive from recordings and publishing. All of these performers have one thing in common: they are all established global brands.

When creating your brand, remember that you are also judged on the products you create. So to be successful you need to provide superior or unique products that create, attract, and excite loyal followers. So the image, perception, and actual products are the vehicles to do this. Remember, just a good idea and brand awareness in themselves do not guarantee success. You have to convince the public and ignite their loyalty to you with the products you create.

To get clarification on this whole idea of the band as a brand, I interviewed several people, the first being Emma Quigley, a senior marketing executive at EMI Music who has also held senior marketing positions at 19 Entertainment (*American Idol*, the Spice Girls, etc.), Universal Music Group, and was one of the key people behind the marketing of U2's *Pop* CD and PopMart tour. Obviously it is still about charismatic artists and having great songs, but **what do acts really need to do to get noticed by a major label and market themselves? Do they need to recognize themselves as a *brand*?** "This could be a very short or long answer, depending on what you're looking for. Basically there are a few things that are important, and it can differ per genre:

"Great songs: anything that will be embraced by radio. Years of artist development is a luxury very few labels can afford, so traction at radio, or the potential thereof, is the real door opener.

"Individual look: if an artist has a unique look, something the kids can aspire to, makes them stand out from the crowd, coupled with the above, you're already ahead of the game: think Lady Gaga, Gwen Stefani, Madonna—who's been keeping it fresh for twenty-plus years—the Killers, the Strokes, U2, Bob Marley, Bjork, Nirvana, Eminem . . . all very different artists, but they are each unique without it ever being contrived.

"Vision: branding has to happen organically; if you try to force it too early it can backfire: think Jessica Simpson. . . . Artists should stay true to who they are but should be very clear from the get-go about what they want. Performing is a small part of what is required from any artist. . . . Exhaustive rounds of promotion, styling, photo shoots, and handing your career over to the professionals are all part of what you can expect once you sign to a major label."

To go deeper into this subject matter, I went to Joshua Simons, the cofounder and president of corporate strategy at itsBANG, the new multiplatform television, Internet, and mobile network that is a true paradigm shifter and the ultimate music commerce destination. Joshua is one of the creators of music sponsorship and branding, going back to his days with Jay Coleman at Rockbill, where they revolutionized the industry by putting the Rolling Stones with Jovan Cosmetics and Michael Jackson with Pepsi.

I asked Joshua to explain his vision of branding. "Music artists need to be able to creatively present their talent, music, image, attitude, emotion, and point of view smartly packaged into one cohesive brand position that presents an original personal experience that is theirs to own, control, and grow over time."

I asked him for some examples of successful models. "Some popular music artists like the Rolling Stones, KISS, Alice Cooper, and U2, along with more recent contemporary talents like Lady Gaga, have packaged themselves with smart, creative, and imaginative original expression that clearly put each of them each into a class all to themselves. And by accomplishing this, they each have won the hearts, minds, and pocketbooks of millions of fans worldwide."

Why and how did it work for them? "What has worked for them is that they learned from the very start how to craft a brand name, style, and position that would establish a clear point of differentiation from their contemporaries. They knew that to be truly successful, they had to produce and market a credible product—*themselves*—to be seen as an 'original' music brand. This required more than just becoming an original music artist who leads, not follows. It takes soul-searching determination to find out what your band has that nobody else has and then package it so it becomes recognized, accessible, and highly respected.

"The qualities these artists built into their brands directly linked to the values of the target market that they engaged. One needs to understand that target market audiences (music fans) place emphasis on different musical talents based on the range of skills related to their performance and production, while other target market audiences might be approached with an emphasis on the music artist's personality or character. It might also be personal qualities that they exhibit, or connections with other artists that they resemble or have been influenced by, that already have strong brand recognition, or a narrative or history associated with their life and experience that is relevant to music fans' own personal experience. It is important to look at branding from many different sides before one decides which road to embark upon."

So how do you do this today, and where do you start? Here is a short list to begin planning your band/brand development strategy:

- How do you describe your music, sound, and performance?
- Does anyone else have what you are presenting to the music-buying public?
- What will be the reaction on Yahoo, YouTube, and MySpace? Will you get thousands of hits?
- What will radio think of your music? Will they like it, understand it, and embrace it?
- What will a music fan think of your music? Will they like it, understand it, and embrace it?
- Does the name you're choosing for your band mean anything now? Will it have relevance in the future?
- What music niche are you looking to enter or possibly own if you're the first to be doing this?
- What are you going to do to get your brand name presented to the consuming public? Are you releasing physical CDs or DVDs? Are you going viral? Do you have a fan club?

Key Items to Know

Creating an attractive brand for your music is one of the most important marketing elements to help gain paying and loyal customers. A bland brand means no sales, and the wrong brand can be a disaster. With a great brand that fits your music image perfectly, your band can soar. But what is a good brand? Is it a nice website? Is it the level of quality in your music? Is it just a catchy name?

It's all that and more. It's everything from the logo on your website to the design of your CD, from the values your music conveys to the way you conduct interviews. The brand is the perceived value and quality of you as an entertainer and its presenter. When you've branded well, you've created a remarkable and distinct image. It's memorable. It's easy to recognize. People know exactly what they get if they're into you—before they even decide they are. Your brand should capture:

- The emotion people feel when they think of your music
- What they achieve from being a fan of your music
- The overall impression that your music projects

Capturing all of these impressions can seem daunting at first, but there are a few tricks that make finding your brand a little easier. By answering some easy questions, you can gain direction toward a perfect fit:

- What feeling do you want people to have when they think of your music?
- What type of personality do you have (e.g., fun, quiet, casual, dedicated, curious, whimsical, scientific, bandit, nerdy, introspective, etc.)?
- What interview technique will you be using, how will you sustain it? How do you make people take notice and see that your music is an honest extension of you?
- What values do you want your music to project? How do you want it conveyed, to whom, and how often?

I spoke with an old friend, radio and television talent and programming expert Cindy Sivak, a founding member of MTV Radio, who was the first female executive in the new medium of satellite radio—as VP of industry and talent affairs/programming for Sirius Satellite Radio, she booked and conducted over 1,100 interviews and exclusive performances for its then sixty music and forty entertainment/talk channels and co-developed its hundred-channel lineup and subsequent specialty programming—and currently owns her own firm, Sivak Entertainment, which works with *The Celebrity Apprentice*, Miss Universe, and others. She offers brilliant advice to artists on how to use media exposure when building their career/brand.

How should a band best prepare and conduct themselves for an interview? "I'm glad you asked that one! Whether you're a brand-new artist or an established act, interviews—radio, TV, print, online—are your chance to promote your career and your music. For a new act, anticipate the questions in advance and think about interesting answers. The worst response to a question is 'I don't know.' If you don't know, how will the interviewer, the readers, the viewers, your fans know? And if you have an unusual band name, be prepared to answer the question for the rest of your career, and other generic questions, such as how did the band form? It may be the tenth or thousandth time someone is asking you that, but it's the first time that interviewer and maybe your fans hear the reason.

"On occasion, you may be interviewed by someone who has not done his or her homework or is, frankly, not a great interviewer. If you're asked a yes/no question (something a good interviewer should never do), don't just answer yes/no. Use that moment to your advantage. For example, if the question is, 'Do you enjoy being on the road?' don't just say yes but explain, 'Yes, because I get to . . .' Or, 'Do you write music or lyrics first?' Don't just say 'Music,' say, 'Music because the melody . . .' Finally, even if not asked, always plug your website, upcoming appearances, new music, etc.

"My one pet peeve: if you do put together a demo CD or add music to your website, make it your best effort. All too often, I get e-mailed MP3s or sent CDs from artists saying, 'My voice was hoarse that day' or that there 'was a buzz in the room' or blah, blah, blah! Not acceptable. Wait until you're feeling better or the equipment is fixed to record.

"My suggestion: when you speak to someone about your music, always introduce yourself and always get their name and contact info. If they've been helpful, you have someone to thank. I use this advice in my own career: either you have someone to thank or know who to blame!"

The more you learn about what impressions you want to convey, what your vision of business represents, and who you are, the closer you are to building your brand. The key to a successful music brand is capturing and retaining loyal music fans who will always stay with you no matter how tired they are of your song catalog, and when you may have not had a great live performance recently. But they are connected to you and what you stand for. That's why bands like the Rolling Stones and KISS continue to thrive after thirty years.

The 360 Deal

Mega-artists are considered ultimate brands, so labels and production companies have now created the ultimate 360 deal. Over the last few years, the world's leading concert promoter—Live Nation, which now owns Ticketmaster, Irving Azoff's Front Line Management, and many other related businesses—enticed Madonna, U2, Jay-Z, Nickelback, and Shakira with huge long-term deals to sign 360 arrangements wherein Live Nation serves as the artists' record label or licensor to another label, and also exclusive promoter, merchandiser, website administrator, and general representative. To attract the artists to their model, Live Nation paid huge advances for these rights, with purported deals of well more than $100 million each to Madonna, Jay-Z, and U2, anticipating that the combined revenue that each of these artists would have as a result would be enormous.

Today's digital explosion has moved the traditional record industry goal-posts. Global physical record sales have fallen in excess of 30 percent since 2004. Digital music, ticket, and merchandise sales, however, continue to grow at a fairly rapid rate. First quarter 2010 ticket grosses broke the billion-dollar barrier for the first time.

360 1.0

From a point of self-preservation, the major record labels have redesigned their contractual approach. As they are owned by multinational corporations and inhabited by a multitude of highly educated financial and creative types, they were not going to be disparaged by the advent of file sharing that many in the DIY movement thought would lead to their demise. One must take into account that a company such as Sony is an established global brand at the fore-front of manufacturing, marketing, and sales, and clearly is not just a record company that will disappear because physical CD sales diminish. According to an article published by Reuters on April 28, 2010, physical sales of CDs fell 12.7 percent globally in 2009, but they still brought in $17 billion. Digital sales, meanwhile, rose 9.2 percent to $4.3 billion over the same period.

What artists must fully realize is that the labels have taken a major role in financing their careers, especially the production, marketing, distribution, and promotion of their recorded product. From the labels' point of view they are a very strong, if not the primary, influence in an artist's success. To them, artists have always been considered products. Artists equal brands and brands are products, so the whole idea of artists as brands is nothing new. What the labels have done now, in light of the decrease of physical sales of CDs, is invent the 360 deal, whereby they participate in all of the revenue streams that an artist generates rather than just the revenue from recorded products. In the 360 contract the labels ask for a percentage of your touring money, they want to administer your website, and they want a piece of your sponsorship income, merchandise income, publishing, downloads, ringtones . . . basically *everything!*

Are they entitled to this? This is the debate. A major record deal means several hundred thousand dollars being invested in your group for recording, promotion, packaging, marketing, and distribution. It is a totally speculative, unsecured investment. There is no guarantee, and the artists are not responsible for this investment other than generating repayment from the products that are produced. And considering the small percentage of bands that have achieved success, it's what would be called a high-risk investment. If you go to a private investor and try to borrow $500,000 unsecured by proven (real, concrete) collateral, are you going to get favorable terms or are you going to pay a premium for money you borrow if, in fact, you can borrow it at all?

Once you've generated substantial revenue and are established as a brand, there will be a significant difference in the terms you can negotiate. But even in the over-$100-million deal that Live Nation made with U2, there was no guarantee that Live Nation would turn a profit. Obviously the risk factor, based on U2's past performance and past sales, is much better than that of a new artist. But in this business success is never guaranteed and unanticipated things happen. Bono's May 2010 surgery caused cancelation of U2's summer stadium tour, which had great impact on Live Nation's anticipated quarterly revenue. So even at the level of superstar artists, there is still risk for these companies.

I am not a huge advocate of blanket 360 deals. In my days as a manager, I would have told anyone who offered me one "where to go." But I'm also the guy who argued with legendary record industry mogul Neil Bogart over an artistic issue in regards to the musical content of a record I was producing for his Buddah label, and was quickly informed that art had no part in the record industry. It was about selling product, he said, as he pointed to the gold records on his wall. I understand the record industry's point of view, but I think there are problems with labels gaining artist support of the 360 model when it's not a mega-deal but rather, for example, a deal for some great new band from Brooklyn that has a big buzz on the net. Until the labels can prove that these deals are beneficial to the artist and not a vehicle to satisfy corporate greed, artists will continue to be skeptical.

Traditionally, major labels professed to be the home of artist development. They justified, with some validity, their share of the pie with the full scale of services, professional guidance, and resources they provided. They offered advances for signing, budgets for recording records and filming videos, tour support, wardrobe allowances, and the other accoutrements befitting a pop star, most of which was recoupable. Artists didn't care. They love when somebody's giving them a limo to ride in or sending a Gulfstream V to fly them to do *The Tonight Show*. Artists were treated royally and executives took even better care of themselves.

Don't forget, even if you are getting an extraordinary royalty rate, that you will still need to generate more than five dollars in gross revenue to pay back every recoupable dollar that the labels spend or advance on your behalf. And remember the word *advance* means a loan against your future royalty earnings. Back in the eighties and nineties it took years of audits and a few amazing accountants, lawyers, and managers to unravel creative accounting practices that permeated some of the labels. It took the Internet explosion to turn the industry—from both the label and artist sides—into something more transparent, where both sides are better informed, are more responsible, and understand their roles. In the past, too many artists believed that having a record deal was the be-all and end-all. Groups depended on the label to do much more for them than just sell records. In some ways the labels' artist development departments helped foster that idea by coddling young artists and catering to an assortment of their career and personal needs. For example, European labels provided bands with tour managers; helpful, yes, but is this the label's role? Not really. It's your career so accept responsibility for it.

A big problem, yet reality check came about when a group's option wasn't picked up, and now without the infrastructure that the label had supplied, the group was left out in the cold and struggled. Smart managers knew that groups had to be self-sufficient, and rather than depend on the label to provide physical support, they made their bands self-reliant. They managed the relationship between the labels and band, thus reinforcing the labels' efforts to maximize sales and exposure of the group's product without participating in the group's day-to-day business, as it should be.

Major record companies are also marketing, manufacturing, and distribution companies that generate revenue from sales and licensing of products that they produce and/or represent. It's not much different than Procter & Gamble, Ford, or IBM. Now that the dollars are tight, the labels want to share in all aspects of an artist's revenue, and they want to convince artists, who perceive they have DIY options, that they need a label's involvement to have major success.

As I mentioned, the labels have issues to overcome in order to convince new bands and their managers that the 360 deal is beneficial. First, every seasoned manager knows that, historically, the record companies had fully staffed departments to oversee marketing, promotion, airplay, and artist development, but bands still needed to hire their own publicists, radio promotion, and other professionals to develop, enhance, and maximize their exposure and take care of them after a record priority release period was over. Another issue is that many bands don't release new records every year, and unless they have catalog that is selling like hotcakes when their current record's priority time is over, the label will divert its attention to catering to other artists who do have new product out.

As good a job as the labels may do, the key emphasis of all of their personnel is to service, promote, and maximize the product they are releasing and, in order to do so, they are relegated to operating at full speed to generate sales, promotion, and marketing of the products that are current. So, yes, the labels do have an interest in an artist's development, and they do add value to and have an interest in marketing and maximizing the group's ancillary revenue (touring, merchandise, publishing, website, etc.), but can we *trust* them to do this all of the time rather than just when an artist has current product that is hot and happening in the marketplace?

Finally, why do the labels need to participate in a band's other streams of revenue now when they did not before? If they wish to participate via the 360 deal, what are the guarantees that they will add benefit to these aspects of your career? It's important that you recognize that the labels definitely understand that the industry and marketplace are changing and they have taken steps to maintain their relevance and competitiveness.

To illustrate this, I asked Emma Quigley, a senior marketing executive at EMI, **How have the labels changed in the digital age?** "The role and focus have changed significantly. Artists are now being signed to 360 deals, and brand partners are no longer just used for touring. Videos, album art, and album launch platforms can all have brand associations. In addition, with iTunes now being the world's number one music retailer, the launch and subsequent campaign for each release has a significant digital focus, from sales to marketing to promotion. We put a huge focus on digital marketing, and labels are exhaustively looking at new ways to expand upon it. Most album campaigns are launched digitally first, regardless of the music genre. Everything from viral tools such as album trailers, video clips, blogs, news stories, and track leaks all happen digitally before the more traditional forms of marketing are rolled out. Promotion plays a large role also. Sessions for Yahoo, AOL, and MySpace are prioritized, as are bonus versions of the album for iTunes—they nearly always receive exclusive content."

Emma's answer attests to the labels' implementation of new technology and methods to market their artists and fully exploit all of the potential revenue streams through branding and various other corporate tie-ins. So I urge that you consider all avenues and make sure that you have proper guidance from your advisors.

Here is a contract proposal that will outline the issues and provide some insight as to how these deals are structured. I'll explain each aspect.

Proposal Between Mock Record Label and Mock Artist for a 360 Deal

EVERY NAME RECORDS, INC.

April 29, 2010
Resurrection Ranch ℅ John Smith
Rockstar Lawyers P.C.
5000 Broadway
New York, NY 10019

Re: EVERY NAME Records, Inc., a division of Big Major Record
        Label, Inc. with Resurrection Ranch/Exclusive Recording
        Agreement—PROPOSAL

Dear John,
I am writing to you on behalf of Every Name Records, Inc., a division of Big Major Record Label ("Major") to suggest the following revised terms and conditions in connection with which Major will enter into an exclusive recording agreement with Resurrection Ranch, comprising Mary McConnell, Junior Wilson, and Henry Bush ("Artist") (the foregoing the "Agreement")

1. **Territory**: the Universe
2. **Term/Product Commitment**
   (a) Initial Period: One (1) Album ("Album One"). Album One shall embody Artist's master recordings entitled "Best Music Ever" and "The Greatest Album Ever Recorded."
   (b) Option Periods: Four (4) separate consecutive one (1) album (hereinafter "Album Two," "Album Three," etc.) for a total of five (5) potential Albums, if Every Name exercises all of its options.
3. **Advances / Recording Funds:**

Album One: $150,000 "all-in" Recording Fund will pay Thirty Five Thousand Dollars ($35,000) as an advance (inclusive of legal fees) promptly following the full execution of an agreement, and the balance, if applicable, upon Delivery of Album One.

Albums Two through Five: Every Name will pay the following recoupable "all-in" recording funds (i.e. inclusive of all advances and fees to be paid to Artist, individual producers and other third parties, all recording costs, subject to a budget to be approved by Every Name). The recording fund for the applicable album will be calculated based upon minimum/maximum formula of 60% of previous album's earnings *(including pipeline royalties and applicable sales with respect to Albums in the form of Permanent Downloads)* or average of the previous two (2) Albums' earnings *(including pipeline royalties and applicable sales with respect to Albums in the form of Permanent Downloads)* whichever is less calculating such royalties of fifteen (15) months, based on royalty bearing sales as reported by SoundScan as follows:

	Minimum	Maximum
Album Two	$200,000	$350,000
Album Three	$300,000	$400,000
Album Four	$325,000	$500,000
Album Five	$350,000	$600,000

The recording funds for Albums Two through Five will be payable as follows:
(i) *15%* of the applicable minimum amount set forth above promptly after Every Name has approved all preconditions to recording (including, without limitation, approving the recording budget with respect to the album concerned) and the recording of the applicable album has commenced,

provided that Every Name may reduce such amount subject to Every Name's standard "back-end" protection provisions; and (ii) the balance, if any, promptly after Delivery of the Album concerned.

4. Royalties: Royalties (all-in, inclusive of Artist, producers, etc.) will accrue on 100% of records sold, paid for and not returned, pursuant to Every Name's standard policies.

(a)   U.S. LPs (on top-line sales through normal retail channels)

(i) U.S. LPs	Basic Rate
LP1	*15%*
LP2	*16%*
LP3	*17%*
LP4	*18%*
LP5	*19%*

(ii) Each of the foregoing album royalties shall be subject to prospective half (½) point escalations at USNRC net sales of 500,000; 1,000,000; 1,500,000 and 2,000,000

(b)   Singles: 10% (but please note that single tracks sold by Electronic Transmission are paid at the applicable Album rate with no container charge and without deduction for free goods)

(c)   Foreign:

(i) **Canada**   90% of the otherwise applicable U.S. Basic Rate

(ii) **Major EU Countries**

Australia

New Zealand 75% of the otherwise applicable U.S. Basic Rate

UK   75% of the otherwise applicable U.S. Basic Rate

(iii) **Japan & S. Africa & Non-Major**

EU Territories 65% of the otherwise applicable U.S. Basic Rate

(iv) **Rest of World** 50% of the otherwise applicable U.S. Basic Rate

(d)   Audio-only Compact Discs and Permanent Downloads 100% of the applicable rate.

5. Mechanical Royalties: Controlled compositions will be licensed to Every Name at the rate equal to sixty five percent (65%) of the minimum statutory rate in effect at the date of "Delivery" (or last date for timely "Delivery") of the master recording concerned with escalations to 75% at 350,000 SoundScan units and to 100% at 700,000 royalty-bearing

SoundScan units. These escalation increases will be on an album-by-album basis. Said rates will be subject to the following caps:

Albums:	11 × the rate (in no event will any digital album be released with more than twelve [12] tracks)
EPs:	5 × the rate
Singles:	2 × the rate

In addition, Every Name will provide so-called "outside song protection" for up to three (3) approved outside songs per album.

6. Websites: During the term of the agreement Every Name will have the exclusive right to create, host, and maintain the "official" artist website. All elements of this website and all artwork, materials, and content to be included on the website will be subject to the mutual approval of Artist and Every Name. During the term of the agreement, Artist will license to Every Name exclusive right to use Artist's name as part of the URL for this official website and Artist also agrees to license exclusively to Every Name during the term of the agreement any URLs owned or controlled by Artist that relate to Artist. If (Artist's Name).com, .net or .org is not available, Every Name and Artist will mutually approve the URL to be used in connection with the "official" artist website in the United States will revert to Artist following the end of the term of the agreement provided that Every Name will continue to have the *non-exclusive* right after the term of the agreement to create, host, and maintain ancillary websites in connection with or related to Artist. Every Name shall have the exclusive right to place "banner" and other advertising links to third party websites on any Every Name Artist websites as well as on any Artist controlled websites.

7. Tour Deficit Support: If Artist tours in the United States in connection with Every Name's United States commercial release of Album One, Every Name will provide "tour deficit support" in an amount to be determined by Every Name (not to exceed **$50,000—the Tour Amount**) subject to Every Name's standard "tour deficit support" provisions (e.g. the tour must be preapproved by Every Name, the tour must include performances in at least fifteen [15] major markets, and all amounts expended by Every Name are 100% recoupable).

8. **Additional Rights Granted:**

   (a) Mobile Materials: In addition to the right to exploit master recordings by transmitting them to an end user's mobile telephone or personal digital assistant (or other personal communication device), Every Name shall have the right to so exploit nonmusical mobile material (e.g. artwork, images, polyphonic [midi] ringtones, voice messages, voice ringers, graphics, "wallpaper" and/or other materials) via mobile phones and/or PDAs and the like.

   (b) Merchandising: In addition to the traditional album and master rights that are granted, Every Name will have (i) exclusive record artwork merchandising rights and (ii) exclusive rights to sell merchandise embodying two (2) exclusive designs per album (to be delivered by Artist) alone and in conjunction with Artist's name and approved pictures, likenesses and other identifications, subject to Artist's approval with respect to such matters as product design and manufacturing. Every Name will pay to Artist fifty percent (50%) of Every Name's net receipts from such exploitation (less a distribution fee of twenty percent [20%] in accordance with Every Name's standard merchandise provisions). With respect to all other available merchandise rights, Every Name will have a right of first negotiation and a back-end matching right with respect to equal or lesser third party offers.

   (c) Touring: Artist shall pay to Every Name five percent (5%) of Artist's gross revenues generated in connection with Artist's touring activities (including, without limitation, box office and gate receipts or guarantees, sponsorship income and advertising revenue, etc.)

   (d) Ancillary Revenue: Every Name shall be entitled to fifteen percent (15%) of all gross compensation received by or credited to Artist in connection with ancillary entertainment-related activities and services related to Artist (other than touring, as described in 8c above) including, without limitation, any interest in endorsements, special marketing arrangements, music publishing, strategic partnerships, etc. Notwithstanding the foregoing, solely with respect to income-generating ancillary opportunities which are presented to Artist by Every Name, Every Name shall be entitled to twenty five percent (25%) of the gross compensation for the opportunity concerned instead of fifteen percent (15%).

9. Major Release Commitment: Every Name agrees to release a record embodying Artist's performance as the first record commercially released under the Big Major/Every Name venture: provided, Artist "Delivers" Album One within the required time period. In the event that Artist "Delivers" such record within such time period and Every Name fails to comply with the foregoing release commitment, Artist's sole remedy will be to exercise its option to terminate the term of the Agreement, subject to the repayment of any and all monies paid and/or incurred by Big Major/Every Name under the agreement, that have not yet been recouped by Every Name.

Please note that the foregoing terms are not a final offering but are **deal points** that will be negotiated and finalized and included in a formal contract to follow.

We at Every Name Records are excited about signing the Resurrection Ranch to our label and look forward to hearing from you soon.

Very truly yours,
Business Affairs

Dissecting the Offer

In dissecting this proposal, I will show you which points you really need to pay attention to and which areas are pretty much standard. Obviously a contract will have an additional twenty or thirty pages of clarifications and specific details, and it is essential that you hire a knowledgeable music business attorney to represent you and negotiate on your behalf. Do not depend solely on information you get from the Internet or your friends or even a non-industry lawyer. Major record contracts are filled with terms that are particular to the industry and are well outside of the range of those not familiar with the specifics.

ITEM I: **Territory: The Universe**—The United States is the number one market in the world. It is common practice when signing a deal with a major U.S. label that they will also look for global rights. The issue with giving these rights has always been one of foreign royalty rates, since the label does have administrative costs and still seeks to earn some revenue from your product because they have made the initial investment. My advice is to agree to the global deal because if you try to make territory-by-territory deals, you will have a hard time maintaining continuity, you may not be able to release the same products in each place, and administration of everything will be an arduous task. What you may want to try to add to this are: guaranteed releases in specific territories, guaranteed promotion and marketing funds, and the same rights of Artist approval that you have in your United States contract. These might be difficult negotiation points but are worthwhile pursuing.

ITEM 2: **Terms, Product, and Commitment**—This is standard and defined further in a formal contract, but you must understand that picking up an option is always the label's prerogative. Options are exercised when a label believes it makes financial sense and/or they expect to have success with a new product even if your current product does not reach profitability. Therefore, a five-album option-based term is an acceptable and common practice.

ITEM 3: **Advances/Recording Fund**—The $150,000 for Album One is quite substantial in today's marketplace. The days of million-dollar advances for new artists are gone. Advances for new artists as set forth in Album One are measured individually, and it should be noted that in order to be in a position to make a major record deal in today's market, you will have to have achieved substantial success, had thousands of hits on your website and social networks, have obvious hit songs, garnered great press acclaim, and have interest from a label that is willing to make a sizable investment. The advance mentioned includes all sums that are provided for your own use and for recording of your first album. In addition to this advance, the label will also need to invest at least an equal amount in your marketing and promotion. In regards to Albums Two (2) through Five (5) there may be some room for negotiation but in this proposal, a basis for a formula to determine how future budgets are calculated is provided as a starting point.

ITEM 4: **Royalty Rates**—This is an example of basic royalty rates, again subject to negotiation, but these rates are a good basis for review. You'll note that each time your option is exercised, your royalty rate, just like your album budget, is increased. You'll also note as you move into section (c) that the rates for foreign sales, as mentioned before, are less than those for domestic sales, and again are subject to negotiation.

ITEM 5: **Mechanical Royalties**—These are royalties for controlled compositions, i.e., the music and compositions that you have written and are used on your record; as well as non-controlled compositions, i.e., other people's songs that you record and use on your record. There is a statutory royalty rate that is paid in the United States for the license you provide—and, in this case, the label is offering to pay a percentage of that rate. Again, this point could be negotiated, and you may possibly be paid 100 percent of this rate rather than the amount offered. Please note that foreign rights are not subject to a statutory rate and that payment is different country by country.

ITEM 6: **Websites**—You really need to examine this one and discuss it with your legal advisors. In this example, the label wants to create, host, and maintain a website on your behalf subject to creative approval that you would grant. But think about it. You should already have your own website that you consider your "official" website. So what are they going to do to add value to your web presence? You've already spent a great deal of time and effort in developing your own site with links to social networks, and you have a good team administering it. Is Every Name Records going to make a better site for you, sell more items, and really interact with your fans better than you can yourself? So even though the record label wants this, it's not a simple yes or no decision.

From the artist's point of view:

- What are they doing that you're not already doing?
- Will they turn off your fans by creating a site that is less unique than your current one?
- What's going to differentiate you from the hundred other websites they administer?
- In this example, they're also asking for rights to sell banner advertising. Is this something you really want, and do you have control over this?

From the label's point of view:

- They want to make sure that you have a professional website that is administered and marketed to ensure the greatest impact and market penetration.

- The label wants to promote your product and draw traffic to the website it has created for you.
- The label wants to be able to ensure their participation in all revenues generated by your website.

A savvy industry attorney can determine for you how to reach a meeting of the minds in this area. Obviously, both sides agree that the digital marketing and representation of your band is imperative and a substantial tool to generate visibility and revenue. So unless you can prove that you have the capability to market, administer, and maximize the impact of your website while providing a participation for the label, you may have to let the label run your website as long as you have artistic control over content and equitable revenue participation. Read this section carefully and question every line.

ITEM 7: **Tour Deficit Support**—The label is offering you money to make up any shortfall you might have while touring. Unless you are already generating a profit from your touring and are satisfied with your current stage production and feel there is no need to upgrade it, you should consider taking the deficit support. It will give you the ability to play new markets and to add needed staff, equipment, and production elements. As we discussed earlier, you need to be able to generate a fan base to become a viable touring act, and touring in support of an album helps with radio airplay, promotion, and marketing of your product.

Be aware that in most situations, tour deficit support is recoupable, so you must do what you can to maximize your regional touring so that you can turn touring into a profit center. Do not become a victim of overproduction. Be lean and mean. In today's marketplace, touring is a major source of artist revenue. This is where you need to enlist professional guidance so that you can achieve the maximum benefit from your presentations. Later we will discuss production managers, business managers, and other support personnel who can help you in this area.

ITEM 8: **Additional Rights Granted: Ancillary Revenues**—These are the areas that are at the heart of the 360 deal, and are all subject to negotiation. As I've stated before, signing with a major label today requires that you allow the label to participate in all of your potential revenue streams in exchange for their financing, marketing, promotion, and distribution of your product. Understanding that their model has had to be amended to compensate for diminishing sales of physical product, the labels believe that in order to protect their investment, they are entitled to this participation and that they are still the best choice and only choice for mass marketing and sales of artists' product. You have only to look at the top industry superstars' terms to see that what the labels say is valid.

There are ways, as a band, that you can manufacture and ship CDs and merchandise on demand so you can offer your fans physical product directly. You can also distribute digital products, obtain sponsorship, do publishing deals, and enter into agreements for other revenue streams. This methodology might work at a level of five thousand units, but could you and your independent sources administer, coordinate, and deliver a million pieces of product? As of today, no! Even Greg Rollett, one of the biggest advocates of DIY, agrees with me that certain mass-market music requires major label participation: "I think in the pure pop genre there is a need for what the major labels offer, not necessarily a record deal, but what comes from being backed by a company with a ton of leverage. If you want to sell out arenas you need help. Britney Spears couldn't get to the level where she is at today doing it DIY. There's no way."

Although this specific contract structure that we're looking at is for an artist deal, there are other models, including pressing and distribution deals, that we will discuss later.

ITEM 9: **Major Release Commitment**—There is always the possibility that the album you record is not accepted by the label. Even major groups like Poison have had albums that the labels did not wish to release. At that point, your contract could be cancelled and you may be offered the options of (1) retaining the master to sell to another label, providing that you reimburse your original label for all costs accrued; (2) the ability to renegotiate your deal, get additional funds, and bring in a producer; or (3) find another remedy to make the record acceptable. Let's hope this doesn't happen to you.

Tips

- To maximize your deal, you need to be in the strongest position possible and create a demand for your product (i.e., your band)
- If you have hundreds of thousands of hits and downloads for your band on MySpace or other sites and have been able to sell out shows in major markets, you have bargaining power
- If more than one label is excited about you and you find yourself in the middle of a bidding war wherein two or more labels are offering you deals, you will certainly be able to negotiate a better contract
- If you have a producer with a track record as a hit maker, you will also be able to negotiate a better deal

Remember, you need to have great songs and a charismatic stage presentation as well as all of the above.

One quick warning: the 360 deal may require your band to be more commercial than you had intended. Perhaps the best option for a new band without an extraordinarily huge buzz trying to sign to a record label would be to follow an independent route and either release product on an indie/alternative label, or DIY. If you just happen to be that one-in-a-million artist that has set the world on fire, you may be able to cut out the 360 elements and possibly even sign your own production and distribution deal.

Be aware that it has been rumored that some of the majors may be contemplating switching their focus away from CDs in light of falling sales and their economic woes and may refocus their efforts on brand advertising and sync licensing. This is a way for them to generate substantial revenue for the songs that you have recorded by licensing them for use in television, film, commercials, games, and streaming radio. In addition, this generates revenue and may also generate increased visibility for you. However, you may be sensitive to the usage and may have issue with the particular entities that are granted this license, and again this is an area where artist approval should be part of the process.

A NEW APPROACH TO A RECORD DEAL

DIY

The digital age has now put DIY into a whole new perspective. Before CDs, independently released records stood out since everyone assumed they were "homemade" and not up to technical standards. The thick vinyl on which small batches were pressed was reminiscent of 1950s 78s, and the packaging, often just white label, was lacking. With the CD and advent of desktop publishing, the factor of a product's appearance quickly disappeared. Digital distribution and file sharing, first brought to us by Napster, Gnutella, and others, started the revolution and opened the floodgates for artists to distribute their music directly to the consumer.

As I've mentioned throughout the book, there are many wonderful web-based services that help with packaging, design, distribution and, most important, promotion. But with DYI, there's a great deal of administrative work and costs that are involved. Several key issues arise about monetization, i.e., making money from the digital and physical distribution of your music and products. Most of this methodology, however, uses digital means to distribute physical product, and many of the services bypass traditional brick and mortar retail outlets for your music. So if there happens to still be a cool record store in your town or you want your records in your college bookstore, you may need to service them yourself. Check thoroughly before you sign up with any distribution outlet to make sure you understand exactly to whom they sell. See if there are any restrictive elements preventing you from selling directly to customers on your website, fansite, at gigs, or at retail locations you may have made contact with on your own.

I asked Greg Rollett of Gen-Y Rock Stars, **Is there a real way to generate income for groups outside of the major label model without the groups needing to make the substantial investment in recording, marketing, and promotion that labels previously provided?** "Yes, there is a lot of money to be made as a musician, and none of it has anything to do with selling records on a major platform or spending a ton of out-of-pocket expenses. Companies like Audiolife will print and ship CDs and merchandise on demand, which means you can offer your fans physical products without inventory.

"Then take a look at digital products, like setting up some PayPal buttons with secure downloads for music, video, PDFs of lyrics, exclusive content, games, photos, and more. All of these approaches offer your fans something of value without any overhead at all.

"If you are starting to develop your fan base you can then start looking at monetizing through a membership site in which your fans pay monthly for some kind of exclusive and intimate access. This creates a recurring revenue stream for an artist. You can look at affiliate marketing, sponsorships, advertising, publishing, songwriting, teaching, speaking, and so much more. If you add these revenue streams together you really have few expenses and a high margin of profit that can benefit any indie musician today."

I believe Greg offers great advice and I agree with his methodology. You should consider using the software, widgets, tools, and services offered by the web services he mentions, or from Topspin, ReverbNation, Grooveshark, CD Baby, the Orchard, TuneCore, Disc Masters, and others that can make it all happen; but you first really need to learn what's involved. You also need to learn the terminology and mechanics of distribution, the differences between physical and digital distribution, the pay scales, etc. In digital, for example, there are aggregators who offer your music to online stores, subscription services, and mobile providers in the same way that traditional physical record distributors offer your CDs to record retailers. The major label system has regional branches that are located around the country. They distribute product only to big-name retailers and record chains. Mom-and-pop neighborhood shops are serviced by independent distributors, one-stops, and rack jobbers who often represent product from several major record companies.

It seems illogical and contrary to artist development, but the majors are geared toward mass volume sales. So as much as you may hear from your product manager or the A and R executive in LA who loves you and signed your band to the major label, if you're not on the radio in Chicago, Boston, or Miami, or there's not a big, designated priority push and contract-obligated marketing and promotion campaign, your record may not even get into many stores. Rather than push your product to the corporate buyers at Walmart, Best Buy, or Target, the major label's sales team would rather push a new Beatles compilation or Justin Bieber record that will guarantee volume sales. Neither the branch that controls the regional sales team nor the stores are in the business of breaking new bands.

Basic distribution is all very complicated and is one of the things every professional artist manager has had to deal with. Part of the reason you may be asked to play an in-store isn't to excite your fans; it's to excite the record store executives and make them fans so they order and stock your music.

Years back, I had an artist with Warners, and when we were on the road touring I quickly learned that if I wanted some marketing help to support my gigs, I needed to get friendly with the people at the WEA branches who were responsible for distributing, marketing, and servicing Warners' product to retail and radio. So now my job became even more complicated. It was like being signed to two labels, and each required that I devote time to oversee their efforts that took me away from my band where I was needed.

With DIY, your job is bigger than before. The web-based services do a great job with your distribution and viral marketing, but what about terrestrial radio airplay and publicity? Doing it on your own makes you more dependent than ever on having a great team behind you. And even though you may have a greater revenue share from the records CD Baby sells for you than you would have with a deal from Sony, which is getting you on the radio or on Jimmy Kimmel or in *Spin* magazine?

You'll need to learn about every single function that the traditional record companies provide, and duplicate them for the most part, with the team that you put together. It's an overwhelming job and it can be very costly. Later we'll be discussing the team you need to build. Meanwhile, I strongly suggest you attend conferences like the New Music Seminar (relaunched in 2009 by industry veterans Tom Silverman and Dave Lory), South by Southwest, and other events where you can attend panel discussions and interact with representatives from labels and DIY sites as they discuss the issues. You can network with a vast array of people from the industry, including other artists, and participate in workshops that will provide you with the tools and methodology that you will need. If you have the opportunity, go to one of Martin Atkins's *Tour:Smart* seminars or lectures. Besides being a great showman, Martin offers real-life touring advice from a musician's point of view that is spot on; no pretense, no bull, just stuff you need to survive and succeed. Also take time to check out musician blogs and Twitter posts that offer a lot of valuable dialogue. Everyone from Dave Matthews to Eminem are posting, *so join in!*

Do It Yourself means fund it yourself. How are you going to pay for everything? Where are you going to get the money to pay for recording, to pay for distribution, to pay for packaging, to pay for marketing, to pay for merchandise, etc.? As much as everybody loves the idea of on-demand manufacturing and distribution, what is it actually going to do for you in the big picture? No disrepect meant but you must understand web-based aggregators may be able to generate some money for your downloads and sell a few records in brick and mortar locations, but to really promote and market an album that's going to have national success, it takes big bucks. I'm not saying that you can't be efficient as hell and record a CD and make a video for five thousand or ten thousand dollars, because you can, but a national campaign and radio promotion costs hundreds of thousands of dollars. Where are you going to get that kind of money if you have nothing? You can't count the triumph of Radiohead's digital campaign, and other major artists' Internet success, to be your model.

Radiohead has had global success and millions of dollars of sales behind them. It was a brilliant move, on their part, to once give away their music and then offer their fans a pricing option. But they could afford to do that. So get it out of your head that you will never need a record label and that the only way to proceed is DIY. Instead, think of DIY as the marketing tool and source for your development and a huge first step on your road to success. Over the course of the next few years, the viability of DIY distribution and services will expand exponentially, and *bravo* to that. Empowering the artist with more control over their product and destiny is a blessing, but it's not an automatic method to achieving success. The labels will have to become more creative in the types of deals that they structure with artists as artists become more successful and familiar with their own new power.

Ken Krongard, the well-respected A and R executive who now sits on the other side of the table as an artist manager, **offered his insight.** "The major label business is undergoing extremely rapid change and the business model is evolving daily. Lawyers who draft these agreements are struggling to keep up, and although some may disagree, no one really knows where it's all going or where today's record deals 'should' be.

"360 deals didn't even *exist* until a few years ago; now they are the norm. However, the *level* of label participation—how *much* they take—varies greatly from deal to deal, and since this is all new to everyone, I say it's a bit like catching a falling knife. Standards have gone completely out the window. The bottom line is that labels are fighting for their very survival, and since they can no longer survive on record revenue only, they are trying to get money wherever they can.

"The paradox is that as labels continue to let go of personnel who actually do the work, they provide less service and take more. At some point, the artist looks at what the labels are offering (including much smaller advances) and looks at other options including the DIY route. Every day, more and more artists are eschewing the traditional major label route and deciding to go it alone."

Is This the Future?

> **"** *I doubt we are seen as a threat; we're just another option, one among many. There are many artists that have viable careers, so no shortage of opportunities for all different approaches.* **"**
> —Terry McBride, CEO, Nettwerk Music Group/cofounder Polyphonic

An extraordinary example of another model that embraces both DIY and major label distribution is Polyphonic. At the center of this new exciting paradigm is one of the music industry's brightest stars, Terry McBride, the man behind

Nettwerk. From its Vancouver-based inception twenty-five years ago, Nettwerk started as a management company representing Skinny Puppy, the Grapes of Wrath, Moev, and other regional bands. Terry, along with his partners, turned Nettwerk into a highly respected international record label, management, and publishing company, discovering and breaking superstar artists Sarah McLachlan, Avril Lavigne, Dido, Barenaked Ladies, Coldplay, and many others, as well as bringing the Lilith Fair concert tour to life. *Wired* magazine called Nettwerk Music Group the "next-gen music company."

A visionary and outspoken critic of the traditional record industry, Nettwerk has taken a staunch stand against restrictive DRM technology that the major labels have put in place to limit the availability on download sites, and has even gone as far as paying for the legal defense of individuals prosecuted by the Recording Industry Association of America (RIAA) for illegally downloading and sharing music. In the last few years, McBride has taken steps to transform Nettwerk away from being a physical CD provider and has set out to create a new industry structure that benefits both artist and fan. In partnership with the MAMA Group (managers of Franz Ferdinand and Kaiser Chiefs) and ATC Music (managers of Supergrass and Radiohead), McBride formed Polyphonic and raised in excess of $20 million to launch the company, which is financially underwriting artists' formation of their own record labels while allowing the artists to both retain their own copyrights and maximize their profits from physical and digital distribution of their music.

In addition, Polyphonic will act as managers and copublishers and oversee the marketing, promotion, and distribution of all aspects and products of the artists they work with. In this model, the artists will have greater control over their own careers, and the business of representation and maximizing revenue streams will be represented in a manner that also positively exploits the new opportunities that have arisen in the changing industry. Rather than take more control from the artist as the traditional industry has always done and as the 360 deals seek to do, I asked Terry, **Will Polyphonic provide the artist with more control over their careers and copyrights?** "Yes. What we will do for the artist is guide them properly as managers and put together a professional team that maximizes all aspects of their careers."

According to Terry, the whole idea of "owning" music is disappearing, and fans really just need to have instant access to millions of tracks rather than to own them. Under this model, for a reasonable monthly fee fans will have "digital valets" and digital apps that will provide them with the music they want to hear when they want to hear it, and will also offer them suggestions of new music similar to what they have already subscribed to. Companies such as Last.fm, Spotify, Pandora, and the MOG Music Network currently provide aspects of this service; iTunes and Google will soon follow.

According to Terry, Spotify, in particular, has generated more income for the record labels in Europe than iTunes and has also been a key to the decline of illegal file sharing there. Although there has been great resistance from North American labels, publishers, and songwriters, McBride believes Spotify will soon make it to our shores. I asked Terry, **Will your method of using digital valets have the potential of replacing income lost from physical sales?** "The valets monetize 95 percent of the digital market, which right now has zero income; so there is no loss, just future gain."

Even though Polyphonic is 360 in nature, it is based on a very different approach than a major label's 360 deal. With Polyphonic the revenue split is approximately 80/20 in favor of the artist. With the majors' 360 deal, the label gets 80 percent of the revenue and the artists get 20 percent if they are lucky. Polyphonic is structured as a management model that uses the expertise and proven track records of its principals. Each artist has his or her own record and publishing company. Polyphonic manages, directs, administers, exploits, and monetizes, in the most positive sense, all of the artist's creative products and assets. In addition, Polyphonic finances the recording and other needs that the artist may have in exchange for an agreed commission and reimbursement of funds it has outlaid on behalf of the artist. The artist maintains the complete rights and control of all of their assets including their music releases, both physical and digital, as well as their copyrights.

I asked Peter Wright to explain his Virtual Label to me, as I thought this was also an interesting new approach. He said, "We describe ourselves as a 360-degree service company. It's basically an à la carte situation. The basis of what we do comes from my realization eight or nine years ago that what was about to be happening in the business was that there were going to be more and more artists who were signed to labels who realized they probably didn't need labels anymore, in the sense that they could probably do better on their own. But the problem artists would have would be access to distribution and access to the services they needed to back that up: the manufacturing, how to manage royalties, whom should they hire to do the press and radio promotion.

So Virtual Label facilitates it as an à la carte situation where there are people that can do everything from soup to nuts for our artists. We have a band that we manage called Rasputina. We do their physical and digital distribution, manage their web store, do their manufacturing, all of their accounting, and even hire their publicist. Some of this we finance, some are joint ventures, and we split the results."

Is there some similarity to Polyphonic's approach? "There are a number of people doing what we do. What we tend to focus on, it's almost like a transposition of the Rykodisc model inasmuch as what I have been looking for and what I built with the company is a catalog that's going to continue to sell one way or another. And we look for artists that we used to call, at Ryko, "bin card artists," artists that are already somewhat established. We have Dan Zanes, who was one of our first artists; we have Sonny Landreth, whose last record was number one for five weeks on the *Billboard* blues chart. Sonny was on the Sugar Hill label and he called me and said he's made more money off of one record working with us than he had off of his last five albums on Sugar Hill."

So you're not taking 80 percent like a traditional label, and like Polyphonic you're taking a much smaller piece, and the artist has, in fact, their own label? "Yes. Ours is a distribution deal, and we take a physical and digital distribution fee. We help people with manufacturing and we have an arrangement where we get a commission."

Another new artist-friendly approach that's making inroads in the New York City area is RethinkPopMusic (RPM), which was founded by twenty-seven-year-old Bob Berman, who earned great experience and gained industry perspective straight from college interning and working at MTV, Epic Records, and various PR firms. I asked Bob, whom I met at one of RethinkPopMusic's showcase events at Crash Mansion in New York City, **to tell me about RethinkPopMusic.** "RethinkPopMusic is an artist-collaborative record label without an album sales business model. Founded in New York City by myself and a group of young music industry experts who were disenchanted with the climate of gluttonous executives, misleading indie labels, and 360 deals, RPM intends to return creative control to the artist and reestablish integrity within the industry. RPM provides affiliated artists with all the marketing, publicity, booking, recording, and legal tools necessary to 'make a living making music.' RPM affiliated artists are under no contractual obligation to sell or distribute their music and retain all rights and creative control of their art. Subsequently, the RPM business model uses experiential and integrated marketing initiatives that partner consumer products and artists via showcases, tours, music supervision and innovative projects."

And how did you come up with the name? "To us pop music is not a genre; it's not a sound. It's simply the ability to appeal to a broad audience."

If I were an artist, how would I find you? "If you just Google Rethink-PopMusic, that's pretty easy. If you watch MTV, you see our videos; you know we're the label from that. Our videos on YouTube have 5,000 to 6,000 hits; one of our artists is top 15 on MTV.com. MTV wrote a big blog about how it's nice to see an independent group in between the Lady Gagas and Miley Cyruses. So we're not really self-promoting, but there is a lot of visibility out there, and as people slowly start figuring out who we are and what we do, it's almost been a snowball effect of support within the industry. Not really with the CEOs or the VPs, who really don't control the day-to-day activities of these giant corporations anyway, but it's the people who control the blogs, who write the blogs. MTV twitters about us, they retweet things that we do; the *Village Voice* the same thing. They like what we're doing and those are the people that are our age who are kind of disenchanted with being constantly bothered by VPs or huge press people. They want to discover something on their own; they don't want it shoved down their throat and told this is the next thing; they want to figure it out for themselves."

Do you finance anything? "In many ways we're consultants, so it depends on the project. We offer the bands various opportunities to generate income to help pay for costs like recording. We do a great deal of PR for our showcases and events. We also offer the bands the opportunity to record at Atlantic Sound Studio in DUMBO (Brooklyn, NY), where we get the studio at a very attractive price. We have engineers, producers, and others to help the bands record their records, and we cross-promote the studio so that they're happy to have us there as we generate business and visibility for them. Also, if a band we work with already has some decent tracks recorded, if need be, we'll mix and master three tracks for them for free."

I told Bob that I knew he'd put together a few albums for some of the artists and that he's using digital and independent physical distribution as well as selling the music at events, and asked, **What would happen if you were approached by a major label that was interested in signing one of your acts?** "If our bands were provided with a deal from a major that was suitable and everybody wanted to sign it, then we would take a back seat as a label and take over as the group's managers."

Bob and his team have a fun model and are fairly innovative. For example, since their bands will be touring in a van and they'll all need to rent trailers for their gear, RPM went and got U-Haul to be one of their tour sponsors. RPM bands that have been making some noise in the marketplace and gaining huge fan support are the Yes Way, the Ambassadors, and the Vanguard. Go to the RPM website to get more info on what RPM does and a list of bands and upcoming events, and learn how they may be of help to you.

Will models such as these spell disaster for the big four (Sony, EMI, Universal, and Warner Bros.)? I think it's naïve to believe that Sony and the others will disappear. Don't count the majors out. They will reinvent themselves, and when they reinvent themselves they will decide what their true business is, where they generate the most revenue, and how to reformulate their models and deploy their assets. This may mean drastic cuts in personnel and a new reinvigorated power base that will use all of its resources to preserve and grow the billions of dollars it generates every year, possibly by buying or investing in new technology and delivery systems, as well as companies that may be leading the digital revolution. In this decade we will see a major shuffling of power and assets, and it's best not to get caught in the crossfire. Just concentrate on your own career path one step at a time.

Now you have an idea of what your options are with your recorded music, physically and digitally, independently or with majors, I've shown you what the 360 models are and I've also exposed you to new paradigms developed by Terry McBride, Peter Wright, and others. Don't be naïve. Don't get caught up in greed. Be realistic and, most of all, do your research before you make any decisions that will tie up your music on an exclusive basis.

RECORD DEALS AND HOW THEY WORK

> *What is the advantage of signing with a major label over DIY? Funding and expertise. If you want to be a very big band there is still no alternative to the major system. If you are happy in a musical niche or operating your career at a certain indie level, then the majors are not the place for you. The wonderful thing is there are so many choices now—not everyone has to fit in one box.*
>
> —MARIA EGAN, SONY MUSIC ENTERTAINMENT

CHAPTER SPOTLIGHT
Types of Record Deals • The Role of the Producer

To help you navigate, here's some history and information on record deals, record companies, and record distribution. You will see that except for the digital model, which has taken physical brick and mortar for a loop, everything old is truly new again. Remember, the distributor's role is to get your recorded music into the stores, *not* to market your music; that's what a record label does. EMI, Sony, Universal, and Warner Music Group are labels and distributors. Physical versus digital may be the battleground that you'll have to maneuver through, so it's best that you thoroughly understand how it all works.

Physical DIY's current major issue is the capacity and financial wherewithal to deal with breakout success. It takes money to create physical product and to promote, market, produce, and distribute it. Whatever you want to believe about digital only, deciding that you needn't manufacture and distribute your product physically is just wrong. Five years from now digital valets like Spotify, Last.fm, and Pandora very well may be the primary medium and CDs, like vinyl, could be subjugated to collectability only. But today you need to make physical product part of your arsenal if you want to make it to the top, and there are some very creative ways to do it. And by the way, vinyl sales are up, according to Peter Wright, of Virtual Label, and many bands are producing them as limited editions that immediately sell out.

Based on today's business model, you will need to hook up with a record distributor at a point in your career. To do that you will need to be a label yourself or sign with one. There are many types of labels and deals that you can sign, depending on your current industry and financial status.

Types of Record Deals

This information is in reference to new artists signing their first record deal.

The Artist Deal

The artist deal applies to deals with the major and indie labels. Some Indies are distributed by the majors and some by independent distributors. The Recording Industry Association of America (RIAA, riaa.com), the National Association of Recording Merchandisers (NARM, narm.com), the National Academy of Recording Arts and Sciences (NARAS, grammy.com), and the American Association of Independent Music (A2IM, a2im.org) are the main trade organizations representing the physical industry. A great deal of information about them, their members, and other industry associations is readily available on the Internet for you, so you can check on the various companies you may be interested in working with.

In an artist deal, the label provides a recording budget and advances all costs. In exchange the label owns all rights and provides you with a royalty and possibly an advance. Sizes of budgets and advances usually differ greatly between major label and indie deals, and can be anywhere from $10,000 to $300,000 or more.

The deals are usually one year with several options that the label may exercise at its discretion, usually determined by your success. All money and expenses advanced, except otherwise stipulated in your contract, are recoupable. Today, as cash tightens, signing advances are usually quite small. In fact, in many instances demo-driven development deals precede actual long-term contracts. But if you have great songs and have used all of today's wonderful tools and widgets and have turned your band into an Internet and touring phenomena, a bidding war between competing labels could break out and you could win big, garnering a huge nonrecoupable signing bonus. It's not a daily occurrence but bands like Duran Duran, Phoenix, and Gomez all reaped huge benefits when several labels fought to sign them.

That's why I urge you to embrace technology and take advantage of all of the opportunities that the web services and DIY community have to offer prior to going after a record deal. The old days of sitting at home and putting all your efforts into a demo are long gone. Getting a deal today that matters requires you having done your homework and paying your dues doing gigs and establishing a substantial fan base.

The Development Deal

A development deal is a precursor to an artist deal, wherein a label provides studio time and expenses for you to record a demo, which can be anywhere from one to several songs. In exchange you grant the label an exclusive option to determine whether they wish to sign you.

In some instances labels might offer you a singles deal or EP deal with a similar album option based on performance of the single or EP. This minimizes the label's initial investment and offers them the opportunity to see whether you can make good records that generate visibility and airplay, and sell product.

Anticipated Royalties for Artist Deals

Today's artist royalty rates on albums are roughly 10 to 16 percent of the suggested retail selling price of your CD, based on 90 percent of the records sold, usually with small escalations each option year. Recording funds on your option years, however, may be subject to a floor-and-ceiling formula determined by the royalties from sales of your previous album multiplied by a preapproved percentage, usually 60 or 70 percent, resulting in either an increase or decrease in the budget provided. However, if your sales are weak, it is very unlikely that a label would pick up your option and use this formula, which in the worst-case scenario wouldn't provide you with enough money to record your next album. Like everything else in the music business, every deal is negotiable. The more in-demand and better represented you are, the better deal you'll get.

We have all heard stories about our favorite rising act signing long-term deals with Sony or one of the other majors for millions of dollars. Don't be a victim of industry hype. The millions referred to are a total of all budgets for the group's long-term contract, and are based on the group's options being exercised every year for the full term. If their first album bombs, the band may get dropped and never even do a second record. So that $5 million deal you heard about and want for yourself was, in fact, only $200,000, with the majority being spent on recording.

The Artist Deal and Record Producers

Labels will stipulate, subject to your approval, that you work with record producers with whom they have had previous success, or who have known creative and administrative track records. Since major record deals allocate substantial recording funds, there is a great deal of influence that labels may exert in this area. It's both to help you creatively during the recording process and to take charge of all of the administrative chores. Unless you can prove that you are knowledgeable in handling both the creative and administrative tasks, don't count on self-producing your album. When you negotiate your contract, make sure you get at least three royalty points and an assigned budget for paying the producer, otherwise their fee and points come right out of your studio budget and royalty rate. You need a great lawyer who knows all the ins and outs of current deals. Reference the deal memo and data that I've provided in earlier chapters for a current point of reference.

As strange as it seems, it is possible to negotiate too good an initial deal. In this case there is a great deal of pressure on you, and your first album has to be a huge success or your options will cost too much to be picked up. I've been there, and it sucks. I thought I had it all when I made the deal. Two labels were interested in my artist and we wound up signing a deal that gave us twice as much as we had ever anticipated, but when we only sold 50,000 copies, the label said good-bye since they needed us to sell at least 100,000 to recoup. In retrospect, a smaller advance and recording budget, less tour support, and a cheaper option would have sufficed and may have kept us on the label. It took two years to get another deal. Lesson learned the hard way, and I never forgot it. Now I understand that my father was right when he told me, "any deal you make had better work for both sides."

Finally, it's important that you understand when you submit your finished album, the label will have final say over what they deem acceptable to release. They'll be nice and friendly when they have you in to meet, and may even offer you more money to fix your album. But unless you're some huge phenomenon of the day, every darn dollar you get will be taken from some other in-house budgets allocated to your project, such as marketing and promotion, and could really hurt your chances for success. A good producer helps prevent these nightmares and other problems like going over budget.

I urge you to be efficient. Don't go unrehearsed to the studio. Yes, some groups even write new songs in the studio and, when the muse strikes, you have to welcome the spirit and embrace it, but don't make a habit of coming to the studio unprepared. Remember, you are spending hundreds of dollars every hour in the studio, maybe even more. It's your money so use it wisely.

The Production Deal

A production deal is a producer-generated deal. Your group is signed to your producer's production company, not directly with the label. The production company negotiates a deal with the label that specifies it will furnish your music and services. The label requires you sign off on a simple side agreement confirming your exclusive relationship with the producer. But your rights as far as direct negotiation with the label are fairly nonexistent.

In production deals, as with artist deals, the label allocates funds for recording expenses and various advances and provides a royalty after recoupment. The label retains ownership of the masters and record copyrights. All payments are made to the production company. Your deal with the production company will be exclusive to a producer but otherwise similar to an artist deal in that you will receive an advance and royalties, usually 8 to 12 percent of retail for 90 percent of records sold, obviously less than what you would have received in a direct artist deal. Production deals are based on the producer's credibility and track record, sometimes even more than on the particular artist.

Successful producers nurture trust or welcome relationships with the label's A and R staff. Many labels including Island, American Recordings, Def Jam, and Atlantic were headed by award-winning producers. For decades, several hit-maker producers have had their own sub-label deals at the majors or guaranteed multi-artist deals that needed minimal label approval to sign acts.

Production deals can be very beneficial for both artist and label. Rather than believe that you don't need a producer to record great music, and that you definitely don't need to pay someone a big piece of your record revenue just to produce your record, I suggest that you first learn what a producer can do for you. In addition, when it comes to new artists, production deals offer record labels some added protection on their investment:

- Labels usually have had previously successful relationships with the producer
- Hit-maker producers know how to help a band transform a song that may be a concert hit into a radio record by using proven techniques in arranging, adding and deleting instruments, formatting, etc. Many producers are also excellent musicians.
- Labels can count on the production company to keep the band on target, administer the budget, and pay all of the recording costs that accrue as needed, ranging from studio time, equipment hiring, and engineers to outside musicians, unions, and other expenses

The Role of the Producer

> ❝ Every producer has something different to offer: ultimately the artist is trusting their good taste. It all starts with writing a good song, but a good record producer can make all the difference in the world in how that song is heard. ❞
>
> —NICK LAUNAY, PRODUCER, ENGINEER, AND MIXER

When I went into the studio to produce a demo (which today I might be able to do at home) I thought it was pretty easy. We were just recording two tracks that, luckily, were each only three minutes long. So to begin with, I didn't need to think about huge edits or arrangements. I knew my way around a sixteen-track Soundcraft desk that we used live, so the studio's Studer mixing console was fairly familiar. Plus I had a great engineer and assistant, so it all worked well. Six months later I had a deal and was coproducing an album. That's when the world changed dramatically.

To begin with, some of the songs needed better arrangements, strings, horns, and backup vocals. I had to find the talent, hire them all, and pay them via the musicians' union. I had to fill out track sheets, studio logs, tax forms, and a host of other documents. I had to deal with effects, bouncing tracks, isolation, doubling, and later mastering. As a novice I might have done OK, but a real producer may have helped a great deal. The problem I had was that the label had given me a famous producer to work with. I was a bit impatient with him and also resisted things he wanted to do to make a record. Because of my band's anxiousness and my inexperience, I was insisting that he was violating the artistic integrity of the songs. It took me several years to realize that a record and a live show just aren't the same.

Producers deal with things like layering and sweetening tracks. They know how to add texture to songs, how to arrange songs for radio, and how to make hit records. But that being said, there is no one size fits all. When using a producer you'll need to find one who suits your musical style and sensibility. Think of your favorite albums and look at who produced them. If you have an artist deal, ask your record company to help you get a producer to work with you. If you don't have a deal yet, contact producers and try to enlist their support and interest.

Producers are creative *and* business people, and many actively scout new artists to work with while others are accessible through their agents or managers. One of the foremost producer management companies is Worlds End. If you're lucky, you may find a great producer early in your career and they may help you with the live recordings I mentioned earlier. They may even offer to take you into a studio on some type of spec basis and potentially offer you a production deal with a label they work with.

To give you an idea of what a producer does and how they work, I spoke with a few I know to get their point of view. One brilliant producer whose work I have admired and respected over the years is Nick Launay. Over the past three decades Nick, who is also an engineer and mixer, has worked on albums with Public Image Ltd, Arcade Fire, the Cribs, Supergrass, Nick Cave and the Bad Seeds, Yeah Yeah Yeahs, and countless others.

Do you ever work with indie or DIY artists, and if so, does it cost a lot to hire you (or others) with your level of credibility? "Yes, I often choose to do low-budget albums/EPs/singles because I like getting involved with new, interesting bands from the ground up. For my costs you'd have to talk to my manager, but if I have a craving to work with someone based on the potential of their songs, there is always a way of making it happen. If there isn't much funding available up front, then promises can be made that if the music we make together is widely appreciated, then favorable compensation can be made when the loot eventually comes in."

What advice can you offer bands about finding a great producer? "Most producers these days have websites where you can contact them or their manager. It's wise to choose a record producer who sees your vision, has similar taste in music, and is enthusiastic to expand on your ideas. Many bands actually contact me directly because they see my name on the back of albums that have influenced them in some way."

How much can a producer help a band create their own sound and make great records? "A record producer can help enormously in focusing what the artist/songwriter is trying to achieve. A good producer will bring in the ability to not only help focus the arrangement of a band's songs and come up with a unique sound, but also to push the musicians into performing the absolute best they can on any given parts.

"It's worth mentioning another important side to the producer's job. There are always personal dynamics in bands: egos, sensitivities, differences of opinion . . . addictions, even! An experienced producer will have the ability to maneuver things to be on track and be productive in the studio no matter what the circumstances are.

"Making music is a very organic thing. There are lots of tricks and clever solutions we producers learn over the years that go far beyond knowing when something is in tune or in time. For me, making records is all about creating a mood for the listener, giving them a sense of attitude, and making something inspiring that has longevity. Every producer has something different to offer; ultimately the artist is trusting their good taste. It all starts with writing a good song, but a good record producer can make all the difference in the world in how that song is heard."

With today's strong DIY movement, do bands still realize how important a producer is, or do many naïvely believe that they can produce themselves? "I think most artists still recognize the importance of having outside ears coming in to help them shape their songs, whether it's from an arrangement sense, getting the best musical performance out of the band, or deciding which sonic direction to go in. I find these days some bands produce themselves up to a point then have someone like me come in at the end to help edit and focus what they have done, then also mix."

Nick touched on a lot of points I brought up earlier in this book, especially things like band dynamics and a band's needing to have a direction that a producer can help them envision or enhance. I also interviewed Scott Harding (professionally known as Scotty Hard), the Grammy Award–winning producer/engineer/musician who specializes more in urban and hip hop. Scotty's worked with Chris Rock, P.M. Dawn, the Brand New Heavies, Wu-Tang Clan, Stereo MCs, and others.

What does a producer really do, and how can they help my band? "A producer's job tends to change depending on the project and type of music they are working on. For instance, if you were producing a hip-hop record, you would probably be wholly or partially responsible for creating the beats, and involved in writing the songs. With a rock record, you would be helping the band with parts and arrangements and picking the songs and keeping the record on track. With a jazz record, the band probably doesn't need help with writing or parts but might need help with arrangements and editing, as well as creating an overall sound. So a producer is there to keep an overall concept in place and to focus the direction of the record, no matter which genre you're working in."

What happens if a band has already recorded three songs, they're on MySpace with more than ten thousand hits, and people seem to like them? Why do they need a producer now? "Because a producer brings a sense of continuity and will help them create even more tracks that match the three tracks they have already done. This way they can give their fans a whole album."

How do I find a producer and how do I pay them? "You can find a producer by checking out who is producing other artists whom you admire or follow. There are many payment options, from flat fees, hourly or daily rates, percentage of earnings or publishing, or a combination of all these things."

Can you help me get a record deal? "Sometimes a producer can help you find a record deal. Many producers have production deals with labels, or have established relationships with labels that will help you get access to labels you may not otherwise be able to contact on your own."

Doing It Yourself

You use CD Baby, Bandcamp, or the other websites I mentioned to manufacture and distribute your physical CDs and download cards and distribute your digital product. (Go to their websites for unit pricing, costs, etc.; they're listed in Valuable Music Web Resources section on page 177.) It's working out pretty well and you are able to meet demand and have a positive cash flow. I'm not saying you should tell CD Baby to bugger off, because they *are* great, but let's say you manage to get on the second stage at Coachella and Daughtry goes crazy about your music and jumps onstage with you. Now it's all over YouTube, you're asked to be on Leno and CNN, and then you go crazy viral. You get huge offers, five hundred thousand hits in two days on your MySpace page. Can you afford to manufacture the ten thousand CDs and T-shirts you'll need to meet the groundswell of fans asking for them? What the hell do you do?

There's still no guarantee that your fifteen minutes of media stardom is going to last. You could be replaced by a talking skunk or smoking baby on YouTube by the time you've borrowed the money to get your product manufactured. CD Baby has a physical distribution deal with Super D, the nation's number one rack jobber; and several of the other sites also use well-established distributors, sometimes even the big four majors, so that means they can get your CDs into the stores that still exist. But with a DIY deal, you have to pay to manufacture your product, and if you can't, your opportunity to take advantage of your big-break-buzz is gone. This is the DIY conundrum.

I know this might be impossible, but a solution could be for each band member to save up a couple of grand just in case or, even better, try to get a few friends to invest some money. You can pay them back with interest from the sale proceeds and don't need to offer them a piece of ownership in the band. I'm not saying who, but someone I quoted in this book told me the indies give advances that are as good as the majors. Well, relatively. Once you show you can sell some records, a few indies have capital, but many operate on a shoestring. So my advice to you is definitely use DIY but, if you have the kind of band that could break out and have mass appeal, consider that there will be a point in time that you may need to make a record deal, either with a major or indie.

Indie Labels

Indie labels are an incredible source of both A and R and of talent. Island, Motown, Stax, Virgin, and more recently Matador were all independently distributed labels before being absorbed by or entering into distribution arrangements with the majors. Actually, Matador severed its ties with Atlantic and later Capitol Records and sold a percentage of its business to Martin

Mills's Beggars Group, England's fiercely independent and proudly alternative label and distribution company whose roots were London's Beggars Banquet record stores, which fueled the DIY movement of the seventies punk era in the UK and who for three decades have led the way for extraordinary alternative music. Their current artists include Vampire Weekend, Adele, and many other great ones. Check out Matador at matadorrecords.com and Beggars Banquet at beggarsgroupusa.com. Matador's heads realized that their music had more of a home at Beggars, and that with Beggars as a partner they would be able to sign and release records whose commercial appeal might be too small for the big four's systems. They've also seen Island, Motown, Virgin, and several of the other historic indies be homogenized and turned into imprints once they diluted too many of their assets by selling off to the majors.

Indies like Metropolis, Astralwerks, and Century Media found a place for themselves by catering to specific genres that included industrial, electronica, and metal. But often the indies like Chicago-based Wax Trax had no choice but to sell off or go belly up. However, it's important that we also see it from the majors' point of view. Giving Seymour Stein a place for Sire brought Warner Bros. Talking Heads, the Ramones, the Pretenders, k.d. lang, and Madonna to enrich Warner's coffers and enhance their own label's A and R. By adding the streetwise, progressive indies, the majors often prospered from these deals.

In the seventies and early eighties Island was the biggest independent label and for a short time had their own pressing plant. Island was founded by Chris Blackwell, a man I believe to be one of the most influential, artist-friendly, and music-loving record producers and industry leaders of all time. Chris exudes sincerity and confidence. He truly supports the rights of artists and I believe he also respects the general public, whom he's provided quite successfully with an extraordinary selection of musical options to embrace. Island exposed us to a vast world of talent and genres, unencumbered by traditional industry restrictions.

Island, under Blackwell's leadership, brought us acts ranging from Traffic and King Crimson to Bob Marley, U2, Grace Jones, and so many more. Island exposed us to world music, ska, Africa Fête, Marianne Faithfull, Angélique Kidjo, Black Uhuru, P. J. Harvey, and Robert Palmer. It nurtured its artists and fostered several smaller independent labels such as Mango, Gee Street, and 4th & B'way, and is also credited with giving birth by way of distribution agreements to Virgin and Chrysalis Records in the UK. It's different today, however.

Chris sold Island in 1998 to Polygram for more than $500 million and now it's part of the Universal Music Group, merely a brand name.

The reason I bring this up is that, unlike industry icon Clive Davis, who rose from within the ranks of Columbia Records, Blackwell did it his own way. Not the easiest route, sometimes even bumpy. When the time was right and the industry was in its initial period of multinational consolidation, Chris sold Island and went on to pursue other interests that excited him, including film and some music under his Palm Pictures banner, as well as real estate and hotels via Island Outpost, his extraordinary luxury small-hotel group. (While recently at Geejam, the private Jamaican hotel hideaway owned by former Gee Street Records head Jon Baker and represented by Island Outpost, I even got to try Blackwell rum—a fine small-batch rum which had just been released to market.)

The record industry has, for the most part, consisted of a few majors and independents. In the forties RCA Victor, Columbia, and Decca, like today's big four, controlled a major share of what was in the stores and on the radio. But indies have always thrived, too, and have spawned new artists and genres that often later became the mainstream. At worst, indies offered alternative artists a vehicle for their product and independent record stores a place to acquire the product.

Chapter

EVERYTHING YOU WANTED ᵀᴼ KNOW ABOUT DISTRIBUTION

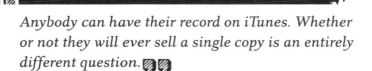

Anybody can have their record on iTunes. Whether or not they will ever sell a single copy is an entirely different question.

—PETER WRIGHT, VIRTUAL LABEL, LLC

Physical Distribution

CHAPTER SPOTLIGHT

Physical Distribution • How Distributors Work • Label Deals • Digital Distribution

Major Label Primary Distribution

The four major labels have their own branch offices around the United States that distribute records regionally. They sell in bulk to chain stores, places like Walmart, Target, Best Buy, and Barnes and Noble, which now account for a majority of brick and mortar sales; and to Amazon, the number one online physical product retailer. They all get steep discounts on their bulk orders, but except for Amazon, they carry a limited amount of titles. Tower, Sam Goody, Virgin, and most of the other major freestanding record chains are disappearing. The whole buying experience has changed. This, too, will help kill the CD. Unless some new model is developed that can provide the consumer with an experience that recaptures their passion for buying music and music-related lifestyle products, physical product will disappear from sight, as the whole buying experience in chain stores is not conducive to attracting music fans and offers little for record collectors.

Secondary Distribution

One-stop distributors like Super D distribute major label and indie label product to chain stores, and to other retail outlets that are not in an area serviced by the major labels' own distributors. In several areas of the country, mostly college towns, small independent record stores have survived. They usually carry a limited and specialized collection of product. They buy from one-stops or indies since the majors won't service them; their sales volume is too small.

Rack jobbers rent or lease shelf or display space in department stores, supermarkets, and convenience stores. They handle only top-name artists on major labels or cutouts (discounted overruns, compilations, out-of-date product). They give small, high-traffic shops the opportunity to sell product on consignment without any risk or special staffing.

Independent distributors handle domestic and sometimes foreign indie label product

These distributors service a variety of retail outlets and specialty record stores. There are both regional and national indie distributors as well as genre-specific distributors. So when the person from Metropolis offers the buyers at F.Y.E. the new KMFDM vinyl collection, it's unlikely he's the one to offer up India Archive's Vilayat Kahn CD. Often indies are headed by people like Peter Wright, who has had an extraordinary career with independent distributors and labels ranging from Dutch East India Trading and Mute Records to Rykodisc. Peter loves music so much and takes great pride in the labels and artists he works with.

How Distributors Work

Distributors get CDs and other product into retail outlets. They all work closely with the record labels they represent to promote and market their CDs and other physical goods. Most publish catalogs listing the labels and titles they carry. Be warned that if you are an indie label, distributors don't pay you up front for your product and will accept it only on a standard 90-to-120-day billing cycle. Major labels may get better terms. Distributors all want "free goods" for incentives for retailers to carry your product, and "promotional copies" to be used in-house by their sales teams and to give away to media and retail staff.

How can you interest a distributor to carry your band's own label? You'll need to show them that you have created a demand for your product and can bring people into stores. Proof of your measured success from your DIY efforts can do the trick. But they'll need a marketing plan, and you'll need to coordinate with them regarding press promotion, tour schedules, radio airplay, special events, and other things that they can use to excite store buyers to carry your product. And the packaging had better be top quality, and the delivery on schedule at your expense. You also need to have posters, display cards, and press and marketing materials to support their efforts best. Initially, for your DIY product, you've been using CD Baby or one of the other services to distribute your product digitally and to their physical accounts. If your product has created a buzz and some sales, this will help you in making your own independent distribution deal with distributors.

Should you consider signing with an existing indie label rather than releasing on your own label? Do you have the time and staff, as well as expertise, to create all of the materials required to maximize your distribution, sell your product, promote your releases, and run your own label, or may it be better to work with an existing indie who knows the drill? Do you feel it's time to distribute your product in more stores than you believe CD Baby is able to provide for you? Can you afford to pay for manufacturing thousands of CDs that will sit in a warehouse for possibly three or four months before you receive any payment? If so, and you are sure the demand will exist for your product and you have the cash flow, the answer is yes. You will earn much more if you release product yourself, and you will have more control over the product you release, the frequency of your releases, and the price you charge consumers. If over the course of time you build up a catalog of your band's CD releases and possibly add solo CDs by members of your group or even CDs by other artists, you will be in a great position but *trust me*, this is no simple task. Selling your own CDs at gigs, online, and through online aggregators is an extraordinary thing and is something you should do until you truly can generate sales of thousands of CDs. But do you really want to devote a huge part of your time and money to selling product and administrating a sales operation or making music? My advice is create a buzz, use CD Baby and the others to their fullest extent, and once things are happening, make a deal with an indie like Beggars Banquet, a major, or with a new entity like Polyphonic or Virtual Label if you can get their interest.

Label Deals

Types of Deals Labels Make with Distributors

Label deals with the majors are typically imprint-only artist deals, whereupon the major gives the artist their own logos on records, creative autonomy, and a larger royalty rate. Very successful artists and producers often try to form their own label deals with the majors. This usually happens when their initial contracts are expiring and the labels, in order to keep them, offer the groups the opportunity of having an imprint and financial incentive. The Rolling Stones had Rolling Stones Records, Led Zeppelin had Swan Song Records, the Beatles had Apple, Madonna had Maverick Records, and the Beastie Boys had Grand Royal. There are many others.

Often these deals are solely for releases by the groups who own them, but in other cases, they actually develop into vibrant labels that sign many artists; such as Led Zeppelin's highly respected Swan Song Records label with Atlantic, which released records by several great artists in the early seventies including Bad Company and Dave Edmunds, and Madonna's Maverick Records label with Warner Bros. in the nineties had great success with Alanis Morissette, The Prodigy, and numerous other great bands. On many occasions the labels were run by the group's managers or other industry vets, but it's not easy running a full-fledged label, and despite their successes, a majority of the labels ran into trouble ranging from a lack of promotion to accounting to other issues with their major label distribution partners. Some still continue selling catalog, but others have shut down or restructured without their founding artist members' involvement.

We must remember that these deals, for the most part, are initially funded by the parent label/distributor. For example, Atlantic had a sizeable investment and distribution with Swan Song, and Warner Bros. with Maverick. What the artist owners gained by having their own labels was more creative control over their product and design, control over marketing and promotion budgets, better royalties, and room to develop either their own solo projects or to sign other acts. It's still a viable model, but for these aforementioned examples, the complications and mechanics of operating a label and expanding their business beyond its core brought about issues that caused them to later extract themselves.

Basic Mechanics of a Label Deal

The **artist label** has creative control and produces and records the music, videos, etc. It controls its own A and R, negotiates all contracts with other artists it may sign, and allocates all budgets as it sees fit. The artist label, in conjunction with the parent label/distributor, promotes and markets the record, overseeing and creating all press and marketing materials. The parent label oversees all manufacturing and distribution. The artist label pays royalties to artists it has contracted, but if it is in fact funded by the parent label, then it is paid royalties by the parent label and subtracts its override before paying anything out to artists. If it is self-funded, then it may pay on a schedule it elects, but in most cases would still pay after it receives its funds from its distributor or the parent label. The artist label may own or co-own the masters it produces with the parent label. However, this is a very touchy negotiation point and subject to many variables.

A **vanity label** is similar to the basic label deal except that it is fully owned and funded by the parent label, which owns all rights to the masters. It is paid royalties and operating expenses by the parent company.

In **joint venture deals**, ownership, all expenses, and profits are split between the label and parent label. However, sometimes in exchange for the label providing the talent, the parent label partner may advance the funds necessary for operation and expenses. Otherwise it operates the same way as a label deal. Obviously the greater percentage of the funding the artist label provides, the better the deal.

In **pressing and distribution deals** (P&D) the artist pays all production costs and provides the label/distributor with finished masters. The label/distributor pays to manufacture and distribute the product only. The artist pays for everything else including all marketing and promotion. The distributor pays the artist from the proceeds of product sold.

In a **straight distribution deal** the artist pays for everything and all the label/distributor does is distribute the product. Obviously distribution deals generate the most income, but you as the artist have the burden of all costs.

Consignment deals are truly old-fashioned DIY deals where you make a direct deal with a store to sell your CDs and other product. You cut a deal with them for a set price, give them your product on spec, and they pay you when they sell the product and return it if they don't. It's fine for DIY and early in your career, but limiting and too much work as you progress, unless you have an attachment for a few very special stores around the country.

If you, as a record label, want to have your product carried by a distributor, you must make sure that:

- Its name is trademarked
- Each release has catalog numbers
- Each release has a UPC code. (The bar code which you see on everything you buy at the grocery store is used for inventory control.)
- You conform to all recognized packaging and shipping standards
- You can consult with the distributor regarding specifics

The distributor also needs ammunition to motivate the retailers to carry your product; therefore, for each release you must provide press, promo, and hype. Remember that you—as a label—have the responsibility to promote and market your record product, and the distributor just gets it in the stores. For them to do their job and get store buyers to carry your CDs, you need to supply the distributor with posters, display items, and backup to promote your band. So make sure you give them the following:

- A concisely developed promotional and publicity campaign to include radio, press, advertising, and all marketing you intend to do
- Your band's bio and press kit, with complete info on the band and stats on their successes both online and from performances, as well as information regarding the band touring in support of their release
- Any special information that can add to your band's appeal, such as guest artists on the record

If you are starting your own label for your own band, you might have problems convincing a distributor to carry your music unless you have already created a big buzz. Distributors like to work with companies that have a stream of product to distribute. It's important that you understand your one-off CD doesn't fit with their business model, so you'll need to convince them that you have the financial resources to support your product with sales incentives, co-op advertising, free goods, and publicity as needed, like the other labels they are used to dealing with. Assure them that you will take an active role in promoting your product. Make sure you include all of your information on physical and digital sales and downloads of your band's current and previous releases on the Internet, and the stats on how well you are selling on iTunes, CD Baby, MySpace, TuneCore, and your own website.

Remember, you must disclose if you have any other distributors selling the same product and realize that most national distributors will require an exclusive deal. So if you sign with them, you are making them the sole distributor of your label or band's product.

There are so many other aspects and costs involved, ranging from packaging, shipping, reserves, returns, and payments, and for this reason it's very important that you get a lot of information before you try to have your records distributed separate of using one of the currently available services I've mentioned. The record industry and record distribution are very complex. For example, royalty rates, which appear to be simple in artist deals, are subject to deductions of anywhere from 25 to 40 percent for packaging, free goods, and other items. Distributors may require that 20 to 30 percent of the money generated from your product sold be held in reserve before paying you. Since the distributors will pay their major clients first, it could take 120 days for you to be paid.

Digital Distribution

There are many aspects to digital distribution. They range from a very simple process whereby you order online from a virtual catalog and then receive a CD or single at home by mail or courier, similar to ordering from a catalog by phone. Then there are digital downloads, pioneered by Apple, where you order singles or albums through digital services while using credit cards, PayPal, and other electronic payment methods. Several digital aggregators (distributors) also provide actual physical distribution for artists and labels they represent to retail brick and mortar accounts, using major label distribution networks.

I think the latter is needed for now, but the situation is a bit ironic. Just think, the digital DIY business is using the facilities of the majors so it can, as is necessary for today, provide brick and mortar physical distribution to the artists. That's why they get the DIY baby-band CDs carried by and distributed through the independent distribution arms of Warner, Sony, Universal, and EMI to chain stores and other outlets. This concept is pretty ludicrous on the surface, but it does truly have great merit when you think about it. I referred to several digital services earlier and each can do an amazing job for you. Check them all out and see which suits your needs best.

I especially like what Peter Wright of Virtual Label does. His model is very different, and in many ways is more like Polyphonic's than that of CD Baby. I've known Peter forever; he's no upstart when it comes to distribution. He knows more about physical and digital distribution than most, so I interviewed him to get some real insight about the history of physical and digital distribution that I could share with you, to clarify all of the data and explanations about distribution and deals that we've discussed. In the interview, Peter also told me about some great smaller distribution companies and an interesting funding option.

Peter, indulge me a little and give me your Wikipedia version of distribution. I understand the majors have their distribution arms. Can you please explain? "There's still, in theory, four major-label distribution companies—EMI, Sony, WEA, and Universal, but within that, every single one of those distributors has their own so-called indie distribution arm. So EMI has EMI Label Services, Sony has RED, Universal has Fontana, and WEA has ADA."

How do they work? "Basically all of those independent distribution companies, to the best of my knowledge, are bolt-ons. They use the back end of the major distribution companies to pack, ship, and collect, and they have their own sales and marketing people on top of that."

Not just their name, but now they're using the same systems? "There's definitely changes happening as the business gets more and more difficult for the majors; there is more consolidation going on in those areas. ADA right now is effectively merged with WEA, and my expectation is that by this time next year, ADA as a distributor may not exist anymore. It may be a label services company that's for the indie labels that will distribute through WEA."

Basically there's another tier. And do they actually help the smaller labels; are they the ombudsmen for the smaller labels? "It's a separate sales staff, so in theory they can focus on their priorities with the accounts."

So they have different accounts? "No, it's pretty much the same account. So, for instance, with ADA, any account that's open with WEA is open with ADA and ADA picks, packs, ships, and collects. So they're also taking the credit risk; they manage the credit."

The one thing they do have is the clout to collect quicker. Are they servicing anything other than major chains and box stores? "They service the one-stops. There's a significant one-stop business, and there's still a significant indie business and also special markets, what people would call Hot Topic or Starbucks or museum shops or specialty children's distributors, specialty ethnic distributors . . ."

One-stops pick up the slack? "A lot depends on what album you are distributing. A good deal of product is never going to get into the big box retailers. Some records will never get into Walmart or Kmart; some records will never get into Barnes & Noble or Borders; but everything is in Amazon. Most things will get into the one-stops and many will get into indie stores."

Is it necessary to have one of these distributors? Say you're doing it all DIY as a baby band and you have a bit of a buzz going, you use CD Baby or one of the others, you have a fan base with a bit of visibility with your physical product distributed by these aggregators. Does it make sense to get a distribution deal with an indie so you can get real distribution out of, say, RED, or can these digital aggregators do it for you? "There are a lot of answers to that question. First of all, the key for anybody who is doing the DIY situation is to know that pretty much anybody can have their record on iTunes. Whether or not they will ever sell a single copy is an entirely different question, whether anybody will actually know that record exists. So unless there is something or somebody to drive customers to the artist's music, it doesn't mean anything. That's always going to be the case; you're going to have to have something to drive that customer and it can be press, a blog, upcoming live gigs, something that gets people to notice you.

"There's always something you can do without going to the level of a Sony or RED or WEA or ADA. You can do the CD Baby thing; there are a lot of distribution options. There's Entertainment One, which is about a $150 million business, almost the same size as ADA or RED, which are $200 to $300 million companies. And then there's a whole bunch of other people: Revolver, Carrot Top, Forced Exposure. These three are kind of smaller distributors that do a very successful business with a lot of smaller independent labels.

And certainly, if a DIY artist has a buzz, they are an entry point. Not so much Forced Exposure, but the others may even do a pressing and distribution deal with a DIY band.

"An example: one of the people we work with is Michael Gira from the Swans. Michael has had his own label for the last fifteen to twenty years. He does it through Revolver, they do all the manufacturing for him, and he does a reasonable amount of business that way. He's comfortable there and the records get into the key stores. He's in Amazon; he's in all the indie stores. He may not necessarily be in Borders or F.Y.E., but he's in enough places where enough people can find him and he's not in a high-risk situation where he's laying out a lot of stock with the potential of it being sent back, because that's the other problem, obviously."

If you're going to do the DIY thing, the problem is, there is a point where you can't afford it if something happens and there's a demand for ten thousand pieces. Do you have $50,000 to manufacture? Are there some indies where you can get some finance? "There are some people like Secretly Canadian who effectively own their own manufacturing plant, and they do a lot of indies for their own labels, so that is certainly possible.

"And everybody should also learn about Rocket Hub (rockethub.com), the grassroots crowd-funding community that might also help them put together a campaign to underwrite manufacturing costs."

So the real key and advice for all of that is that you do your research, talk to people, and find out what's going on out there; you shouldn't just depend on one simple DIY thing that is going to promise you everything? "I agree. You have to concentrate on physical and digital and use every method you can. Selling music at shows is just as valid as selling through retailers. Actually, you make a better margin on it. I was talking to Garry West, who owns Compass Records, three or four years ago. They do a lot of Americana-type genre acts, and the biggest growth part of his business was selling CDs to his artists to sell at their own shows, and he had to get a bigger warehouse to deal with it. The only thing that was stopping the cap on it was how much product the artists could carry, either in their bags or on planes."

So what is the cost to press a record and put it in a jewel case with artwork? "The actual manufacturing cost for a CD should be about one dollar, not taking into consideration your cover artwork, design, and mastering. But the actual manufacturing cost should be about one dollar."

So if you prorate recording costs and sell a CD to a boutique account, what's the retail price? "It's all over the place, but indie stuff is about $12.98 as the recommended level. The wholesale is probably about $8, maybe, less distribution fee, say 25 percent off of that and less discounts, so you're maybe making $5.50 going back to the artist."

That's substantial. So artists just need to be able to deal with fronting the cost to the manufacturer, waiting on getting paid, figuring on 120 days... "At least sixty to ninety days. Then there's advertising and marketing, which the artist/label pays for 100 percent. There are co-op advertising deals, sometimes with Amazon and some of the one-stops. It's become less expensive, interestingly, over the past couple of years, what the chains were able to charge. Best Buy is still charging an arm and a leg for advertising in their stores. But at Barnes & Noble and Borders, the cost of in-store advertising has come down 50 percent in the last couple of years."

Are their sales declining, too? "Yes, and what's happening in those places is the amount of space for CDs is getting smaller. Barnes & Noble hasn't taken the space away, but the amount of space they use for DVD product has gotten bigger."

The stores are limiting what they're buying, so are there little tricks that you have to work your product from a point of press and PR to generate numbers? I'm not saying corrupt or bad tricks, but I assume you have created tools to enlist your distributors' help in marketing your product to their store buyers. "Yes, exactly! You can't just go and say this is a great record. That doesn't sell anything. You have to provide materials and give them tools to help promote your product."

I've heard some industry experts say that there isn't a direct relationship between radio airplay and record sales anymore. Is it different than it used to be? "I mean, honestly, I think that there's a whole bunch of other discussions about that. I don't know that there's a direct connection on the indie level—college radio doesn't really sell anything, Sirius may sell some stuff, Pandora may sell some stuff. Those to me are things you should be working because of the royalties that you could generate from SoundExchange for that airplay—obviously that should be part of your game plan.

"There are probably a few things that really drive sales on an indie level. NPR still drives sales, and the key programs *All Things Considered* and *Morning Edition* will have an impact. The *New York* and *Los Angeles Times* can still, amazingly, sell music, that will have an impact, too; and *Rolling Stone* and *Spin*, definitely. Then the key blogs like the Aquarium Drunkard, PopMatters; most important, obviously, Pitchfork, which gets instant results."

And again that comes down to the music or a combination of . . . "Yes. A couple of years ago we had this Joe Higgs record that we sent around to a couple of the blogs. One of the blogs picked up on it, and then *Rolling Stone* ended up running a review. That album then sold a lot and he didn't spend a penny on promotion. That's just physical sales, and we did more digitally. And just thinking about organic, we also work with a Brooklyn artist called Julianna Barwick; and we help her out and she just signed to Asthmatic Kitty. She put out two records on her own, which we helped manufacture, and some people at Pitchfork found out about her and fell in love with her and she's probably sold three or four thousand. We did a thing on the eMusic Discovery thing and she made about five or six thousand dollars off of that."

What real advice can you give artists to make it happen today? "It's about teamwork. Everyone has to be committed to do everything they can to work together to get the result."

HOW YOU MAKE MONEY

> *There are currently too many digital income streams and not enough monitoring yet. Hopefully there will be changes soon so that the artists are protected and receive their due share.*
>
> —JOHN TELFER, BASEMENT MUSIC

CHAPTER SPOTLIGHT
- Publishing and Licensing
- Songwriters
- Merchandise
- Sponsorship
- Touring

Publishing and Licensing

Historically, publishing has been the most lucrative area of the music business. Publishing can be defined as the administration and commercial exploitation of your songs. This is done via licenses that pay you royalties. Mechanical royalties are paid by a record company for using a songwriter's song on one of its records, digital downloads, or ringtones. Performing royalties are paid by broadcasters—television, radio, or Internet—for playing a song publicly, in full, as entertainment. Synchronization royalties are in exchange for a fee to have part or all of your song used as background in film, television shows, or advertisements. There are other royalties, such as print royalties derived from sheet music and reproduction of your songs and lyrics in publications.

When we talk publishing, we talk about copyright. You, as the songwriter, have written a song and own the copyright to it. The publishing industry, through some historical agreement that no one seems to know the origin of, has established a mechanism whereby you as the writer and copyright holder have now turned over the rights to use and generate money from your songs to a "publisher." The basics are as follows: 50 percent of the ownership of a song is considered the writer's share; the other 50 percent is considered the publisher's share. This does not preclude you from being the publisher as well as the writer, but often the publisher's share, which is also called the "administrative share," is sold to a professional publishing company who can then market the compositions so other artists can perform them and generate substantial revenue. The actual percentage of ownership is subject to negotiation. You should note that the major record companies own publishing companies, including EMI Music, Sony/ATV, Warner/Chappell Music, and Universal Music Publishing, which, for the most part, have been very profitable over the years.

A music publisher promotes songs and licenses them for use by other recording artists, including for use by television, films, and advertisers. A good publisher is in tune with the songwriter so that the use of these songs by others is in keeping with the artist's sensibilities. John Telfer, manager of such bands as the Proclaimers, Joe Jackson, Everything but the Girl, and the well-respected publisher and owner of Basement Music, says, "Publishing has become more important than ever before. A good independent publisher helps and advises their writers and catalog owners. A publisher can often be more objective than the other parties involved in a musical career. A manager, label, or agent sometimes will be building up their companies through the writer. The income of a publisher depends on the success of the writer and their success with the label and concert performances. The publisher tries to get all parties working together for the advancement of the writer."

Publishers also monitor a song's usage so that it is properly reported to ASCAP (ascap.com), BMI (bmi.com), SESAC (sesac.com), SoundExchange (soundexchange.com), and the Harry Fox Agency (harryfox.com). These are the performing rights organizations that keep track of airplay on all terrestrial and digital radio, television, and Internet formats, as well as in live performance and in print, and collect payments for usage. Songwriters and publishers designate one or more of these organizations to act on their behalf and pay them a small licensing fee. BMI, ASCAP, and SoundExchange are not-for-profit organizations, while SESAC and the Harry Fox Agency are commercial. All of these entities offer very interesting programs for songwriters and provide additional support for their members. It makes sense to go to their websites and decide which organization suits you best. They are easy to join and are there for your benefit. You can also get information as to how they operate, how they make payments, their fees, and the current statutory fees paid to them by broadcasters and other users. A rule of thumb, however: you can anticipate revenue collected by these organizations at approximately ten cents per play, so if you're lucky enough to have a record that reaches the top 10, it's possible to make several hundred thousand dollars. The money is paid directly by the performing rights organizations, half to the songwriter and half to the publisher.

The songwriters in your band need to take measures to protect their compositions and make sure that they don't sign away their rights prematurely. Your manager will, I hope, advise you in generating a publishing deal that may even provide you with a sizable advance. You should also take some time to look at the websites of major publishers like Warner/Chappell Music (warnerchappell.com), EMI Music (emimusic.com), and many other companies out there to see what they do, whom they represent, and learn as much as you can in advance of making any deal. When the time is right, you may want to ask around and do some research to associate yourself with a publisher that you believe is sensitive to the type of music that you create so you can reap the greatest reward and benefit from your compositions. There are many great smaller firms like John Telfer's Basement Music (basementmusic.co.uk) that have distinguished reputations and impressive international client lists. These firms can serve you well and give you some individual attention.

The most important function a music publisher can do for you, other than collecting the basic income I've just spoken about, is to promote your songs and license them to others to use in ways that earn you money. This includes talking to record labels to get other artists to perform your songs; talking to music supervisors and others responsible to get your music into films, television shows, video games, ringtones, commercials, etc.

According to John Telfer, "there are currently too many digital income streams and not enough monitoring yet. Hopefully there will be changes soon so that the artists are protected and receive their due share."

Two common terms you will see in record company contracts are **controlled composition** and **non-controlled composition**. Controlled compositions are the songs that you write, own, or participate in. Since this is an area where you generate personal money from every CD sold, record labels try to negotiate with you so they have to pay royalties only on a percentage of the songs that are considered licensed to them for your records that they release.

There is a standard rate known as a statutory rate that is a minimum for controlled compositions. But you will note in the mock agreement in chapter four under mechanical royalties that the rate is equal to only a percentage of the minimum statutory rate at the date of delivery of the master recording. According to ASCAP, the current statutory rate is 9.1 cents per composition times the number of CDs sold. But in our example, as the artist has more sales, the mock record company, as an enhancement, has decided to pay 100 percent of the 9.1 cents. Additionally, the mock record company has defined the maximum number of songs per album, EP, or single that they will pay for. So even if you have twelve songs on your album, they will pay for only eleven as per this proposal; and if you have six songs on your EP, they will pay you for only five. Additionally, as you'll note, the label has specified "outside song protection." What does that mean? This has to do with non-controlled compositions. These are songs written by outside songwriters, e.g., you cover someone else's song or that of anyone else who is not a member of your band and signed to the record label. Being that the record company has no control over these writers, you need to make an agreement with the songwriter whereby they are paid a royalty that conforms to your contract, or else you will be charged for the overage.

Say you have a CD with eleven songs:

Eight songs are written by you, the artist

($65\% \times 9.1$ cents $\times 8 = 47.32$ cents)

Three songs are written by outside writers

($100\% \times 9.1$ cents $\times 3 = 27.3$ cents)

Total mechanical royalty charged is 74.62 cents.

Total mechanical paid by label per album

($65\% \times 11 \times 9.1$ cents $= 65.065$ cents)

The net amount difference between what the label pays per your contract and what the actual rate is for this recording is 9.55 cents that you *owe* for every album that you sell. The mock record company has to pay the statutory rate of 9.1 cents (unless a different rate is negotiated) for the use of the songs on these albums. In this case, you have negotiated with the label that you get paid only 65 percent of the statutory rate on controlled compositions; but since your album also contains non-controlled compositions that are paid 100 percent of the statutory rate, each and every record of yours that is sold, as per the math above, has *a deficit of 9.55 cents which the record company will charge back to you.*

Publishing companies have administrative and creative departments. Many even make an effort to assist in artist development for those wishing to have careers as performers. One should note that in 2010, EMI Records was on the verge of bankruptcy, while EMI Music Publishing was extremely vibrant and lucrative. You must make sure, before you enter into any publishing deals or agree to give away any rights to a label or manager or sub-publisher, that you are well advised by someone who knows the current industry dynamics, is knowledgeable, and has experience in the field. Artists of past days were often handed twenty dollars in a bar for songs that later generated millions of dollars. Don't be like one of the great soul men and get ripped off, because the sharks are still out there and they are looking to take advantage.

Songwriters

Throughout this book we have been dealing with career options for bands. However, another very good career option for musician/composers is to follow the path of legendary songwriters like Jerry Leiber and Mike Stoller, Doc Pomus, Bobby Charles, and others. Many singer-songwriters sign contracts with major publishing companies whereby they are given advances, similar to record deals, in exchange for a percentage of their publishing rights, and are provided with studio time to record demos for their own catalog and for the publisher to license to others to perform and use. This is a respectable way to generate income and can lead to a lucrative career. Desmond Child and Kara DioGuardi are two of America's top songwriters. They do not currently perform live but they generate extraordinary income from the songs they've written for major artists. Desmond, who in the seventies performed in New York City with his band Desmond Child and Rouge, has penned hits for Bon Jovi, Meat Loaf, Carrie Underwood, the Jonas Brothers, Mötley Crüe, and others; while Kara has written chart-toppers for Pink, Kelly Clarkson, Rascal Flatts, and LeAnn Rimes, among others.

To get some perspective on this issue, I interviewed Keith Cooper, who has a long track record in artist management and publishing. He is currently head of Express Entertainment, and along with several other music industry veterans is developing the Fourmula, a new industry concept for publishing, management, production, technology, marketing, and promotion. He has represented multiplatinum-selling acts P.M. Dawn, Stereo MCs, Finley Quaye, Aphrodite, Jurassic 5, and several others.

Are there many songwriters who don't wish to be performers, and if so, are they of interest to you? "If they write good songs, I'm definitely interested. I believe most songwriters have had desires to be performers at some point. It may be that they exhausted that route, sometimes successfully, but then as things tailed off, they transitioned into just writing. Or maybe they were not so successful as artists and their songs became more popular with other artists performing them, which then led to more songwriting work. I guess each writer and artist has his or her own path."

What are the career possibilities/potentials for songwriters? Can they make money? What kind of deals can they make and how does it break down? "Songwriting is really the backbone of the music industry. Without a successful song nothing else matters, so a great songwriter will always be in demand. A songwriter is largely remunerated through music publishing royalties (mechanical, synchronization, performance, and print), of which performance is rapidly becoming the most important through radio and online broadcasting and synchronization, the use of a song in film or TV, etc. A successful song can earn its writers a great deal of money. A writer can typically sign two types of publishing deals:

"**Administration**, whereby an administrator has the exclusive rights to collect royalties generated for a small amount of time (typically three to five years). The writer retains copyright to their compositions. The administrator usually charges a fee between 10 and 20 percent.

"Or a **publishing/copublishing deal**, whereby the writer assigns the copyright of the song to a publisher for a period of time often up to the life of copyright, or even in perpetuity, depending on the levels of advances paid to the writer and bargaining position of the writer. The publisher will charge a commission from 20 to 50 percent depending on the income type (different types attract differing rates) and territory.

"There are other income sources that writers can sometimes earn, such as 'arrangement fees' or 'vocal production fees,' depending on the type of writer and experience levels. Also the '**grand rights**' is a separate right normally excluded from standard publishing and administration deals that involves the adaptation of songs for musical stage performance—such as Green Day's *American Idiot*."

How do you find the songwriters you work with? "Any means necessary! Typically one good writer or producer will attract others, too."

What tips or advice can you give young songwriters to launch their careers? "Try to work with producers or songwriters you love by sending them material and developing a working relationship."

What tips or advice can you give young songwriters to find you and people like you to work with? "Networking in industry events, online, and other connections."

What are the "musts" to avoid, to save them from making bad decisions or signing the wrong deal? "Today the Internet provides everyone with easy (and mostly free) access to all the information you need. If in doubt, don't be afraid to ask other writers, artists, lawyers, or rights societies for help before making any big decisions."

Should songwriters join a performing rights organization? Why? When? "As soon as a song is being performed or broadcast to the public, then royalties are being attracted, and it is in a writer's best interest to sign up with a PRO [performing rights organization] in their territory. Most charge a small fee and it can be done online. Often writers leave this for many months or even years. However, the longer you leave it, the harder it can become to retroactively collect your royalties."

Licensing for Film, TV, and Games

More advertising agencies, television shows, and film companies than ever before are using popular music in their presentations. Obviously, artists have street credibility, artists are cool. The producers and agencies want to appear as though they are, too. So they choose music already publicly known, like the song "Walking on Sunshine," attempting to match contemporary music with contemporary brands. It appears to be a moneymaking match made in heaven for both songwriter and product. This is the lucrative world of music licensing.

The producer of a film, TV show, or commercial requires a **sync license** from the songwriter or publisher to "synchronize" the song to the film, TV show, or ad. The producer also needs a **master usage license** whereby they obtain a license from the person or people who own the recording of the song. If you are signed to a label, your label owns the performance of your song as recorded for the label, but you as the composer/songwriter most likely own the actual copyright, and your publisher, if it is not you, will work to represent you to get your music licensed to these other formats. If an advertising agency or producer wishes to use your song for a television show, film, or commercial, you must have a **master use license** from the label unless you are going to adapt and rerecord the song specifically for a new purpose. Fees paid for your music will vary greatly depending on the actual usage.

If your song is playing in the background of a TV show, say on a jukebox, or being performed by a bar band in a scene of a show, a performance royalty is made and you and your publisher receive a fee for a short-term license. If your actual recording is used and/or if it happens to be a hit song that's being used, you would receive more, depending on the amount of the song being used and the placement of the song. A song used as a film's theme music can be worth anywhere from $20,000 and up, but if you're lucky enough to land your song as the theme song in a major hit TV series or yearlong, nationally broadcast commercial, you might earn $500,000 or more. The song "Happy Birthday" was written in 1893 and still generates $2 million annually in licensing fees.

Moby's album *Play* had every track licensed to film, television, and advertising, making huge money for the artist, publisher, and his label, Mute Records. Artists are now seeing increased sales and downloads based on their tunes being used for these purposes. Television still has the largest audience of any media. Have you ever used Google to see what music was being used in a TV show or commercial?

And let's take *CSI*, Jerry Bruckheimer's extraordinarily successful franchise of three hit television shows, which use classic Who songs for their themes. The music is both apropos for the edgy show as well as immediately recognizable to the over-forty set. *CSI* has exposed a whole new audience to the Who's music. In fact, when the Who played the halftime show at Super Bowl XLIV in February 2010 many young fans were heard to say, "Hey, it's that band from *CSI*." Jerry Bruckheimer and his writers understand the power and influence music has on viewers in today's culture, and as I'm sure you've all seen and heard, music plays a substantial part in the overall show. This is known as "musical architecture": music supports the mood, the environment, and the action. To accomplish this, several TV shows have also gone out of the industry's typical safety zone and used music by Nine Inch Nails, Rammstein, the Cocteau Twins, Sigur Rós, Radiohead, and others. An additional cross-pollination has been the appearance of several music artists as actors in episodes of TV series.

Another major source of music sales and publishing revenue is coming from the games industry. While recently playing a Nintendo Wii *Ferrari Challenge* with my nine-year-old nephew, he told me that the background music was Muse's "Uprising," and the same song was used in Tom Cruise's 2010 movie *Knight and Day*! Artists as diverse as Paul Oakenfold, Metallica, Barenaked Ladies, and Fear Factory have licensed their tunes, or extensive soundtracks, for games. Games music is so popular now that it has even become part of university curriculums.

Several artists have written music specifically for games. Some have even taken starring roles in the games themselves. Many bands that would not otherwise be heard on radio or television are gaining new audiences through music placement in this format. It has often been said that classic rock bands such as Aerosmith have seen more royalties paid for their music used in *Guitar Hero* than they have from recent record sales. In most cases, artists see huge increases in the sales of their music as a result of the exposure garnered from use in games.

Labels earn royalties from games sales, but much to the chagrin of the majors, they claim that their royalty payment for music use is too low. But bands are also paid for use of their "image," and these deals designate substantial revenue as well as visibility for your band. The "music for games format" has risen dramatically and will continue to do so. The *Guitar Hero* and *Rock Band* series have sold over thirty million units and have generated over $2 billion in retail sales in the United States alone.

With a multitude of shows available on television, untold numbers of commercials airing daily, and hundreds of films and games being released annually, there is an enormous demand for content, and all content needs music. Producers of these shows, films, advertisements, and games would love to use, but often cannot afford, music by major stars, so they are turning to the Internet to find music. Music supervisors, licensing agents, publishers, and music and booking agencies are just a few of the people you can approach to try to get your music considered for use in these mediums. Invest time, do research, and initiate contact either by yourself or through your lawyer, agent, or label. But before you send anything to anyone, make sure you do your homework. Make sure that everything is presented in a professional format with track listings, publishers, clear copy, and contact information.

Merchandise

> **❝** *Most artists know that they're no longer going to get rich off of selling their recordings. Their money comes in waves and is usually spent before they bank the check. Today it's all about building a brand that crosses over and generates income beyond just music. That's why you have so many artists selling their own fashion items, perfumes, and branded gear.* **❞**
>
> —Maureen Baker, itsBANG

According to *Pollstar*, the concert industry's trade publication, 2009 licensed concert merchandise sales exceeded $3.2 billion in the United States, with an additional $1 billion in estimated bootleg sales. This represents an increase of 14 percent over 2008 sales. In 2009, rock legends U2 and Bruce Springsteen generated an average of $18 per head in concert merchandise sales; country music star Taylor Swift generated $15.50 per head, while lesser-known touring acts generate an average of $8 per head.

The music industry's leading licensed merchandisers—Bravado (owned by Universal), Musictoday and Anthill Trading (owned by Live Nation), Signatures Network (owned by Live Nation), Richards & Southern, and a few others—control over 70 percent of the touring artists' brands and trademarks for licensed merchandise and are also responsible for maximizing merchandise sales outside the concert hall, including sales in brick and mortar retail, online destinations, and catalogs. Companies like ReverbNation and Cut Merch are there for the early stages of your career and can manufacture and provide merchandise in small batches on demand as needed. But once your career is fully established and successful, you will probably be looking to have one of the majors work with you.

It's pretty much the same as doing your record DIY, and at a point in your career you determine that it makes sense to sign with a major label. A major merchandiser may serve you better because they take from you the burden of financing the production and overseeing sales of the merchandise. Merchandiser deals are structured in such a way that the company provides you with an advance against future sales; provides all of the costs for the designing and manufacturing of products to be sold subject to your approval; and takes complete control of marketing and selling the products. You receive a percentage of the sales. You should also understand that they have substantial costs, beyond the cost of manufacturing, in doing business. Venues usually take a percentage of sales in the area of 20 to 35 percent, and in the summer of 2010, a major backlash from band managers driven by high venue fees will have, I hope, resulted in a reduction of these fees charged by venues.

And let's not forget retail sales in major department and specialty stores. The number of hip-hop, rock, and pop music stars now creating custom-branded labels is growing and improving overall licensed merchandising sales for traditional retail outlets. Artists with clothing, jewelry, and cosmetic lines include Madonna, LL Cool J, Jennifer Lopez, Rihanna, Gwen Stefani, Justin Timberlake, and Nickelback, to name a few. By example, J.Lo's clothing brand, which launched in 2001, has seen revenue skyrocket from $130 million in 2002 to over $440 million in 2009.

Merchandise is an important aspect of your career today, and just as with publishing, it's imperative that you don't sign the wrong deal. Get professional advice before you sign on the dotted line or you may be giving away millions of dollars that you and your bandmates could otherwise be sharing!

It may surprise you but you can get a recoupable advance of $50,000 or more from the major merchandisers if you have an album coming out and a tour scheduled. Plus you can earn upward of 30 percent of the gross sales, and the bigger you get, the better your deal will be. This is why merchandise is so important. It generates income, and even if your physical record income decreases, your combined merchandise and touring revenue will pick up the slack. But to make the best deals you need a good manager who knows the players, understands the specifics, and has the company's respect.

Sponsorship

Sponsorship comes in many ways. For example, a corporation such as Pepsi or Coke underwrites a band's tour in return for a fee paid to the band. The company would be allowed to put up signage at a band's show, have a logo on the band's advertising, or have their products exhibited in various ways. Other sponsorship options include artists appearing as spokespeople for products or endorsing products—like *American Idol*'s judges' Coca-Cola cups. This is a multimillion dollar area of the industry that has helped many bands underwrite their touring operations and their careers in general, but others have not wanted commercialization as part of their artful presentation.

You have the choice. Twenty years ago I would have said no way, but today things are very different and corporate tie-ins are almost expected. When you look at a website and there isn't any advertising or streaming on it, you think something's missing, and perhaps that it is homemade. In some ways, all of this banner advertising is innocuous and we've somehow all learned to live with it. Wearing a shirt with a big tampon company logo or an erectile dysfunction drug company logo might not be so appealing, but does a Nike logo on the side of your band's hat really bother you? NASCAR or Formula 1 would not exist without sponsorships, nor would the European soccer leagues. Sports fans have learned to live with corporate logos and, fortunately or unfortunately, music fans will see more and more company names linked to the artists they love.

To get some perspective about sponsorship, I asked two of the industry's pioneers a few questions. Lee Heiman and Joshua Simons, whom I've mentioned before, along with Jay Coleman, were at a company called Rockbill that is credited with inventing music sponsorship, as we know it, in the early 1980s. The company initially put Journey with Budweiser then went on to put the Rolling Stones with Jovan Cosmetics, Michael Jackson with Pepsi, and paired many other acts with major corporate sponsorships, generating millions of dollars in revenue and benefits for the artists, the companies, and their own firm. All three of Rockbill's principals continue to be paradigm shifters.

I asked Lee, **What changes have you seen today in regard to actual sponsor dollars for bands, including promotional tie-ins?** "The whole landscape has changed on the sponsorship scene. Before it used to be 'hang up a banner, have a meet and greet, give every artist *x* amount of dollars; put them in some print advertising, some TV, and thank you very much.' Now it's a lot more discretionary, a lot more integrated. There are not as many sponsorships as there were before, and the sponsorship dollars are highly integrated right now.

"When I started this over twenty years ago, there were two disparate cultures: corporate America and the eclectic musician, and I was the one pairing both of them with a common goal. Each one was a brand. Each one was an asset. The ability to put them both together was fairly unique. Today publishers, record companies, sales promotion companies, advertising agencies, and booking agencies are all involved in the process. Everyone is going after it to act as a broker on a deal; the middlemen putting the deal together, those days are more or less gone. Everyone wants a piece. It's called ancillary income, so now for record companies, when they are doing their 360 deals where they cross-collateralize all the assets—the merchandise, the sponsorship, the touring, the publishing—sponsorship is one component in that marketing mix. So it *has* changed. The dollars are there but the integration, the opportunities, and the entitlements are greatly different than the entitlements of ten years ago."

Then I asked, knowing he'd worked with Pepsi for more than a decade creating sponsorships and also producing their events, **How are these deals being made today, and who is making them?** "The booking agents now have their own departments, so when an agency signs an act, they're already on the phone to Procter & Gamble, to Coke and Pepsi, talking about the artist's tour and how they can leverage it. It's not only about the money; it's about how they can extend the artist's brand. And your brand, the band's brand, and the product itself have to create opportunities. It has to be synergistic. One has to be an extension of the other; otherwise the sponsorship does not work. Bands need the visibility. They need the exposure, so sometimes the money isn't that great, but the exposure on TV and radio and print and on a digital campaign can be enormous for the artist.

"But even early in your career, your band can earn money or offset costs via cooperative web ad programs that you can attach to your sites. You can also get musical instrument manufacturers to provide you with goods in exchange for endorsements. You should explore this area further. Discuss it with other bands that you know who may have some sponsorships or product endorsements. Have your manager and agent look into it for you, and go online to see which web services offer help. I know TuneCore does and I also know that RethinkPopMusic and Gotham Rocks do. In addition, make sure you also enter manufacturer contests, event contests, and battles of the bands that may offer endorsements and sponsorships as prizes. Right now the New Music Seminar has a huge search for the Best Emerging Artist contest and the winners get a host of great prizes including contracts, equipment, sponsorship, high-profile gigs, and extraordinary exposure."

Touring

"For any artist, indie or major, the most important thing is to have a tour support, marketing, and promotions budget. The amount of your budget is not what matters. What matters is that you take the allotment you have and use it wisely and to your best ability, even if this means you only do shows locally. It's what you build with what you have that is key."
—HENLEY HALEM, PRESIDENT AND FOUNDER, HRH MUSIC GROUP

Touring is the heart and soul of your band's career. It's the place where you engage your audience one-by-one *live*. It's where you feed off their response; it's your lifeblood, giving birth and legs to all of your other income streams. I've addressed putting your initial shows together and getting your first gigs. I've also mentioned how everything you need to do must be complemented by building your fan base online and in person. We know we need to create incentives for our fans—create merchandise and have CDs, download cards, and other items to sell—but what do we do when we start seeing some results for all of our effort? What is the next step and where is the payoff?

This book is geared to bands, real bands; bands that perform live onstage, bands that record, bands that engage their fans. From the first chapter, I've explained how important it is to put together a good performance. By taking the necessary steps (writing, rehearsing, playing potentially crappy gigs, and recording), as well as using all of the modern technologies and media to present your group to audiences around the world, your perseverance and efforts will pay off and you will be able to generate income that will drive your career by doing what you always dreamed of: performing to a venue full of enthusiastic fans. Today's top tours gross in excess of $100 million, and many young artists break through every year as a result of their efforts and the demand of the audiences for new live music.

There are a huge number of unsigned bands in the United States, maybe more than ever before; and there are scores of independent promoters, hundreds of clubs, and many websites that are all seeking these bands to perform in the shows they present, represent, or are somehow connected to. Obviously there are key venues that national acts perform in, recognized clubs like the 9:30 Club in Washington, D.C., the Metro in Chicago, and the Whisky a Go Go in Los Angeles. All of these great clubs have an extraordinary history and have established their reputations over the years through their owners' hard work, perseverance, and desire to provide great talent and often introduce extraordinary bands to their towns and cities. These clubs should be on your list of places to play, just like CBGB was to punk bands from all over the world. But when trying to get gigs at these venues, you had better be ready to rock with the best of them and understand that you will be judged at a higher standard.

Are you ready for this now? Are you ready to go out on the road, spending nights in a smelly fifteen-seater van pulling a U-Haul trailer, or in a Motel 6 if you're lucky? When I say that, it's because by now you should have already made it through the first part of your journey, squeezing into someone's car, crashing at a new friend's or admirer's apartment, sharing gear with local bands, eating three meals a day at Waffle House or Wendy's. I went through it and I've been to plenty of Piggly Wigglys to use their john to take a whore's bath. Remember, it isn't purely for fun anymore. You are on a mission and you are committed to reach the top of the mountain, but you first need to learn how to climb one careful step at a time . . . *except in the music business we always look for a way to ride to the top rather than crawl!*

So you stick out your thumb and hope a Sherpa comes by with a mountain goat that you can mount, and look behind every rock for a hidden elevator, and reach for the top without whining. As I said before, get out there and call every club you can imagine, use every website that offers help, gig with every band you can make friends with, and push every button and contact you can on the Internet to get your music and stories in front of fans until they are yours. While doing so, may I suggest you go back to Barnes & Noble (or to barnesandnoble.com) and buy Martin Atkins's *Tour:Smart* book. It's packed with great guerilla touring tips that work, like "tour east of the Mississippi because that's where the majority of the gigs are." And once you've paid some of these dues and have your mojo, it will be time to work with a booking agent to help you take it all up a notch. In the next chapter I'll explain how to find one, how to work with one, and what they do.

Remember, real touring is to promote album sales and make money from selling tickets, merchandise, and sponsorship. Not much has changed with this model, and you'll see that even today promoters and agents look for you to have product out and either have radio airplay or Internet download activity in the marketplace to ensure you have some fans out there who will buy tickets. I've shown you how to use Grooveshark and other services to stimulate local activity and provide some analytics. In the upcoming chapters, when we discuss your team, I'll explain how, even without tour support or promotion from a major label, you can get your indie product on the radio, in stores, and written about in local and national publications.

YOUR
EXECUTIVE
TEAM

> *You have to have done everything. You have to have put out your own records, booked yourselves, managed yourselves—you have to do all of these things so you have some idea and perspective on what other people are supposed to be doing.*
>
> —GERRY GERRARD, PRESIDENT,
> CHAOTICA BOOKING AGENCY

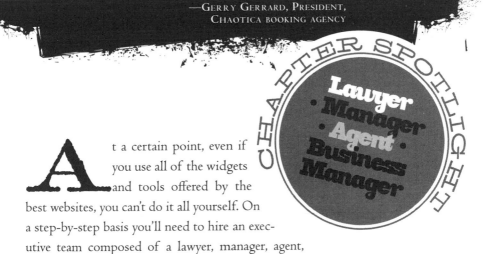

CHAPTER SPOTLIGHT

- Lawyer
- Manager
- Agent
- Business Manager

A t a certain point, even if you use all of the widgets and tools offered by the best websites, you can't do it all yourself. On a step-by-step basis you'll need to hire an executive team composed of a lawyer, manager, agent, and business manager. You'll also need a support team including a tour manager and production staff, as well as other personnel such as your publicist, independent promotion, and marketing people. Each step of the way costs you money, and that requires you to generate more income just to survive.

I did some work for the Jacksons' Victory tour, which was run by Peyton Wilson, a consummate pro. I remember being backstage at Dodger Stadium with more than two hundred workers and scores of ten-wheelers. The production area had earned the name "Jacksonburg" because it was the size of a small city. At the time this was probably the biggest production in history, and the fifty-thousand-plus who attended the concerts each day were thrilled by the king of pop and his family. But how much net profit was there for the group, considering the production costs, taxes, and commissions paid?

It's great to have an extraordinary and over-the-top presentation, but lean and mean is the way to go if you can. If you're the kind of band that requires excess, at least be as efficient as possible. Just think of the difference between a Madonna and a Springsteen stadium sellout. Whose show nets more? I'm not knocking big productions. If they are good, the audience gets what they've paid the big bucks for and the artist wins by adding fans and, I hope, selling more CDs, merchandise, and future tickets. But you need to be wise, and that's where a lot of your advisors' expertise comes into play.

Lawyer

Musicians need help, they need a team. I think they need smart and influential people around them, working with them to get them to the stage they want to be on.
—GREG ROLLETT, GEN-Y ROCK STARS

This might seem fairly unorthodox, but I believe 100 percent that the first professional member of your team should be an experienced music industry lawyer. They can advise you in regard to a lot of the early business decisions you'll need to make. They can help you structure your operation—and your band is an operation, it is a business. They can help with things like copyrighting your songs but, more than that, a good music business lawyer has contacts throughout the industry and can help you find a manager with a reputation that has already been tested. It's no surprise that many music business lawyers are different than traditional lawyers in that if they are excited about your group, they may be willing to structure a financial relationship that makes working with them affordable from early on.

You need to be very careful in choosing a lawyer, and you definitely don't want one that your manager uses if you already have a manager. *I hope you've hired a lawyer prior to hiring your manager and used them to negotiate your management contract!* To find the right lawyer, you must first understand that lawyers, like doctors and athletes, are specialized, and whomever you use must be experienced in the music business. Hiring a great real estate lawyer to represent the band will cost you money and may cause you to miss opportunities, and even lose deals you may be offered.

What can a lawyer do for your band? There are lots of good lawyers and lots of sharks, so you must be careful in choosing one. And FYI: at certain points in your career, you may hire several different lawyers to do different things for you. You don't need a $500-an-hour hired gun to do your band agreement, but one is needed to negotiate a major record contract. Don't be afraid to engage a lawyer, and don't think that hiring a lawyer in itself is going to be astronomically expensive. In this cutthroat music business that I love so dearly, even more so than in standard application, the classic phrase "he who represents himself has a fool for a client" applies, and you'll soon see that many music business lawyers can offer you advice and support that will greatly benefit your career beyond just writing contracts or simple agreements.

In order to illustrate an attorney's role in your career, I decided to interview Brad Rubens, a highly respected Philadelphia-based entertainment lawyer who has represented many major recording artists and record labels including the Roots, *America's Got Talent* champion Bianca Ryan, rappers Whodini, Luther Campbell, and Beanie Sigel, and multiplatinum artist the Bloodhound Gang. The reason I chose Brad over countless well-respected New York City and Los Angeles–based attorneys is that Brad is an example of someone who has his own firm and is not one of hundreds of lawyers at a mega-firm. Brad, and a handful of other lawyers like him around the country, are knowledgeable, experienced, and accessible, and they are approachable early in your career. You don't need to go to New York City or Los Angeles to find good representation. You've heard of superstar lawyers Joel Katz, Allen Grubman, and John Branca, but at this stage in your career, you have nothing to offer them that is of great interest. What they do is make mega-deals for mega-artists. So finding somebody who is right for you today requires putting everything into proper perspective, because there are great lawyers out there, like Brad, who can put you on the highway to success.

I asked Brad, **How does a developing band find a good attorney and when is the right time to hire one?** "There are a lot of resources people can use to find an entertainment lawyer—some obvious and some not so obvious. One thing to do is to talk to other artists and find out who the knowledgeable entertainment lawyers are in your region. People build up reputations in a particular market, and those reputations start to filter down to the people who can use those services. You can also speak to your local bar association, you can speak to NARAS. I would talk to folks at the local studios, promoters, clubs even, because again, even in a market like Philadelphia, you can probably count the people who are doing the real work with real clients on one hand. You might also speak to non-entertainment lawyers who may know who the entertainment lawyers are. So it's just a matter of trying to network any of those points I mentioned."

What are the main qualities one should look for in a music business attorney? "Certainly experience, and even on a more basic level, experience with the kind of music you do as an artist, producer, or writer. Lawyers who handle Broadway or classical are specialized; they're not necessarily doing something that the average person who might be representing rock bands or rappers is doing. There is a little bit of specialization in that regard. You'll definitely want somebody who is in your ballpark and familiar with what you are doing.

"In addition to experience there's reputation, and that goes back to your first question. As you're networking around, ask people whom they think is good, whom they think is fair. One thing I would advise artists when they're looking to work with an attorney is to ask them what kind of deals have they done in the last eighteen months. You want somebody who's current, who knows what's going on today, who knows what the new developments are.

"You want somebody who has a working relationship with people in the industry, whether at record companies, publishing companies, agencies, or web services. Somebody who is active is more likely to have those current relationships, because again, people at the record companies could change every week. The other thing I would suggest is that you should be careful when making a decision since, unfortunately, there may be some unscrupulous attorneys out there who will make promises that they cannot fulfill, while asking you for fees."

When do you need a lawyer? "You need a lawyer when there is something to lawyer! Whether someone has given you a management contract, or a studio has given you a spec agreement, or you need to put together an agreement among the members of your band, all those things will probably trigger the need to find a lawyer. If you don't have any of those triggers, until you do, in my opinion you'd be a lot better off putting your money into recording, getting yourself on the Internet, doing local shows, buying equipment. There are a lot of things that you can and should be doing prior to having a lawyer when there is no specific need for one." (That's why I like Brad. He's an honest lawyer!)

What about band agreements? "A band agreement is a good thing and should be done ASAP. What the lawyer can do, should you choose to use one early—first and foremost, if there is not a particular agreement to negotiate—is to get the artist organized by putting together a band agreement, getting copyrights filed, searching the band name in terms of trademark rights, and possibly filing a trademark application if the band has the money or has some kind of investor that is giving them money to handle these expenses."

Do today's music lawyers offer contacts? Do they do more than just negotiate contracts? "Many music business lawyers have extensive contacts and try to link their artist clients with other people who can help launch their career: managers, producers, studios, publishers, record companies—it's definitely something that lawyers in the entertainment business, and the music business in particular, do."

So you're saying that lawyers actually do artist relations work, to some extent? "Absolutely. Many entertainment lawyers are truly interested in developing talent, sometimes to the extent of being managers, so it's not uncommon for music business lawyers to work with clients on spec. Most lawyers are not going to take somebody on if they don't believe in the artist, unless it's somebody coming in on a strictly fee basis for a specific job."

I get from your statements, and from my own experience, that a truly professional music business lawyer wears multiple hats. Beyond their proficiency in traditional "lawyering," they also play a major role in career development. "That is certainly my experience. And that is of great benefit to the artist. And yes, we're a cog in the creative development process, we're not just lawyers."

With the whole paradigm shift in the industry, is the role of an attorney more important today than it had been in the past? "I think it's always been important. It's certainly important today because as artists are trying to do things on their own without the backing of a label, there's a lot more for them to deal with and consider. So a lawyer is extra important in these times, when the artist needs to be way more knowledgeable than they had to be in the past."

Should a band hire a lawyer before they decide on a manager? "Yes, it makes sense because the more that you have going on in your career, the more you will understand what the manager's true role is, and where you may need a manager's expertise and guidance. And you'll also be able to determine who is right for you."

Give me some tips on what people should avoid. "Don't sign any contracts with managers, record labels, publishers, agents, or merchandisers, or anything else of major value, without first having a lawyer review it. *Don't give away your publishing.* Be very careful in negotiating a 360 deal, and understand that major labels will request one. Labels and production companies these days are taking a very aggressive stand in terms of getting additional rights, so you have to try to negotiate those provisions. You have to be pretty damn careful to craft those as favorably for yourself as possible, because you're giving away streams of income that you never gave away before. Those streams, in large part, were ones that a lot of artists were living off of, so you must be properly represented by someone who understands the ins and outs of the 360 model so that they have the least impact on your revenue streams."

Manager

> *A good manager has always had to manage and direct every aspect of their artist client's career. The job is to help the artist realize their goals and maintain their creativity and integrity . . . and to be careful how you spend the money!*
>
> —MARK KATES, OWNER FENWAY RECORDINGS, MANAGER OF MGMT, THE CRIBS, DOVES, MISSION OF BURMA, AND OTHERS

Other than you, your fellow musicians, and your attorney, your manager is going to be the most important person whom you will work with. They will provide you with career guidance, business and emotional support, structure, and the advantage of their experience to help you negotiate the complex intricacies of the music business and garner the maximum results in the presentation of your band, both creatively and financially. The manager becomes the chief executive officer of your group, and the four or five of you, if you're equal partners, become the board of directors.

Managers receive anywhere from 15 to 30 percent of your gross earnings and it is important that you understand that *you are not employed by your manager, he or she is employed by you.* However, you need to know that in order for a manager to provide the best advice, it's very important that you establish a relationship where you trust each other and create an environment where communication is frank and honest and all sides are considered when making important decisions.

A manager must bring value. Having some energetic person act on your behalf and represent you in the industry can be a good thing if that person is knowledgeable and is also a fan of what you're doing. If they don't like your music, don't understand where the music fits into the marketplace, and have no experience with your particular genre, WTF are they going to do for you? A bad choice can do you more harm than good.

As I mentioned in previous chapters, in the early stages of your career, each band member needs to take on additional responsibilities, and one of you has been designated as the tour manager. I specifically said *tour manager* rather than *manager* so that you would understand that this person was an assistant and not the one in charge. Many bands have a friend assume this role who, as time passes, learns to become their manager, and this friend may be able to offer an extraordinary amount of help. But at a certain point of success, they will be overwhelmed with work, and their lack of experience may cause your band to miss some very important opportunities.

Ken Krongard says, "In the early stages, 'managers' are the artists themselves or friends, presumably without real music business experience. As an artist's accomplishments grow, they can begin to approach the industry and have a higher expectation of a response. It follows that the greater the artist's achievements, the higher the level of managers they will be able to attract."

You need to be very careful in the beginning whom in your band you designate to oversee these duties. Make it clear to them that you are all working together and that they are just lending their support in this area, whereas you may be lending your efforts to your website and someone else may be dealing with other matters, and it's agreed among all of the band members that at the right time, you will need a professional manager. It will be a lot easier to find a professional manager once you have obtained a certain level of success. And during these initial periods, your lawyer will be able to guide you and, at a point, even introduce you to prospective managers.

There are millions of horror stories about bands that signed deals with managers without legal advice early in their careers. These managers often did nothing for the groups and disappeared into the woodwork until the groups became a success under another manager's efforts; then they reared their ugly heads with lawsuits and demands for millions of dollars, and in many cases won. Don't be one of those bands! The key advice here is to manage yourself as long as you can and then, after careful advice and consultation from other professionals whom you have met along the way, you'll be able to find someone who has the experience and credentials to really help your band succeed.

I asked Ken, **With the major changes in the industry, has the role of a manager and one's support team become more important than ever?** "With labels doing less, managers are the ones stepping in and fulfilling more of the roles traditionally handled by the record companies. Because of that, there is also beginning to be a power shift in favor of the managers, who with the new tools available can accomplish more than ever before on their own. This is especially true at the developmental level. Whereas major labels used to have the time and resources to work 'baby artists' and bring them to a level where they are truly ready to launch, they no longer do and managers (as well as indie labels) now bear this responsibility."

What do you need from a manager? First, your band wants to unburden themselves from all of these additional roles you've had to assume. You want somebody who can take on all of your responsibilities, other than writing and performing music. You want someone who can run your business so that you are free to pursue the creative path, but you also want someone who can take the band to the top.

Once you're successful, managers will be pursuing you. It is important that you know exactly how they work, what they're supposed to do for you, what their reputation is, and how they are paid. It is more than just promises and enthusiasm, and it is more than yesterday's success. It is finding someone who knows the business and is respected by his or her peers in the industry. You need someone who knows what's going on today, who loves music and loves your band. You've probably heard of and might contact Irving Azoff's Front Line Management or Coran Capshaw's Red Light Management; both are very successful, extremely professional management companies headed by industry icons who have many superstar clients. Both have stables of young managers who work in conjunction with them in breaking new acts and can deliver. I'd also seriously consider Terry McBride—his Nettwerk Group has fostered some extraordinary artists and his new venture Polyphonic could be a real game changer. And I really like Mark Kates, Henley Halem, Ken Krongard, Dave Lory, Bob Berman, and a host of other managers I know who really care for the artists they represent and are in touch with today's industry and all of the new platforms and options available to maximize the results they obtain for their clients.

A manager is probably the most important person you will hire to work on a daily basis with your group. Today, unlike the old days, you have the potential to learn a lot about these people through the Internet. If you are generating a buzz, there will be a lot of people offering to help you network and find the manager that's right for you. Today's young generation of managers are in tune with the digital industry, have worked in the physical industry, and possess skills that lead to future success. But some of them may not have the global contacts, experience, or understanding that a superstar artist's business requires, and for that reason it is not uncommon for them to have alliances, at some point, with superstar management groups.

So when it's time to enter into an agreement with a manager, you'll need to work with a knowledgeable attorney so that you can negotiate the right agreement, and you'll need to make sure that whomever you work with will give you the attention, priority, support, and respect that you require. You must also respect their abilities so that you and your band will be able to take their advice.

The most important thing is that you and your fellow bandmates have a vision for your band, and that the image and values that you seek to present are not compromised out of a desire for success. You should always be open to the possibility of enhancing them as a result of input from others.

Keep one thing forward in your mind at all times: your choice of the right manager will have great impact on your future. Be wise, be careful, and be sure that the person you choose will be someone you can communicate your vision to and that they are someone you trust to act on your behalf to make your dreams a reality. From my point of view as a manager, I believed that:

- Communicating with a band was the number one element so I could provide creative and practical support based on my experience
- The band's operational and technical areas should be brought into a professional format

- I should use all of my contacts to maximize the band's position and presence in the industry, in recording, touring, marketing, promotion, and media, to generate the maximum financial and creative results

Agent

The next key member of your initial posse of professional advisors is your booking agent. Agents will work with you and your managers to develop the proper touring strategy and book the shows that will guide you on the road to successful touring. Choosing wisely will allow you to reap the rewards and benefits that I am sure you are all dreaming of. As I addressed earlier, there are many options available to you on the Internet to assist you in identifying and booking your initial gigs. It's imperative that you have used these resources to the max, have already established a performance reputation and developed a strong fan base. This should all have been done in conjunction with your use of web services to initially distribute your music both digitally and physically so that it is available for download and, if possible, for sale in stores in the regions where you are looking to perform.

If in fact you are at this stage, then it's time to get a proper booking agent. My advice here is corroborated by Gerry Gerrard, whose Chaotica Music Agency represented such acts as Nine Inch Nails, the Prodigy, the Chemical Brothers, and others.

I asked Gerry, **When is the right time for a band to get an agent, and how can they find a good one?** "From an agent's point of view it's changing, especially in England, where the agents are taking on acts without record deals, but here in the United States I don't think much has changed yet. You need some kind of a record—I'm not saying a record deal, but if you don't have a physical or digital record of some kind out there that is available, that is being marketed and promoted, then you're too early for an agent, because in this country you need everything going for you that you can trade off of.

"As for finding a good agent, an act needs to be persistent. There are a lot of unsigned acts out there that I wasn't particularly interested in, but they kept on calling me once a week or every couple of weeks. They were always very persistent, very polite and smart when they were on the phone. To me it's just as important how smart a musician is about marketing and the business. So persistence is key when it comes to getting hold of an agent. Never lose it, never get angry, never get upset—just keep pressuring in the most polite and intelligent way you can, because a band needs to understand that their timeline and mine are very different. I have other acts that need my attention that are generating income and, although I'm never really looking to sign new acts, we always want them, but it is very difficult in the early days to tell who is going to make it and who isn't. That's why it's really important when a band calls that they get their point and their personality across to the agent quickly. Please remember not to call us every day, but you can call every week. We appreciate people who show us how committed they are to their careers and success."

I asked him, **Would you consider working with unsigned bands that had already established themselves on the Internet and in the DIY market, bands that had garnered action and had proof of a substantial number of downloads and high visibility on MySpace and YouTube?** "In the old days, no, nor would any other national agent, but these days definitely yes. Obviously it depends on how big the buzz is they've created, and it's really important they've booked themselves extensively and that they've done it themselves. It's important that they know what to do; therefore they know what their agent should be doing, to a certain extent. It's really vital in the early days that someone in the band, or the manager if they have a manager, is doing a lot of the donkey work, because nobody's going to put as much time into them as they put into themselves. And as a result of this hard work, they'll work together with an agent and be able to maximize their efforts. As an example, you've played thirty gigs in the eastern region over the last six months and you've developed great relationships as well as good pull in New York City, Philadelphia, Providence, Boston, and Washington, D.C. I need you to give me all that information; I need you to work together with me. First of all, maybe we can get you into a bigger venue if it makes sense, but most important, we won't take any steps backward, because you want to show the promoters and your fans that your band is gaining momentum in the marketplace."

Another reason why your agent is important is that your agent is respected in the industry as a professional who has a track record, who has long-term relationships with venues and promoters ranging from clubs to stadiums and has a direct interest in their success as well as in his or her own commission. Therefore, when you sign to a credible agency, especially with someone who believes in you, they are putting their seal of approval on your band, and that goes a long way in the industry. More than just attracting the promoters, it also means a lot to managers and to labels.

Even though I've mentioned how important it is for you to use the sites and services available to you on the Internet, they only help you to a certain point in your career if you're on a path to stardom. What the gig sites do for you is extraordinary; I wish I had had those resources. The only things that where available when I was there were *Billboard* guides and the information I got from other bands. There was no mechanism to get my band's name out there other than calling every single market and every single venue one at a time . . . which is something you should still be doing, by the way! But what the web services do is put you in front of some talent buyers, help promote the name of your band, and put your band in categories with other similar bands, helping you identify the right venues in particular markets. For the most part, they don't prioritize by presenting your band relentlessly to individual promoters like an agent will. You are part of the website's subscriber base and you do not get personalized attention. Some of them offer banner advertising, so you might get more visibility through that, but it's an added cost.

I asked Gerry, **How does a good agent work with a band or manager, and what does a band need to know to get the maximum result from working with you?** "They need to have a definite plan. You know, an agent is just that, they're the band's agent. So an agent's real job is to do what the band wants and to interpret what the band wants. Although they put in a lot of ideas themselves and use their experience to help the band, if the band doesn't have a plan, then it's not going to go anywhere. The manager doesn't just call up an agent and say, 'Have you got any gigs for me?' A professional manager should call up and say, 'Have you got any gigs?' and if the agent says no, then the manager has to say, 'Well, how about we do Vegas again? It worked really well last time.' So it's a two-way street with lots of input coming from the band, and that's the same, in my opinion, across the whole industry. Everyone seems to think it's the record labels, agents, and managers who have all the ideas, but it's not; it's the artist. All the other persons' jobs are to interpret what the artist wants, so if the artist doesn't have a plan, then everyone's in trouble.

"Your team is really your support mechanism, but you have to have a set of objectives, your plan, how you're going to do it, ideas for your artwork, the clever ideas, the little gimmicks. I don't think people realize how much of that actually comes from the artist. Generally for an artist to get noticed they've got to do a lot of work before the agents and managers ever notice them, and that work shouldn't stop just because they get a record deal. A lot of people think that once they get a record deal, the record company takes over. That's not true at all. It becomes even more important, because if you lose it with the record company then people say *you* failed, not that the record company failed. So really, everything comes from the artist. *You have to have done everything: you have to have put out your own records, booked yourselves, managed yourselves—you have to do all of these things so you have some idea and perspective what other people are supposed to be doing."*

How do you book a tour? "When I book a tour, I go to the right clubs and generally the promoter takes my word for it. They may not have heard of the act, but they'll book them because I tell them they should! One would hope that once I tell them who the band is, they go out and do their research. In general when I call up, they listen. For example, I was working with the Streets when no one in America had heard of them, and I had a whole tour for them without any of the promoters knowing who they were. But by the time the tour happened, the band had already created a huge buzz and all the dates sold out. So the promoters absolutely depend on the agents in the early days."

The situation is no different in Europe. I asked Rob Berends, whose Paperclip Agency in Holland represented acts including Nirvana, Helmet, Hole, and Soul Asylum, and who books acts into concert halls, clubs, and festivals throughout Europe, **When is the right time for a band to get a booking agent?** "This very much depends on what the artists want to achieve. If the intention is to reach stardom, an agent is almost irrelevant up until the moment that those financing the artist (these days, that's not necessarily the record company) have secured enough momentum. At that moment, live shows are in order, and agents will line up. If the intention is to develop a healthy career with a good balance between creativity and economics, an agent should be found as soon as possible, since the trick is to play as often as possible. In this case, an agent should be found as soon as the agent can actually add results (in terms of number of shows, or quality of the shows, or height of the fees) to what the artists themselves can achieve. In the early days of a career, artists should do as much as possible themselves."

In order to get an agent, is it important to have a record deal, or is a substantial presence on an Internet music site enough? "In Europe, like America, physical distribution through a record company/label is nowhere near as important as it was. But a substantial presence on the Internet is not enough either. Marketing and promotion are still as important as they were, and it's best if you have some type of product in the marketplace that people can buy. But it doesn't have to be on a major label; indies are fine."

I asked Rob, **What effect has the changing role of record companies had on touring, and does it impact club gigs for new, developing bands, and opening or support slots on tours?** "There are several effects. Financial tour support has, for the most part, disappeared. Contrary to popular belief, tour support was used not only by artists who did not really need it, but also by artists who did. This is one reason why it is more difficult to tour developing artists. (Other reasons include the increasing dominance of festivals and the continuing shift of ticket-income to major events, shows, and festivals, rather than to smaller gigs.) This (and the reasons mentioned earlier) affects the development of new talent in a negative way, and therefore it also affects the club circuit in a negative way.

"Another effect is that especially promoters, but also agents and others in the live music industry, need to increase their promotional efforts. This of course requires a bigger cut for these operators, but this is often not acknowledged. Artists must also focus more on earning additional income while on tour. Selling merchandise has never been so important, and an increasing part of merchandise sales comes from selling recorded product on location."

What is the best way for a group to generate your interest? "Best is to make sure that people in the business who know me tell me about the artists. All agents need a good network all over the world. This network includes managers, agents on other continents, record companies, and so on."

Remember, to find an agent, talk to all the other bands around you, talk to your advisors. Also, do some research to see what agencies represent the bands that you like, then make an effort to contact them. Be persistent, as Gerry says, and send them your press kit, your CDs/downloads, and any analytic or statistical data on gigs you have already done in markets where you have a following. You need to impress upon them that your band has already made a name for itself and uses all the tools that are out there. Show you can generate ticket sales and, most of all, be professional.

When I asked Gerry **what bands can anticipate earning when starting out,** he replied, "It depends on where you are. In New York City or Los Angeles I'd say that initially you're not going to earn any money because generally the clubs don't pay until you have a substantial following. At that point you can get a good piece of the door and eventually a guarantee. But it's essential that you have a strong mailing list and you build up a large fan base so you can get everyone to come out to your gig.

"In the San Francisco Bay Area, where I started out, there were plenty of bands without record deals that actually made a living playing the local circuit. Even twenty years ago, they were making good money. So it depends on where you live. Initially, however, I believe a band trying to make it on a national level should consider that if they are breaking even, they are doing well."

That's why the deficit tour support that was provided by the major labels was so important. Today you need to be ingenious and generate that additional money through sponsorships, merchandise, downloads, and any other way you can possibly think of. As I've stated before, the key elements for success are confirmed by multiple professionals: you must use all methodology to establish your band as a touring entity, and having a strong, loyal, and committed fan base is essential.

Here are a few points that will give you a little perspective on agencies. According to Ray Waddell from *Billboard*, a majority of the top tours are booked by only eight major agencies, which include all the big names you're familiar with, like Creative Artists Agency (CAA), William Morris Endeavor, International Creative Management (ICM), Paradigm, and The Agency Group. But also placing high on that list was the Howard Rose Agency, which has a very small roster including Elton John and Jimmy Buffett. And then there were boutique agencies like Marty Diamond's Little Big Man Booking, which is now part of Paradigm; Chaotica, which was taken over by William Morris; and Ian Copeland's Frontier Booking International (FBI), all of which reshaped music over the last thirty years. These agencies were the forerunners and were absorbed by the big eight just like so many great indie record labels were absorbed by the majors. So do your research, go to *Pollstar* and *Billboard*, and subscribe and buy their guides. Talk to other bands and managers, and make sure you hook yourself up with someone who can deliver for you. There might be some great young agent at one of the big agencies who will kick ass for you, but don't go to an agency just because of their name and what you presume they can do.

In several states, including New York and California, agencies must be licensed since they procure employment. In addition, most major agencies are signatories with labor unions, specifically the American Federation of Musicians (AF of M) and the American Federation of Television and Radio Artists

(AFTRA), and therefore their rates are governed. But in general, booking agencies charge between 10 and 20 percent, with AF of M–regulated agencies charging a maximum of 15 percent of the gross fee paid to the band.

There are several types of agreements you can enter into with an agency, and during your initial period and prior to a substantial record release, you may consider working on a limited, nonexclusive, short-term basis with a regional agent, if in fact they are excited about your band and offer you work. By the time you're ready for the major agency, you will have your product out in the marketplace and are capable of generating an audience in every market you go to, so you'll want to be with a major or boutique national agency. If they agree to sign you, it will be for exclusive representation and usually for a specific time period.

Whether you like it or not, all major labels and most indies are also signatory to agreements with the AF of M and AFTRA. As a result, once you record a record for a label and it is released, you've joined the union, and they require that if you have an agent that they are signatory as well. So at that stage in your career, you're limited to working with substantial recognized agencies or you'll be subject to penalties. Don't bother joining the unions prior to this time; there is no need. Don't worry when you hear about the unions going on strike; it's never about rock bands, it's always about Broadway show musicians or symphonic orchestra agreements, so joining the union has no downside for you. In fact union membership may offer some benefits, so check out their websites.

Business Manager

❝Stay involved so you know what is happening with your finances and don't wake up one day to discover that you have no money.❞

—Mark Donenfeld, business manager

Early in your career, it is fine to work with your family's accountant or to use software and financial management packages from resources such as BandCentral and QuickBooks. But once your career has taken hold, it makes much more sense to connect with a business manager, specifically a *music* business manager, most of whom are CPAs themselves or who employ CPAs in their firms. What a business manager does is enhance your band's daily, basic financial management systems if you already have them in place, or set them up if that's still needed. This means your daily operation and accounting needs, ranging from managing your bank accounts and establishing credit to budgeting band expenses with band income and making sure that all tax and employment filings are dealt with. But more than that, the business manager is familiar with and takes care of your royalty statements, your tour budgets, and the operations needs that are specific to the music business.

Just like an experienced lawyer or manager, a respected business manager has the relationships with the labels, agencies, and promoters you will be working with. He or she knows how payments are structured and should be made, what specific royalty deductions might be legitimate, what tour vendors charge you, and a host of other items that can save you money and maximize your income. To give you more insight, I contacted Mark Donenfeld. I have known Mark for fifteen years and he represents several major international superstars.

When is the right time for a group to hire a business manager, and what do they need to know to select one who's right for them? "In general the time to hire a business manager is when the group is being signed to either a record deal or publishing deal and advances are going to be paid. At this point in time many groups do not have in place a formal structure that could be beneficial to them, e.g., either a corporation or a limited liability company. Often the money gets paid to one of the band members who then pays the other band members, and while this can work, it is not efficient and can lead to problems.

"The group should do their homework when choosing a business manager, just like they did when choosing a manager or attorney. They need to be comfortable and know that they are putting together a team that will work for them to make sure that their finances are in order."

How do they find you or someone as good, and is there any standard? "Usually the business manager is referred by the artist manager, or the attorney who is helping to either negotiate the contract or shopping for the deal on behalf of the group."

Is it expensive? "The norm in the industry is that the business manager gets paid 5 percent of the gross income. If the group makes money then the business manager makes money, and the group feels that you are part of the team."

Does a business manager also help create revenue and opportunity beyond basic financial planning and management? Do potential opportunities

arise that you bring to the artist or their manager's attention? "While it is not the job of the business manager to help create revenue streams for the group, if the opportunity arises, then certainly we bring that to the artist or their manager's attention. Alternatively, we can help them reduce costs while going on tour, for example, which will have the effect of increasing the bottom line. A big part of this is all about proper planning and budgeting for the tour."

What can an experienced business manager do for my band that my local CPA can't? "An experienced music business manager is someone who specializes in the entertainment area, and as a result deals with record royalty statements or publishing royalty statements as a matter of course, whereas your local CPA does not normally handle that. The business manager today has to deal not only with the IRS and state and local governments for groups on tour, but must also understand what it means when the group goes overseas and what taxes will be like. Many foreign artists who tour in the United States are surprised to find out that the IRS knows they are coming and that if they do not apply for a central withholding agreement (CWA), they will be faced with withholding of 30 percent of their guarantees for any work they are going to perform, which is a lot of money that can adversely affect the cash flow of the tour. Most of your local CPAs will not know about the CWA program or that you can apply for a reduction of taxes on the state and local level. In addition, they will not be familiar with the elements of a touring budget, e.g., the weekly cost of a tour bus, payments for the band and crew, or cancellation insurance."

Do you have any basic advice for a developing artist regarding setting up their systems of accounting, etc., early, and what not to do? "A developing artist, or any artist really, should create a good team including their manager, agent, attorney, and business manager, who will work together to help them be successful in their career. Let each of them do their jobs, but always stay involved so you know what is happening with your finances and don't wake up one day to discover that you have no money."

TOURING
OPERATIONS

Right after your executive team, the most important group of people you have is your tour and operations staff, headed by your tour manager. Your tour manager, as we have discussed, might have initially been a member of the band, but as soon as it's feasible, you'll need to bring in a professional. Most top tour managers have broad-based production and managerial skills. Many have been production coordinators, production managers, travel coordinators, tour accountants, and assistant tour managers, so as well as managing the operations of your tour, they also play a key role in hiring all of your touring staff.

Tour Manager

I interviewed Alia Dann Swift to provide some insight. Alia has worked in all of the roles mentioned above and has been on tour with Peter Gabriel's WOMAD (World of Music, Arts, and Dance), *Lord of the Dance*, Art Garfunkel, Rubyhorse, R.E.M., David Gilmour, Pink Floyd, and many other artists and events.

From your point of view, what is the role of a tour manager? "The tour manager has a number of roles meeting the needs of the management, the band, and the tour. They are in overall control of the touring budget, show settlement (if there is no tour accountant), and are accountable to management, and ultimately the band, for tour finances. They represent management in their absence and are responsible for liaison with the local promoter, press, media, marketing, sponsors, record labels, and one-off events as required. They work very closely with the production manager on production costs and logistics and often are responsible for hiring the production manager.

"The logistics of the tour are also in the tour manager's hands, including accommodation, transport—both commercial and private—immigration, overall security, and daily scheduling. Finally and most important, the tour manager is babysitter and arbiter—they are responsible for making sure the band meets their tour commitments individually and as a group, and they are the one that everyone comes to with their complaints.

"While there is a growing trend to see the cost of everything and the value of nothing in the touring world these days, a good tour manager is of serious value to a band. Apart from the obvious fiscal savings they can achieve, they also crisis-manage daily, ensure the smooth overall running of the tour; they often set, and if necessary lift, the mood and can bring about a coherence and team spirit which is essential to a long tour. They are fundamentally team leader, wine steward, and den mother."

How important is a tour manager for a new band that is just beginning to gig? Can they hire a friend, or could one of the band take on the role? "A good tour manager as early as possible will be an asset to the band, providing coherence, experience, and someone impartial whom the members can rely on. Very early on the manager may provide this service, but the manager has other duties and cannot always tour with the band. Even if they do, as the band grows so, too, do the responsibilities of the manager, and a tour manager will eventually be needed.

"A friend of the band could possibly take on the role providing they are a proven tour manager, or have the skills outlined above and a good working knowledge of live touring. They need to understand that the bottom line is that the tour manager represents the band's *business*—they are not there just to mix drinks. In addition, a tour manager needs to be evenhanded and fair, so if they are a 'friend of the band' they need to be equally friendly with each member of the band, not one or two members, and they also need to be 'a friend of the manager'; otherwise their loyalties will be compromised. The tour manager has real and serious responsibilities, and while the tour manager may appear to be hanging out with the band, their first priority is to make sure everyone gets home without incident!"

When is the time to hire a tour manager, and how can you find one who suits your band's needs? "The best time to hire a tour manager is as soon as you can afford one. As previously mentioned, a tour manager can save you money and give the tour and band some direction and coordination on the road. Finding one, admittedly, can be hit-and-miss sometimes, but the management usually hires tour managers whom they work with regularly. It's usually a word-of-mouth thing based on either personal experience of the tour manager or references from others."

Is it expensive? Can they help find other crew in the beginning, and can they do multiple jobs like mix sound or lights? "The tour manager is the person with the overall day-to-day responsibility of the tour, and so their fee would have to reflect the level of their responsibility; so yes, relatively expensive, but having a good tour manager should be considered an investment, not an expense.

"When starting out, a band has to do what it can afford—usually the tour manager and production manager roles are combined, and sometimes the tour manager will also mix sound or lights. However, being a good sound or lighting operator does not necessarily qualify you to be a good tour manager. Also a tour manager has other responsibilities that are usually performed during the show such as show settlement."

Does the tour manager report to the band, manager, or both, and do they eliminate the need for a manager early in one's career? "The tour manager is usually hired by the manager and therefore reports to the manager, but ultimately both work for the benefit of the band. A few bands have a good understanding of the business side of the music industry, but that's not their primary job; they are primarily performers and 'creatives,' which is why they have management and a tour manager on the road to take care of business and logistics. Sometimes people forget it's a job—a band is basically self-employed and a tour manager represents the band's own business interests.

"A tour manager doesn't replace a manager at the beginning. It is more likely to be the other way around, with a manager taking on tour manager responsibilities until the band can afford a tour manager. The reason being that the tour manager's usual scope of responsibility is live and promotional touring, whereas the manager is accountable for all aspects of the band's business."

Now you get what the ideal tour manager can do for you, but how does that all fit into the bigger picture, because right now you're only the opening act?! Just to give you a little bit of a taste of what's coming up for you, I interviewed a good friend, Thomas Reitz of Entertainment and Concert Promotion, Inc. (ECPI), who is a tour manager, production manager, and site manager, having worked with a vast array of major artists including Luciano Pavarotti, the Three Tenors, Rihanna, and Madonna. In this dialogue, Thomas represents the headliner and your band has achieved a huge buzz and has been asked to open for a supergroup at the Meadowlands Stadium.

I'm really excited about the opportunity to open for your act. What do we need to know? "It's very important that you send us your technical requirements as well as your rider. Please be aware that you are not the headliner and do not demand things! Always ask for what you want in a kind manner; then we will help where we can. You have to understand that the headliner always comes first, so if for any reason there are any technical problems or the headliner is running late, your sound check will be cut short or cut out."

How early do we need to arrive at the venue; how much space will we have for setup? Can we give your crew our stage, light, and sound plots; use our drum riser, backdrop, or production? "You need to check with the production manager and stage manager about all details including load-in, production, and performance times, and note that the band should arrive at least an hour before they are due onstage. A lot of stress can be avoided if you talk to the production manager, and he will tell you all about what production is allocated for you and using your own production and space, etc. As a nice gesture, give him and the headliner some presents (a favored drink, perhaps) and remember, if you want to use the headliner's touring crew, make sure you are prepared to pay them, since it's their downtime. Again, check with the production manager and they'll see if any of the crew wants to make some extra cash helping you. Also make friends and compensate the sound and light crews for best results."

Do we get any spotlights, specials, sound checks, etc.? "Again, all of this will be determined by the main act's production manager."

Do we get any guest list, backstage passes, catering, dressing rooms, or parking permits? "All of these details should be in your contract and made by management, label, or agent, and should not to be discussed with the tour staff."

Remember that the headliner is depending on you to be there to warm up the audience. Sometimes the audience is still coming into the arena and the house lights are still on during your set. But it doesn't matter. If you play well and grab some new fans you are a winner. So whatever you do, don't arrive late, because you'll get thrown off the tour and lose your big opportunity. In Europe opening and support acts pay huge money to headliners to get on tours, so cherish the chance and blow everyone away.

I had a band I comanaged, the Only Ones, opening up for the Who, and I went and asked their legendary tour manager, Big Jim Callaghan, what the rules were. His answer still lives on with me to this day, and I think it is the best answer to any question I've ever asked in my whole life. I had asked what are the rules we need to follow and what is the procedure in regard to guests? He said, "You know what's right." By saying this, he accomplished a lot of things. He tested me, of course, and also gave me an ego boost as well as enough rope to hang myself. We were in Los Angeles and the Who's shows were all pretty much sold out, so having the power to have a guest list was a huge responsibility. Everyone my band or I had ever met or even sat next to on a city bus crawled out of the woodwork and somehow knew we had tickets! But we were smart and didn't tell the label, so they took care of tickets for the press and their own needs. We had a band meeting and set our own limit at two guests each per night. We proved we were responsible and passed the test. If we had abused the opportunity, we might have even been thrown off the tour. Working with the Who, Big Jim, and their manager, Bill Curbishley, was an extraordinary experience, and they still are a first-class, state-of-the-art organization.

Production Manager and Stage Manager

As I mentioned early on, your tour manager will be wearing many hats. But once your band is generating cash flow doing substantial touring, headlining clubs, and getting ready for the big stage, it will be time to consider hiring a production manager. Initially your production manager will also be your stage manager, and for the purposes of this book, I'll keep it simple and have them assume both roles. When you become a mega-act headlining stadiums, your needs will multiply exponentially and you'll be adding more and more support personnel and departments. At that point, you can e-mail us if you need further guidance, but I think it will be safe to say you'll already be in good hands and you'll know what to do. But remember that for right now, even if you don't have a dime for crew, draw a stage plot that you can use for every show you do and provide it to the club's stage manager or representative prior to performance.

Production managers are hired by your manager or tour manager. They are the people responsible for all of the technical aspects of your band's presentation. If they are any good, they really benefit your show and your touring operation. Peyton Wilson, Michael Ahern, Keith Bradley, and Mike Sinclair were some of the best when I was on the road.

When I was putting together a ballroom tour for PiL, one of the first things I did was consult with Mike Sinclair at See Factor Industry in Long Island City. (Mike is now one of the owners of Audio Incorporated, a concert sound and staging company based in New Jersey.) I knew Mike was a great production manager and I had worked on many events using See Factor, which was one of the best lighting companies, and later sound and lighting companies, in the business. I actually first met Bob See, the owner, when we were both working on Alice Cooper's historic Brazil tour. Meanwhile, with PiL, we needed to put together a simple yet effective stage set quickly and efficiently for our first show, which was coming up in a few weeks at Roseland, New York City's legendary ballroom.

See Factor had a great facility and could help us design our set and also provide any sound and lights we needed. I knew that John Lydon and Keith Levene from the band and Bob Miller, our studio engineer and live soundman, would get along with Mike. They'd respect Mike's expertise and creative skills and, on top of that, he had a great personality. Together all of us came up with a beautiful, simple set, more like a backdrop, that encompassed John and Keith's design. It resembled a subway station, and Mike helped build it for a great price. It worked for Roseland and could easily be set up and broken down for use in other venues, so all of our shows would have a unique stage look.

Although we didn't use Mike's skill as a production manager on the road, his experience was key to getting our production organized for touring. The production manager works with the band, its production team including sound and lights, its manager, and its business manager in developing and designing the production, then budgeting it based on the size of the venues a band will be performing in. They will contract on your behalf, subject to approval, all technical items necessary for your presentation including sound, lights, instrument rentals, and staging. Later on, when you are doing major venues and can afford a production manager full time, they either oversee the full stage production you carry with you or arrange that you have what's needed in each venue. They also are the head go-to person in charge of all the technical aspects of your presentation, and they report to the tour manager and manager.

I interviewed Steve Swift, the production manager for Leonard Cohen and other major acts, and asked him, **When do you need a production manager, and in the early stages of your career, can someone else, like the tour manager, assume the role?** "Yes, it is common for a tour manager to assume the role of production manager as well, in the early stages. Once a band moves into bigger venues and requirements begin to become logistically complex, these roles will then need dedicated practitioners."

Does the production manager design a band's stage plot, and how important is it to have one? Should I have one early on? "Yes. All bands need a stage plot and it needs to be kept up-to-date. A stage plot is a detailed plan of where everything is onstage for a performance: where the players stand, what monitors they use, where their backline gear is placed. The other key piece of information to go with a stage plot is a line input list."

How does the production manager interface with the band's crew, the other bands' crews, and the local venue staff? "In general terms, an artist's production manager will advance all logistical details for a performance with the venue and the promoter. Such details as what time the crew will arrive to set up for the show; what facilities are required on the day; how many local crew are required for the bump in and bump out; how much power is required; the amount of bus and truck parking required. It will also be the production manager's responsibility to make any alterations to the band's production to fit into a given venue. The production manager will also be responsible for the health and safety of the band, the crew, and the various contractors used to make a show happen."

What is their role and how do they differ from a stage manager? "A production manager is responsible for all production aspects of a tour or performance. And on any given day, a production manager is advancing the act's next show or series of shows in a region. A stage manager is responsible for the day-to-day setup for performance and the running of the crew at each venue. A stage manager concentrates on the here and now. It should be noted that a rock-and-roll stage manager is not the same as a theater stage manager. Their roles are quite different."

The **stage manager** is the person in charge of everything that takes place on the stage except making music. Basically, in the "premier league," the production manager runs the technical and the stage manager runs the stage, stage setup, stage crew, and keeps it all moving. The stage manager reports to the production manager and both report to the tour manager, who takes care of the band and lets them know when the stage is ready for them to play. But first the stage manager makes sure the lights and sound and house and stage monitors are ready, and that the stage crew and all of the other technical departments are ready, too.

Sound Engineering

I mentioned before that it's a great idea to learn how to run a PA and mix sound yourself. In small clubs you might have to, and sometimes you might even have to bring in your own small PA system. In my early days, we used Shure Vocal Masters. They were hundred-watt, six-channel power mixers with reverb and had two tower speakers. We also had, at best, something similar for onstage monitors, but often none at all. You may still find some of these systems in clubs or rehearsal studios.

Today for the most part, once you pass from hundred-seat clubs to bigger rooms, you'll find that most have good PAs, stage monitors, and knowledgeable operators. One of the attractions CBGB had was a kickass sound system run by Charlie Martin, a guy who was totally committed to making the bands sound good. And to many groups, CB's was the first place they got that jolt of energy that a powerful PA provides.

As I mentioned earlier, with PiL we created a special bass sound effect (B-EFX) to go with our music, and today with computers and digital effects you can really have fun and create a unique sound for your band live. Let's call it your "sound architecture." In general your sound engineer sets up and mixes your sound in the venue for the audience, and your monitor mixer sets up and mixes the sound the band hears onstage.

As soon as you are playing medium to large clubs and can afford to hire a sound engineer, do it. As mentioned, most clubs have one and if you treat them nicely, and maybe even give them a gift, they'll do a decent job for you. However, as you develop you'll want your own person so they can add enhancements and special touches where you want them. But always have a mic plot and give it to the soundman in advance of your show or, at the latest, when you first arrive on show day. As per the monitors, initially there may be a small console on the side of the stage that you preset and one of you or your fellow bandmates can adjust as need be. Later, the house engineer may control the monitor mix and you'll need to communicate with them, but one day soon you'll have a great multichannel monitor system with an operator on the side of the stage, and each band member can have the monitor mixer make adjustments as needed. When you are playing larger venues, for the most part you will be working with hired PA systems from local sound companies. It will be very important that your soundman provides complete microphone charts and audio riders that list all of your audio requirements so that the sound company can meet your specifications. A sample stage plot and microphone input list are on pages 222 and 223, respectively.

Lighting Crew

Lighting is pretty much the same way. Familiarize yourself with lighting equipment and boards. Study other bands and see what you like by way of colors, types of lights, and effects. Talk about lighting with the other bands you know and see what they do. Talk to the lighting crew at various clubs and venues and see if you can enlist some help to design lights for your show, as well as a lighting plot for setup and a lighting chart listing the various lights you want used, and how and when you want them used during your performance. In some rehearsal spaces you'll have lights to practice with, and as you gig more, there will be clubs with more lighting available to use. Initially their lighting people will provide some general lighting for your show, but by talking to the lighting crew and providing them with your lighting plot and some encouragement, you'll get them to help you as needed. Early on, however, in small clubs there may be some lights available and no one to set or run them. So once again, try to enlist some friends or family and/or have your manager or tour manager ready to lend an effort since lights, as we all know, add some dramatic support to your performance. And it's easy to aim lights, so don't hesitate—climb up that ladder in the club and gently aim the lights (cans) so they illuminate the stage to cover your setup. Also slide the gels you want to use under the lighting unit's front plate if you need color. If there are only a few units, make sure you aim lights (specials) on the lead singer, lead guitar, or keyboardist, and maybe just a nice wash on the rest of the band.

When the time comes to play as a headliner in clubs and you move to bigger venues, having your own lighting crew is essential, but again everything costs money and it's a step-by-step process. Remember to do a lighting plot and light chart right away so others can help you prior to having your own crew.

It's obvious that everyone understands the role of your sound system and having good sound people, and I personally have mixed hundreds of shows, so the perspective and information I provided is all firsthand. But with lighting as a real creative part of presentation, I went back to Steve Swift, who besides being a great production manager is also well known as a lighting director for concert touring, corporate theater, dance, opera, art and architectural installations, broadcast, and film.

What is the role of the lighting designer? "Lighting allows us to view a live performance in three dimensions. Lighting links the performers with their environment. Lighting brings together all the elements of a production and provides an emotional context for an audience to better appreciate and understand the performance. The lighting designer's role is to bring all these elements together in a cohesive form. The lighting designer can then provide your lighting director with a complete schematic that you can use in whole or part wherever you play."

How soon should a band consider hiring a lighting director? Can someone else, like the tour manager or manager, do lights early on, or should a band leave it to the house light man? "Generally speaking, a band will need a lighting director once it is headlining its own shows and has reached a level where it is carrying production. Leading up to this level, a lighting designer can provide an act with design elements that will help the act gain attention and assist an act in defining themselves visually. They can assist an act to make best use of available equipment and provide a guide for a tour manager/production manager or house lighting person to work from."

How important is a lighting plot? How soon can one be used, and what if you're limited by the headlining act or venue? What are the minimum essentials one must plead to get? "A lighting plot is a plan of where lights need to be placed and what type of lights they are. In the early stages of a band's career, flexibility is the key. A band capable of flexibility in setup can position themselves on a headline act's stage to take best advantage of existing lighting."

How do you figure out or design lighting to go with a band's performance and the types of lighting, colors, effects, specials, etc.? Do you work with the bands on design and in rehearsal? "A lighting designer will produce his or her best work when provided with a brief. Generally the production manager will give a lighting designer a budget to work to. The lighting director may also be restricted to an amount of truck space and the number of crew that can be engaged. In some instances, a lighting director will work with an act or band member to come up with a suitable design. Usually a design is conceived by the designer working in his or her studio. The designer will then attend rehearsals to devise the programming and operation of the lights. Programming will take place at production rehearsals."

Are lighting directors expensive, and should you try to buy any of your own gear or at least get some gels? "Yes, a lighting designer is expensive. One should consider lighting design as an investment in the artist's future. Good lighting design helps develop a reputation for good live performance. The decision to buy or hire equipment needs to be based on a number of criteria. How long will the act use the equipment for? Does it have the crew to put it up and pack it down? Can it be transported, and can it be stored when not required? If an act is using house systems, it is worth investing in gels to ensure some consistency."

A simple sample lighting chart is on page 224.

Road Crew

From day one, you've hired friends or relatives to help you with your gear, and by now either they've garnered some great experience or you've enlisted professional help. You need the crew to maintain, set up, break down, and transport all of your equipment to venues, studios, and rehearsals. Roadies will tune your instruments, make repairs on your equipment during performances, help you with changes that might take place onstage, and be there to deal with any situation that might arise. Make note that once you have more equipment than you can pull in a trailer behind your van and are doing a substantial number of gigs, your roadies will travel separately from the band with your gear and get to gigs ahead of the band to set up. So make sure whomever you do hire has a clean driver's license and is responsible, because if the truck goes off the road or the driver has a problem, there goes your tour.

A typical five-person band with guitar, bass, keyboard, drums, and lead vocalist needs a minimum of two crew people at the side of the stage. One should be positioned on each side, with one of them taking care of guitar and keyboards and the other drums and bass, and with both assisting the vocalist as necessary. A third would be even better. In general you need all of these people, but they all cost money. That's why you have taken great efforts from day one to put together a budget and enlisted help and even possibly investments from your friends. That's also why you've put a great effort into your Web status and invested in tools to build up your fan base.

As you progress, you'll keep track of your cash flow and determine how much money you have, what it costs to operate and to achieve the goals you've set. Your team will grow organically with people offering assistance, people who want to jump on your moving train, and at times you'll also need to take risks and invest in tools and items that are necessary for your growth.

Should I tell you what everything and everyone costs to hire? No. I'm not going to do that, because even though that great roadie might have been paid $1,500 a week by Band X, he might for some reason offer his services to you for peanuts because he loves what you're doing and wants to get involved. You can't afford to pay for me or most of the great people I've worked with, and you won't be able to pay for us until you're making $15,000 or $20,000 a night. But guess what: We might want to work with you because we see something that's great. *So first of all, make great music, don't be an asshole, and let everyone catch the passion that your commitment to your art exudes.* You'll find the people you need to work with one by one. And when the time comes, most of all, be honest. If you decide you can pay everyone full travel expenses, $250 a week, and a small per diem on the road when you first start touring, don't be surprised that you'll find some help. Later the $250 becomes $750 or $1,500 or more. I used to get four times that back in 1989, but like Nick Launay, the producer, said, sometimes you figure out how to get paid later.

Chapter 7

PROMOTION AND PUBLICITY

Radio Today

CHAPTER SPOTLIGHT

Radio Today • Indie Radio Promotion • Publicity • Webmaster

Because of the Internet and viral media, the role of radio as the key vehicle for exposing your music to the masses has greatly diminished. Terrestrial radio in many ways has caused its own demise since it has not been friendly to new music, college stations aside, and mainstream radio (contemporary hit radio, or CHR) has limited the exposure for new and developing artists. Satellite and Internet radio have opened the door somewhat, but more and more people are relying on MySpace, iTunes, YouTube, Pandora, and the like to find the bands they want to hear and for their listening pleasure. A major hit record still requires terrestrial radio airplay, and there are now avenues to get even DIY music on the airwaves. Remember, if you're touring, it really helps to have your music on stations in the markets where you are performing.

Records get on radio because somebody has a relationship with the program director and has serviced them with product. In the traditional industry, the label's promotion reps deliver your product to radio and if there was any type of priority on your record release, your label employed independent promotion people. The history of independent radio promotion is riddled with intrigue, including the huge payola scandals of the last generation where famous DJs were caught accepting bribes from unsavory promotion people to play records and where the charts were rigged. But today, especially with the corporate takeover of radio stations and the ownership of the major labels by multinationals, it's a very different game.

Before getting into specifics, I thought it would make sense to interview broadcast radio veteran Cindy Sivak again to provide some perspective on what's going on in radio today. She's been at the forefront of radio for a good many years, employed in key positions at United Stations, Dick Clark Productions, MTV Satellite Radio, and Sirius Satellite Radio. **With the advent of Internet radio stations like Last.fm, Pandora, and Live365, are the days of traditional broadcast (and even satellite) radio numbered?** "I believe there will always be a place for terrestrial (AM/FM) radio. It's too embedded in our culture. However, since the current generation has, and future generations will have, so many broadcast options available, its importance is slowly shifting. Think even twenty years ago. Most kids had a favorite FM radio station and could name their favorite DJs. Now? Not so much."

Have the changes in radio benefited new music and bands and provided opportunity for bands to get airplay, or do you think the top 40 mentalities might eventually permeate the new models as well? "The changes have provided an opportunity for many more bands to get their music out there to the public and, ultimately, to consumers. Just compare 1970 to 2010. Once only a handful of artists got signed each year to only a handful of record companies. Now, due to the availability of quality, affordable home audio and video recording equipment, artists can DIY and get professional results, and release it on their own labels and websites.

"The big difference is that while the pie got bigger, there are more people taking a piece of that pie. With the audience fragmented, artists may be successful yet on a smaller scale. Back then, with only a handful of radio, TV, and print outlets, if you made it, you made it big. Since satellite and Internet radio stations can be sliced and diced into specific music genres, they *are* playing *new* and *more* in their own little niche. If someone creates a new genre of music, there will be an Internet site somewhere playing it."

Do you have any advice for new bands, and possibly even unsigned or DIY bands, to get the attention of programmers and get radio airplay? "These days, traditional radio is the last to break an artist, so a new artist should exhaust all opportunities to get exposure, especially new media. Sean Kingston, Lily Allen, and Panic! at the Disco all had huge MySpace followings that attracted attention, while Justin Bieber was discovered on YouTube. Build up success stories like winning a local talent contest, have a great website or social media page with lots of 'friends,' and network. Be aware of what's the *next* Facebook or MySpace. With budget cutbacks, managers/labels are looking for anyone who already has a bit of a following or track record. Become the biggest thing in your school, your town, your county, your state, and you will attract someone's attention."

Are the label and indie promotion people still in control? "Label promo guys and indie promoters still only care about radio airplay—that's what they get paid to do—so they control their niche. A smart artist manager, however, realizes that their artist can gain exposure not only through traditional radio but syndicated/network radio, satellite radio, print magazines (yes—some still exist), online music sites, social networking sites, TV shows, cable networks, and of course touring."

Indie Radio Promotion

But how do you get on the air, especially if you don't have a record out on a major label? I interviewed Howard Rosen, the National Association of Record Industry Professionals top radio promotion executive of 2009. I've known Howie for more than twenty-five years and his clients include major record labels, indie labels, publishers, producers, managers, and artists including Justin Bieber, Nickelback, Jason Mraz, and many others. His company, Howard Rosen Promotions (howiewood.com), is one of the few that can get you on the radio, and they can also help promote your video as well as assist you with other services, so check out their website.

What is the role of an indie record promoter? "We act like any record promotion department of a record company would. We promote the records to radio, we do an open-ended interview with the artist, and we serve as a sounding board for anything that the artist might need. We give them information on music business attorneys, publicists, marketing people, record manufacturers, major company and independent distributors, talent agents, stylists, and artwork for their album covers. Essentially we are a source for all they need. Once they sign up for record promotion, we do everything we can to help them to get to the next level."

Who hires you, the labels or the artists themselves? "Major record companies, independent record companies, artists, publishers, producers, and managers."

What is the best way, and when is the best time, to capitalize on getting added to a radio station? "There are many times of the year that are better for your record to come out. The beginning of the year is always a great time for many reasons. One reason is the major record companies, for the most part, are owned by organizations in foreign countries; consequently, their fourth quarter is our first quarter. Thereby, they only have 25 percent of their budget left to go to battle in the beginning of the year. Another reason is that major companies release their biggest artists for the end of the year to take advantage of the holiday sales; due to this fact, the beginning of the year has less major artists with first singles. As the year approaches April, many of the record companies get their new budgets and start preparing for their new artists to impact radio. Some record companies feel that having two singles out in the calendar year, the second of which peaks in the fall, is a very positive situation because so many records are sold at this time of year and everybody wants to be on the charts at the same time."

Is it more difficult to get records added as a result of companies like Clear Channel owning scores of radio stations? "Clear Channel owns only 9 percent of the radio stations in America, which is hardly a monopoly, so there is plenty of opportunity for airplay. What's more, we do get airplay at those stations and every Clear Channel station is not as rigid musically as people would have you believe. So if one of their stations gets an enormous amount of phone requests, e-mails, and texts on a song that might not already be a national hit, the program director might tell the parent company or one of their sister stations that aren't playing the record and it could be added station by station."

Any advice you can give artists as to what they can do to make their music, and themselves, attractive to radio stations? "To begin with, you must understand that to comply with traditional broadcast formats, your songs should be no more than three minutes long. College and satellite radio may play extended album cuts but eventually it is top-40 radio that you need to have a huge national hit. Stations are attracted to artists making a buzz in their market, so national and localized press, gigs, and Internet activity have influence in getting your record added. Any kind of Internet presence wakes up radio stations. Hire independent promotion and provide them with materials to present to radio that can be sent along with your music. These should include an open-ended prerecorded interview (which we will help you produce), professional pictures of the band, press clips, and if touring, include that information as well.

"I don't believe in starting radio promotion regionally, because it's a damned if you do, damned if you don't opportunity. If you do well in the area, people say you should because you're from there. If you don't do well, people say you don't have the goods. The best way to go at a record is do a total U.S. campaign because it is difficult to know where your record will shine first. When it does pop and do well, you can always take it, bottle it, and move it to the next area. An artist should also keep note of the airplay information we provide them with as well as any chart information. If they do not understand any of the information we provide, they can ask us to explain. And they should be sure to keep us informed of any new press, shows, and sales—those are all useful tools for us to use."

Do indie DIY artists hire you, too, and does promotion now include more than just terrestrial radio? "Yes. With our company it does include terrestrial, Internet, and satellite radio, as well."

Publicity

A publicist is an important part of your team. In chapter one I interviewed Pam Workman, who told you how it is important to work with a publicist very early in your career because they are the ones who will help you in developing your public image. The publicist generates and manages your press and publicity. They either operate independently or as part of larger firms and they really serve as the bridge between you, the public, and physical and viral media. As Pam explains, your publicist will work with you in writing your press releases, finding the right photographer for your press photos, and helping you generate interest in your band from both the media and fans. Refer back to our discussion of stage presence and public image for some details, but understand that every film, every record, every play, every event that involves celebrities and public figures has a publicist directing the media flow.

Record labels will tell you they have publicists to help you, but you need your own because the label's publicist will work your record only when it's current, and you want to take your careers long term. Use a publicist on an as-needed basis and later on, when you can afford it, on a more regular basis. A publicist also puts you in position to generate press and promotion, so don't be surprised if your publicist wants to take you to an A-list party or comes up with offers to play on Letterman or Jimmy Kimmel. They're the ones who really work with you and figure out every angle to generate the buzz. Pam Workman offers more insight now.

Do publicists do more than just get press, and how do they do it? "It's all conditional on the type of publicist you have. In my opinion the best publicists cross media, mediums, and platforms. And that means that they move seamlessly not only across media, mediums, and platforms but industries as well, so that the best publicist has relationships in almost a 360 fashion."

What are the realistic expectations clients should have? "I think the realistic expectation is to hope for the best but plan for the worst. And the worst is that no one is going to listen to you unless you work hard and put one foot in front of the other, go after one fan at a time, one blogger at a time, one sound engineer at the local venue at a time. And you keep putting one foot in front of the other until that break happens. The funniest story is, and you know this as well as I do, that all of these bands seem like overnight successes based on the public perception. The reality is—I'll never forget this with the Magic Numbers; they were everywhere, everybody loved them. They were being reviewed in every credible music place, every music site, they were on every late-night show and they were asked, 'How does it feel to have this sudden success?' They were like, 'No one realizes we have been working together on this for ten years!' That to me is the story and the takeaway that every young artist who has been struggling should look to."

What's the best way to find a publicist? "I actually think the best way to find a publicist is through references where people say 'I worked with this person and they delivered.' The thing about publicists is that we're all good talkers."

Webmaster

In today's world, the newest member and one of the most important in your support team is your Webmaster. Each professional in every area of the industry that I interviewed throughout the book confirms that you must take advantage of websites and social networks. It's where you do your initial research, find tools to get your band organized, generate visibility, and create a buzz. You establish a fan base, build on it, and interact with your fans every day. You can find help producing, manufacturing, and distributing your music both physically and digitally. You can also find help with booking and touring as well as design, development, and manufacture of your merchandise.

Utilizing everything available to you will help kick-start your career so that the industry takes notice of you. But you need to find someone to help you do this from Day One. As we said, in the beginning it might be one of your bandmates, friends, or family, and that's fine, but remember, with the right person you can achieve great rewards, generate income, and succeed. You're lost if you are Luddite. You may as well just give up. The business is not the same as it was last year, and who knows where it will be next year? Find the most qualified person *now*, one with extraordinary computer skills and ahead of the technology curve, one who loves your band, your music, and your sensibility, and who knows, they could be your little sister! So make them a member of your team today.

EPILOGUE

Congratulations! You've read or at least scanned nearly two hundred pages of text and interviews with experts, and hopefully you've absorbed a good deal of information from the many facts and materials throughout the book. In "band think," you've achieved the equivalent of your BA degree and now you can truly go out into the real world prepared, but while pursuing your dream, you'll quickly realize that a master's degree would be even better.

Don't hesitate and waste time worrying about what you can't do. Be empowered by all of the knowledge you've gained, and make sure you keep your eyes and ears open to learn as much as you can from your upcoming experiences and from those you meet on your journey. This is how you earn your master's degree. There is nothing better than real-life experience, and if you digested all of the information we provided, you'll now be working with a great team of people who will help you make the right career decisions to proceed. Don't forget to keep this book handy so that you can refer to it whenever you may have a question, and you can also contact us at our website (rockininthenewworld .com) which will be continually updated to keep up with the constant changes taking place as our industry is reinventing itself.

As so many of our experts have said, it's all about the music you make. And that should be your primary focus. And while you are busy creating your symphony, you'll be confident in the knowledge you've already gained, and will happily anticipate what will come in the future. You'll be on a great creative path and will see results. Your endeavors will be enhanced, your success will be shared by the members of your team, whom you love and respect, and it will all work. Why? Because knowledge is power, and you and your bandmates are learning new things every day. You can achieve greatness because you understand what it takes and what needs to be done each step of the way. You're involved in every aspect of your career and your team is in sync with you and your values.

Remember the checklist you put together when you first started out, and how you charted your goals and progress every step of the way?

You should be up to at least page twenty-five by now, and you know the list will keep on growing with things you want to accomplish and things you have already achieved. You can taste success and that's good, but don't let it fill your head with crap. Stay clear and focused, stay away from the vices that are now brought forward by newfound wannabe friends. It's not the time to sit back and rest on your laurels; more than ever, it's now the time to plan your next move so your rocket to the top gains momentum and prepares to hit warp speed rather than spiral back to earth.

I've seen too many bands unwittingly blow it at this juncture in their careers, but they had no resource to refer to for advice. But today there is so much infrastructure and support to draw on. Let us help you. We've been through the mill and want to save you from yourselves.

You don't have to be celibate or a teetotaler, but excess of any kind will destroy you. Whether it's food, drink, sex, or drugs, abuse destroys your health, creativity, and friendships. It will kill your band. Success can also kill you if your head's not screwed on right. You need to learn to live in the spotlight and not become a victim of it. We have too many examples of great talent whose lives were cut short by their vices, or whose fortunes were lost or absconded as a result of bad advice, gold-digger spouses, and general screwups. Be smart, be prepared, and always get a prenup.

For additional resources, tips, blogs, free music, links, news, and a sounding board for your music, go to our website: rockininthenewworld.com

Valuable Music Web Resources

AffordableRecording.com
affordable-recording.com
Low-cost recording.

Allmusic
allmusic.com
Research and listen to music on this comprehensive reference source.

Amazon.com
amazon.com
Online store.

Aquarium Drunkard
aquariumdrunkard.com
Audio blog featuring daily music news, interviews, features, reviews, MP3 samples, and sessions.

ArtistData
artistdata.com
Updates your band profiles across MySpace, Facebook, Twitter, and other sites.

ArtistForce
artistforce.com
Booking widget, interactive press kit, live entertainment business network, career support, performance feedback, eight thousand venues.

Artistopia

artistopia.com

Membership-based independent artist portal with industry news, music, charts, and shopping.

Audacity

audacity.sourceforge.net

Cross-platform sound editor.

Audio Incorporated

audioincorporated.com

Sound system installation, sales, and rentals, New York City area.

Audiolife

audiolife.com

Drop-ships merchandise, CDs.

Avid Audio

avid.com/US/products/family/Pro-Tools

Pro Tools audio creation and production software.

AWeber

aweber.com

Dedicated e-mail marketing system helps you build e-mail lists and stay in touch with your contacts.

Bandcamp

bandcamp.com

Easy tools to share your music. Shows where your fans are, what they're listening to, tracks they're obsessed with, and which they're skipping; streaming and downloads.

BandCentral

bandcentral.com

A communication, organization, and management tool for bands, enabling bands, crew, and management to communicate, store files, and manage gigs, social networks, finances, and fans.

Band Metrics
bandmetrics.com
Analytics. Identify fans, measure social engagement, find hot markets, track radio plays, discover trends, gauge attitudes, get in-depth reports, and more.

Band Name Maker
bandnamemaker.com
Name your band.

Band Promote
bandpromote.com
Band promotion and marketing, music industry relations.

Bandize
bandize.com
Take control of your career, get organized. "A suite of DIY tools all available and packaged in one smooth, cohesive web application."

BandVista
bandvista.com
Easy-to-use tools for bands and musicians to create and maintain websites with industry-level features.

Bandzoogle
bandzoogle.com
An all-in-one musician marketing platform that helps bands build their websites, promote their music, and sell it online.

Big Live
biglive.com
Films concerts of emerging and unsigned bands and broadcasts them on the web. Also uses its social network for virtual concert events.

BigChampagne
bigchampagne.com
A digital media measurement (metrics) firm, the digital-industry equivalent of Nielsen SoundScan.

Tracks digital airplay, streams, and downloads. Publishes Ultimate Chart (ultimatechart.com), the week's most popular artists and songs; integrates data from song and album sales, radio airplay, online audio and video plays, and fans.

Billboard magazine
billboard.com
Music industry Bible.
Note: Billboard *and* MySpace's *new Dreamseekers chart is made up from aspiring artists culled from the web. The chart appears weekly in* Billboard *magazine and on the* Billboard *website.*

Blip.fm
blip.fm
Twitter-like music sharing and recommendation network.

BobDigital
bobdigital.com
Mobile recording truck (New York City area).

Bravado
bravado.com
One of the world's leading concert merchandise companies owned by Universal.

Cakewalk
cakewalk.com
Audio equipment and software. Leading developer of powerful and easy-to-use products for music creation and recording.

CD Baby
cdbaby.com
CD Baby is the largest online distributor of independent music, providing digital and physical distribution; DIY musician blog.

Champion Sound
championsound.com
E-mail marketing, Twitter and Facebook integration, guest list management, MP3 track storage, and distribution.

CreateSpace

createspace.com

Free online publishing tools help you complete and sell your work. Distribute on Amazon, your own website, and other retailers without setup fees or inventory.

Cut Merch

cutmerch.com

Smaller-batch, on-demand merchandiser.

Disc Makers

discmakers.com

Everything you need to copy, print, and package CDs, DVDs, posters, and postcards. A sister company of CD Baby.

Donenfeld Management

donenfeldmgmt.com

Financial services; business management, tour management.

ECPI

ecpi.cc

Thomas Reitz's Entertainment and Concert Promotion, Inc. represents artists and events and provides services to major and upcoming touring artists.

Eventric

eventric.com

Provider of software and online services for touring, offering "Master Tour," a system to help you plan, manage, and track your touring operations.

Express Entertainment

expressent.com

Keith Cooper's artist management and music publishing service.

Facebook

facebook.com

World's number one social network that allows you to create a band profile, set up an artist page, and add your music from other sites. Use it!

Fanbase

getfanbase.com/

Music fans get the latest content from their favorite bands in one download. Interactive platform.

FanBridge

fanbridge.com

"We make managing e-mail lists, mobile lists, and social networks fun, easy, and effective. . . . Get more fans, excite and track fans, keep fans engaged."

Fanscape

fanscape.com

A social media marketing agency "fostering targeted word-of-mouth conversations with the individuals, influencers, and gatekeepers who inhabit the online social-media landscape."

Fenway Recordings

fenwayrecordings.com

Mark Kates's artist management (not a label).

Foursquare

foursquare.com

Location-based social networking. Use to interact with your fans and maximize your appearances.

Gen-Y Rock Stars

GenYrockstars.com

Greg Rollett's fantastic resource guides and blogs for the independent musician.

Gigleader

gigleader.com

Find venues and events; get gigs.

GigMasters

gigmasters.com

Database of live bands; helps you book gigs throughout the United States.

Go Daddy
godaddy.com
Domain name registration.

Google Analytics
google.com/analytics
Google Alerts
google.com/alerts
Stats from your website; get e-mailed whenever you are mentioned online.

Grooveshark
grooveshark.com
Online music search engine, music streaming service, and recommendation software application allowing you to search, stream, and upload music; offers ways to share and promote your music to fans; Grooveshark artist dashboard offers tools for creating and managing merchandise sales, licensing new music, and making deals with labels, producers, film, and TV.

Gotham Rocks
gothamrocks.net
New York City's modern rock showcase series. Prizes, endorsements, marketing, terrestrial and Internet radio, plugs, interviews; websites and web content; television ads and shows.

Guitar Center
guitarcenter.com
Ultimate place to find instruments, amps, and other band gear.

Home Recording
homerecording.com
Blog offering advice and equipment for home recording.

Howard Rosen Promotions
howiewood.com
Independent radio promotion. Gets your music on the radio.

iContact

icontact.com

E-mail marketing solution allowing you to capitalize on the revenue generating power of e-mail marketing.

Inadaba Music

inadabamusic.com

"Network and make music together through online collaboration . . . Tools and services from networking to education, to production, promotion, and distribution."

IndieHitMaker

indiehitmaker.com

"Provides your live show sales numbers" to SoundScan to help get your indie band charted on Billboard's indie charts.

Indie Band Manager

indiebandmanager.com

Helps with gigs, promotion, and merchandise.

Indie on the Move

indieonthemove.com

Venue details and ratings from across the United States.

Invisible Records

invisiblerecords.com

Martin Atkins's website. Label, Tour:Smart programs (see also toursmart.tstouring.com*), tips for touring, videos, music, and forums.*

iTunes

itunes.com

Online store.

JamBase

jambase.com

"The largest database of show listings and ticket information, authoritative content, community, and personalization tools for fans."

KMFDM
kmfdm.net
KMFDM band website.

Last.fm
last.fm
A music service that connects you to people who like what you like.

LawDepot
lawdepot.com
Basic legal agreements; see especially lawdepot.com/contracts/bandpartner/.

Live Nation
store.livenation.com
Big merchandise company owned by the world's largest concert promoter.

Library of Congress: U.S. Copyright Office
copyright.gov/forms
Copyright forms. File online.

Live Music Machine
livemusicmachine.com
Get gigs.

Loud Feed
loudfeed.com
Promote your music on websites, blogs, social networks, or on your Loud Feed site.

Mobile Roadie
mobileroadie.com
"A turnkey platform to quickly and inexpensively build and manage mobile apps."

MoFuse
mofusepremium.com
"Makes it easy and affordable for any business to build and manage a mobile website."

Music and Technology
music-and-technology.com
"Resources for the recording musician."

Music Arsenal
musicarsenal.com
Manage and schedule upcoming projects, plan tours, and find places to promote your music.

Musician's Friend
musiciansfriend.com
Gear, lighting, accessories, and effects.

Music Submit
musicsubmit.com
Submits your music to genre-specific radio stations, online music magazines, directories, blogs, podcasts, indie record labels, and other electronic music media.

MySpace
myspace.com
Leading social network offering music, videos, and products. A social entertainment destination that includes a mashup with Facebook, providing customization of interests that allows the subscriber to follow artists or celebrities they like and lets them establish a personal entertainment stream on their profile. Also provides artists with a vehicle to sell their music, list performance calendars, and promote their band via MySpace Dashboard.

Nettwerk/Polyphonic
nettwerk.com
Terry McBride's companies: labels and management.

New Music Seminar
newmusicseminar.com
New Music Seminar: a conference for the next generation music business. Go there!

Next Big Sound
nextbigsound.com
Tracks analytics and provides a centralized place to monitor all the behavior and activity happening for artists both online and off.

Nimbit

nimbit.com

One place to easily manage everything about your business; direct-to-fan e-mail marketing, MP3, CD, merchandise, and ticket sales, as well as management tools for marketing and analytics.

1212

1212.com

Database of music-industry-related web information in over fifty countries.

The Orchard

theorchard.com

Music and video distributor that drives sales across more than 660 digital and mobile storefronts in seventy-five countries, as well as physical retailers.

OurStage

ourstage.com

Music discovery and community for all genres, with iPhone app for connecting with artists on the go. Owned by AOL.

Owngig

owngig.com

Provides software and services that help you manage gig booking and promotional and administrative needs.

Pandora

pandora.com

Online streaming radio in all genres allows indie musicians with physical product available on Amazon to be in their rotation.

Ping

apple.com/itunes/ping

iTunes-based social network for music. "Follow your favorite artists and friends to discover the music they're talking about, listening to, and downloading."

Pitchfork

pitchfork.com

Killer commentary, music and tour news, and reviews.

Playlist
playlist.com
Discover and listen to free music online; create and share playlists.

Pollstar
pollstar.com
Worldwide concert industry news and reviews.

PopMatters
popmatters.com
Music news, reviews, blogs, and tour dates; also film, TV, and pop culture.

PulseAMP
pulseamp.com
Get your band organized, from your contacts to inventory to press.

RecordLabelResource
recordlabelresource.com
Resource site with info on general business, recording, touring, promotion.

RethinkPopMusic
rethinkpopmusic.com
Marketing, publicity, booking, recording, and legal tools to "make a living making music," utilizing marketing initiatives via showcases, tours, music, and innovative projects.

ReverbNation
reverbnation.com
A central site for tracking, promotion, on-demand CDs, download cards, merchandise, and distribution. "Fan collection features, gig tools, stats tools, opportunities to earn money."

Richards & Southern
richardsandsouthern.com
Country music's top tour merchandise company.

RocketHub
rockethub.com.
Helps artists promote and fund projects via Internet crowdfunding.

Shoutcast
shoutcast.com.
Radio directory with over 47,000 free streaming Internet radio stations.

Section 101
section101.com
Web-based publishing platform "provides artists with an easy-to-use environment to intuitively create, deploy, and manage their digital persona, while providing integrated tools to organize and leverage their fans via branded communities and viral content."

SongCast
songcastmusic.com
"Release[s] music into major digital retailers including iTunes, Rhapsody, AmazonMP3, eMusic, Napster, MediaNet and all of their respective international stores such as iTunes Europe and Amazon UK; . . . link[s] social networking into the retailers."

Sonicbids
sonicbids.com
Create EPKs, book gigs, get analytics, and other tools.

SoundCloud
soundcloud.com
Online audio distribution platform. "Takes the hassle out of receiving, sending, and distributing music for artists, record labels, and other music professionals."

SoundOps
soundops.com
Online mastering studio.

Spotify

spotify.com

On-demand music streaming, in both free and premium services, and now claims to have more than six million users in Europe.

StarPolish

starpolish.com

Business advice.

Super D

sdcd.com

The nation's number one rack jobber, a wholesaler with "the world's largest selection of music, movies, and games."

Tech-9 Music

Tech9music.com

Concert promotion and booking at Live Nation, AEG Live, and Six Flags venues and others on the East Coast in conjunction with Gotham Rocks.

Topspin

topspinmedia.com

Services ranging from full-service marketing and site development to web design; pick, pack, and ship custom merchandise.

Track Entertainment

trackentertainment.com

Lee Heiman's website. Lifestyle marketing, event management, technology.

TubeMogul

tubemogul.com

Automates video uploads and gets them posted to YouTube, Facebook, MySpace, etc.

TuneCore

tunecore.com

Digital music distribution, promotion, manufacturing, registration, product.

Twitter

twitter.com

twitter.com/tweetforatrack

Use Twitter and Twitter music apps to connect with fans.

Unsigned Band Web

unsignedbandweb.com

Free music: unsigned bands.

Virtual Label

virtuallabel.biz

Digital and physical distribution; manufacturing, marketing, publicity, touring, business management; artist management. This is Peter Wright's new company. Make sure you read his interview for some great insight on distribution.

Wanduta

wanduta.com

Insurance, equipment deals, travel, events booking, and management.

WordPress

wordpress.com

Content management system.

Zazzle

zazzle.com

On-demand merchandise.

zZounds

zzounds.com

Musical instruments, amps, and recording equipment.

Music Performing Rights Organizations

American Society of Composers, Authors and Publishers (ASCAP)
ascap.com

Broadcast Music, Inc. (BMI)
bmi.com

Harry Fox Agency (HFA)
harryfox.com

SESAC
sesac.com

SoundExchange
soundexchange.com

Record Industry Trade Organizations

American Association of Independent Music (A2IM)

a2im.org

Organization of independent music labels that promotes business opportunity, provides advocacy and representation, as well as networking opportunities for the independent label community.

National Academy of Recording Arts and Sciences (NARAS)

grammy.com

The Recording Academy® sponsors the annual Grammy® Awards. NARAS members include artists, musicians, songwriters, composers, engineers, and industry professionals. Offers all types of arts advocacy and outreach programs to positively impact the lives of musicians, industry members, and society at large.

The National Association of Recording Merchandisers (NARM)

narm.com

Not-for-profit trade association that serves the music and entertainment content delivery community in a variety of areas including networking, advocacy, information, education, and promotion. Members consist of music wholesalers and retailers, including brick-and-mortar, online, and mobile music delivery companies. Associate members consist of distributors, record labels, multimedia suppliers, technology companies, and suppliers of related products and services. Individual professionals and educators in the field of music are also members.

Recording Industry Association of America (RIAA)

riaa.com

Trade group that represents the U.S. recording industry to foster a business and legal climate that supports and promotes members' creative and financial vitality. Its members are the record companies that comprise the most vibrant national music industry in the world. RIAA members create, manufacture, and/or distribute approximately 90 percent of all legitimate sound recordings produced and sold in the United States.

Conventions and Festivals

Afro-Punk Music Festival (several cities)
afropunk.com

Billboard Events (several cities)
billboardevents.com

City Showcase (United Kingdom)
cityshowcase.co.uk

CMJ Music Marathon & Film Festival (New York)
cmj.com

The Cutting Edge Music Business Conference & Roots Music Gathering
(New Orleans)
cuttingedgemusicbusiness.com

DIY Convention (Los Angeles)
diyconvention.com

Independent Music Conference (several cities)
indiemusicon.com

International Live Music Conference (United Kingdom)
ilmc.com

Mid-Atlantic Music Conference (North Carolina)
midatlanticmusic.com

Millennium Music Conference (Harrisburg, Pennsylvania)
musicconference.net

New Music Seminar (New York, Los Angeles)
newmusicseminar.com

Noise Pop (San Francisco)
noisepop.com

RedGorilla Music Festival (Austin)
redgorillamusic.com

South by Southwest (Austin)
sxsw.com

Dictionary of Terms

Advance: Money paid by a company to an artist or band pursuant to a contract that is deducted against future royalties. The usual case is a signing advance by a label, publisher, or merchandiser that is recouped by future earnings.

Analytics: The science of analysis used in the digital music space to track the airplay, downloads, sales, and general activity of digital music product.

A and R: An abbreviation for *artists and repertoire*; record company staff or independents in charge of selecting new artists and overseeing their recording for the label. Traditionally A and R executives selected songs (repertoire) for singers or bands, but today many artists write their own music, so that aspect of their role has diminished. They do select artists, however, based on hearing songs they believe can be hits.

Arrangement: The organization (i.e., the structure) of a musical composition for performance.

Artist manager: The CEO of the artist's team. They direct the task of developing an artist's career. The artist manager typically consults with and advises the artist on all business decisions and attempts to promote the artist through all available means. They are the artist's voice and liaison to the business side of the industry.

Assignment: The transfer of rights to a song or catalog from one copyright owner/publisher to another.

Backline: Musical equipment, such as guitar and bass amplifiers, needed onstage for a live performance. It is technically the line of equipment forward of the drum riser and behind the lead singer/musicians' performance space.

Biography: A concise account of an artist's or group's experience or background for use in press and promotional purposes.

Booking agent: Represents artists and books gigs for them at clubs, concerts, and events.

Business manager: Financial advisor, usually CPAs who oversee and manage financial aspects of artist's career.

Cans: Studio term meaning headphones.

Cartage: The technical term for the transport of your equipment from one point to another.

Catalog: The term for the collection of songs that you've written.

Clearance: The granting of rights to play an artist's song publicly on radio, TV, or in film.

Compulsory license: Statutory mandate given to a copyright owner to permit third parties to make sound recordings of the copyright owner's song after it once has been recorded.

Consignment: An arrangement through which a retailer is provided an artist's product, such as CDs or merchandise, and pays after the inventory is sold.

Console/board: The audio desk or control panel for mixing and recording live and in studio. Also refers to the lighting desk.

Controlled Compositions: Songs that you write, own, or participate in. Since this is an area where you generate personal money from every CD sold, record labels try to negotiate with you so they have to pay royalties only on a percentage of the songs that are considered licensed to them for your records that they release.

Co-op advertising: Advertising that is split or partially paid for by a record label, distributor, sponsor, or artist and the retailer.

Copublishing: The joint publication of one copyrighted work by two publishers.

Copyright: In the United States, it is the exclusive rights granted to authors and composers for protection of their works registered with the U.S. Copyright Office.

Copyright infringement: Stealing or using part or all of somebody else's copyrighted song without permission.

Cut-outs: Record company term for overruns, discounted compilations, and out-of-date product.

Digital distribution: Online Distribution of product and content.

Distributor: The firm that sells and ships a record company's product to retail outlets and one-stops.

Engineer: Operates the mixing consoles for performance and recording. Mixes the sound levels for PA systems and recordings. Works with technicians in selecting and coordinating proper use of microphones, baffling, and other sound elements to maximize and obtain proper balance.

EQ: An abbreviation for *equalization*. Electronically boosting or dampening the level in certain frequency ranges relative to other frequencies from the same source. Equalizers are processing units that adjust the strength of specific frequencies.

Fader: A control knob or slider on a console or amplifier that changes the strength of a signal. The most basic example would be the volume control knob on a stereo. Turn it up to 11 like in *Spinal Tap*.

Free goods: A fixed percentage of product deducted from the total in a shipment to account for "giveaways" and promotional copies distributed for free. Note that no royalties are paid to the artist for "free goods."

Gels/color gel: Transparent colored material used to color your stage lights, placed in front of a lighting fixture in the path of the beam. Gels are cheap and easily installed and even if you are doing small gigs, use them and you can have the colors that you want onstage.

Grand Rights: Rights normally excluded from standard publishing and administration deals that relate to the adaptation of songs for theatrical stage performances such as Green Day's *American Idiot.*

Groupies: Male or female fans who seek relations with band members, sometimes leading to catastrophic results to either themselves or the band. You might not want to take one home to meet Mom.

Humpers: Personnel hired by venue staff to assist with loading and unloading gear.

Indie: Unaffiliated record labels and artists. The term, like *alternative*, is not as truly independent as it once was.

Lead sheet: A musical notation (written) version of a song's melody along with the chord symbols, words, and other pertinent information. Not as fully detailed as a complete score.

Liggers: Hangers-on, basically people who are wannabe band fans or entourage members who want to travel with the band and be part of the operation, but bring no value and perform no duties. Not to be confused with groupies.

Lighting plot: A diagram showing the stage, placement, and type of lighting used for performances.

Marketing: Generating public interest in an artist's music/career through various promotional means, including print, television, radio, and the Internet.

Master: The original recording from which dubs/copies are made. It is the finished recording of a song from which CDs/records are manufactured.

Master use license: A license granting permission to use existing recorded material, including but not limited to: vocals, music, TV or film dialogue, speeches, and sound effects. For sampled material, a master use license is required regardless of the length or amount of material that is used.

Mechanical license: A license granted by a copyright owner for the use of copyrighted material on a recording. Mechanical licenses are required any time a copyrighted composition is used.

Mechanical royalties: Monies earned for use of a copyright in mechanical reproductions, most notably records and tapes.

Mix: The final audio product combining all the elements into one stereo composite soundtrack. This is placing and balancing all of the tracks and mixing them down to stereo or mono.

Monitors: Onstage sound/speakers for band to hear themselves while playing, allowing them to adjust their instruments/vocals accordingly.

Music publisher: The individual or company who represents the rights of various song titles on behalf of a songwriter and gets them commercially recorded; exploits the copyrights; protects the copyrights; collects income from performance, mechanical synchronization, and printing rights in the United States and in foreign countries.

Non-controlled compositions: Songs written by outside songwriters, i.e., you cover someone else's song or that of anyone else who is not a member of your band and signed to your record label.

One-stop: Wholesale record dealer that sells the records of several manufacturers to local record stores and jukebox operators. Distributes major label product in areas where the major labels do not have their own distribution teams and to stores that the major labels do not sell to.

Per diem: Money given to performers and crew when on tour to cover daily expenses of food and other personal incidentals.

Points: A percentage of royalty money artists and producers earn on records sold.

Production manager: Oversees and coordinates group's overall production for concerts. Is the band's liaison with promoters, local venue staff, unions, and vendors.

Program director: Radio station employee who determines which songs shall be broadcast.

Promoter: Concert and event producers. Live Nation and AEG are the biggest in the United States.

Publicist: Press agent. Coordinates press and visibility for artist. Often is involved in helping to develop a group's image and media persona.

Publishing Administration: Usually referred to as administration of a copyright. This involves the supervision of all copyright, financial, and contractual aspects of either an individual song or an entire song catalog.

Rack jobber: Independent companies that distribute product on behalf of many record companies to small record stores, drugstores, coffee houses, supermarkets, etc.

Record producer: Works with band and engineers in studio to maximize recording process. Often assists with arrangements. Producers oversee the creative and administer the business/financial aspects of recording.

Recoupable: Money advanced to you against future earnings that must paid back to the label before you see any profits.

Rider: Additional terms attached to a performance contract that includes specific details such as numbers of free tickets, hospitality, technical details, security, and other items.

Rigger: Technicians who set up and hang all flying gear: backdrops, light rigs, pipes, that hang over stage and in venue.

Riser: Raised platform onstage, usually for drum kit.

Roadie: Various tour production personnel who assist band on the road. Can be stage techs, equipment techs, and various other production assistants.

Rough mix: A basic recording sound mix, a work in progress. Used for reference but not final distribution.

Spec: Short for *speculative*. Usually referring to services made available in advance with payment deferred until the project sells. Bands like spec deals on recording studio time.

SEO: Search engine optimization.

Show settlement: Final collection of payment due following a performance. A full settlement includes a breakdown of all expenses incurred by the promoter and all income received from ticket and sales of other items.

Stage manager: Oversees group's production onstage. Works with production manager.

Stage plot: Diagram showing the instrument, equipment, and microphone placement onstage.

Strike: Break down. Refers to tearing down the set/gear after a show.

Sync rights/sync licenses: A fee paid to a label to have part or all of your song used as background in film, television shows, or advertisements.

Tour manager: Oversees and coordinates the staff and details of an artist's schedule including concert tours, recording, etc.

Helpful Forms

Artist Personnel Information
CONTACT

Full name
_____

Stage name
_____

Home address
_____
_____

Phone numbers
_____

E-mail
_____

Date of birth
_____

Social Security number
_____

Emergency contact [name/phone]
_____

Country of birth
_____

Country of citizenship
_____

Passport number
_____

Issued
_____

Expires
_____

Arrested? When, where, why?
_____
_____

Driver's license number
_____

Issued by
_____

MEDICAL INFORMATION

Allergies
_____

Medication
_____
_____

TRAVEL PREFERENCES

Frequent flyer airlines and numbers
_____
_____

Seat preference

Special meals

FINANCIAL INFORMATION

Business manager

Accountant

Address

Phone

E-mail

Your business name

Tax ID number

Bank

Address

Phone

Account name

Account number

Routing number

SWIFT code

PUBLISHING INFORMATION

P.R.O. affiliation(s)

Publishing company name

Address

Phone

Sample Tour Itinerary Page

FRIDAY NOVEMBER 16, 2010
WASHINGTON, D.C., MCI CENTER EASTERN TIME

TRAVEL by Bus from Philadelphia: 140 Miles

BAND departs Philadelphia at 11am and arrives at venue at 2pm for Sound check

CREW departs Phila after show 11/15 and arrives at D.C. venue at 7am for Load-in

VENUE	**SHOWTIMES**
MCI CENTER	Load In: 7am
601 F Street	**Sound Check: 2:30pm**
Washington DC 20004	Doors: 7pm
TEL: 202 555 1212	Showtime: 8pm
FAX: 202 555 1313	Curfew: 11pm
PROD: 202 555 1414	

CTC: JOE SHOWMAN
PROMOTER: 202 555 1515
Rockin' In The New World
P.O. Box 43416
Montclair, NJ 07043
TEL: 973 555 1212
FAX: 973 555 1313
Mob: 973 555 1414
CTC: Bob Tulipan

AFTER SHOW TRAVEL
BAND AND CREW BY BUS: Washington, D.C. to New York City
HOTEL: XYZ HOTEL
1500 Broadway
New York, NY 10000
212 555 1212
CTC: Joan Hotel

Sample Artist Itinerary Daily Page

[Your Band Name Here]

DATE OF SHOW   CITY

DATE:

VENUE:

ADDRESS:

PHONE:

FAX:

ADD'L NUMBERS:

OTHER BANDS ON BILL:

HEADLINE ( ) YES ( ) NO

MORNING TRAVEL:

Depart from/@ Time:

Traveling to:

Distance:

Estimated Arrival:

LOAD IN:

SOUNDCHECK:

DOORS:

ON STAGE: SET LENGTH:

CURFEW:

TICKET PRICE:

CAPACITY:

HOTEL:

ADDRESS:

PHONE: FAX:

E-MAIL:

CONTACT:

PHONE: MOBILE: FAX:

E-MAIL:

NOTES:

SECURITY: _____

PARKING: _____

ROOM SERVICE: _____

DOCTORS: _____

24 HOUR PHARMACY: _____

PROMOTER: _____

PROMOTER MOBILE: _____ E-MAIL: _____

PRODUCTION CONTACT: _____ MOBILE: _____

PRODUCTION NUMBERS: _____

AFTER SHOW TRAVEL: _____

DEPARTURE TIME: _____

BUS: _____ LIMO: _____

AIRLINE: _____ FLT#: _____

Finance Breakdown Work Sheet

ARTIST: _____ DATE OF SHOW: _____

PROMOTER: _____

E-MAIL: _____

PHONES: _____

LOCATION: _____

CAPACITY: _____

TICKET PRICES: $_____ X _____ = $_____

$_____ X _____ = $_____

$_____ X _____ = $_____

$_____ X _____ = $_____

TOTAL GROSS POTENTIAL: $ _____

LESS TAXES: $ _____

TOTAL GROSS AFTER TAXES: $ _____

Limousines _____ Ushers _____

Catering_____Door guards_____

Staging _____

Sound + lights_____Ticket takers_____

Advertising _____ Security _____

    Radio + TV _____ Police _____

    Print _____ Private _____

    Internet + other _____ T-shirts _____

    TOTAL _____ Firemen _____

Rent _____ Utilities _____

Spot lights _____ Electrician _____

Spot ops _____ Medical _____

Setup _____ Insurance _____

Cleanup _____ ASCAP/BMI _____

Piano tuner _____ Licenses/permits _____

Forklift _____ Runners _____

Ticket printing _____ Generator _____

Ticket commission _____ Riggers _____

Box Office _____ Chair rental _____

Stagehands _____ Equipment _____

Loaders _____ Stage manager _____

Payroll _____

EXPENSE TOTAL _____

Artist guarantee _____

Support act _____

Production _____

Total fixed expenses _____

TOTAL FIXED EXPENSES _____

Artist guarantee _____

Total variables _____

Total expenses _____

Promoter profit _____

Variable additions _____

Breakpoint _____

Band will receive % _____

Sample Contracts

Sample Contract (small venue)

ROCKIN' IN THE NEW WORLD.COM
P.O. Box 43416
Upper Montclair, NJ 07043

SAMPLE PERFORMANCE CONTRACT*

PLEASE NOTE: Various Venues and Agencies may have variants of agreements that may be more detailed and this draft is merely for reference and possibly for your initial use at small-level venues; but it's always best to write out all particular details and have both Purchaser and Artist agree to all terms.

Agreement made this date _____ between YOUR BAND (hereinafter referred to as "ARTIST") and COMPANY (hereinafter referred to as "PURCHASER").

It is mutually agreed between the parties as follows:

The PURCHASER hereby engages the ARTIST and the ARTIST hereby agrees to furnish the entertainment presentation hereinafter described, upon all the terms and conditions hereon set forth, including those on the reverse side hereof entitled "Additional Terms and Conditions."

For presentation thereof by PURCHASER:

(a) Name of Artist/Group: YOUR BAND

(b) Number of Musicians: (   )

(c) Place of Engagement and Capacity: BIG CLUB   cap. 300

                                                          I MAIN ST.

                                                          YOUR TOWN, USA

(d) Contact Info John Promoter

                         tel #

                         e-mail

(d) Date and Time of Engagement: 1/7/11   8pm

(e) Duration of Engagement: (1) 60 MINUTE SET

(f) Fee and Terms: $1,500.00 + 60% of gross ticket receipts in excess of $2,250.00 after applicable taxes if any. Purchaser will supply Sound + Lights and professional operators without fee to Artist.

Payment of 50% as deposit by wire and signed within 7 days of contract and attached contract rider agreement. Balance of guarantee payment is due in cash at venue at least 2 hours prior to performance. Final payments to be made in cash to Artist Tour Manager immediately after show. Purchaser will provide all receipts and box office statements. All payments are made without any deductions whatsoever unless agreed in writing prior to performance.

(g) Total Gross Potential

Ticket Price: $10.00 Gen. Admission x 300 tickets = $3,000.00 Gross

Artist Bank Wire Information:

YOUR ACCOUNT NAME

YOUR BANK

YOUR WIRE INFO

YOUR ABA NUMBER

X_____   X_____

    PURCHASER   ARTIST

    BY REPRESENTATIVE

DATE:_____   DATE:_____

THE ABOVE SIGNATURES CONFIRM THAT THE PARTIES HAVE READ AND APPROVED EACH AND ALL OF THE "ADDITIONAL TERMS AND CONDITIONS" SET FORTH HEREIN.

Sample Rider Contract

RIDER TO CONTRACT DATED _____

BY AND BETWEEN _____

("PURCHASER") AND _____

("VENDOR") FURNISHING THE SERVICES OF _____

_____ ("ARTIST")

Any contract returned by Purchaser with any portion of the contract or rider deleted, detached or modified in any way shall be, at the option of the Vendor, null and void and neither the Artist not Vendor shall be liable to the Purchaser for failure of the Artist to complete or perform the proposed engagement.

Any and all proposed modifications of Contract or Rider must be discussed with Vendor's representatives.

I.   BILLING

A.   Artist shall receive 100% (ONE HUNDRED PERCENT) top line sole star billing in all manner and terms of advertising and publicity, lights, displays, marquees, posters, newspaper ads, and programs. No other act shall appear on the same show or on any advertisements for the engagement without the prior written consent of the Vendor. When Artist is playing with other acts, no other act's name shall appear in larger type than or on the same line as the Artist's.

B.   Artist shall control choice of opening act, which shall be paid for by the Purchaser.

2.   PAYMENT

All deposit payments as agreed by contract hereunder shall be made payable to _____or by Bank wire to (YOUR BAND) C/O YOUR BANK, YOUR CITY, ACCT #
            ABA ROUTING #:   Balance of fee if called for in contract MUST be made on the night of performance prior to show in CASH unless otherwise MUTUALLY AGREED in writing at least (I) One week prior to engagement.

3.   PERSONAL APPEARANCES

Purchaser shall not schedule any interview, appearance or other promotional or publicity activity purporting to involve Artist without Vendor's prior written consent.

4.   ADVERTISING

Purchaser will provide Vendor a complete budget and advertising proposal for the presentation a minimum of 45 days in advance of concert date All advertising to be mutually agreed upon by Vendor. It is understand that a minimum of 25% of budget will be used for viral marketing, street teams and fly postering.

5.   MERCHANDISE AND ARTIST'S RIGHT OF PUBLICITY

Purchaser shall have the right to use the name of the Artist solely for the exploitation of the performance hereunder. The performance hereunder shall not be sponsored by or tied in with any commercial product or company. Vendor shall have the exclusive right to advertise, promote, disseminate and sell in and about the place of engagement and elsewhere souvenir program books, pictures, articles of clothing, jewelry, recordings or other articles of merchandise bearing Artist's name or likeness and to collect and retain for its account all proceeds thereof or, at Vendor's option, to refrain. If there are any venue fees associated with ancillary sales at the show they CANNOT exceed 25%. This is NON-NEGOTIABLE.

6.   RECORDING OF ENGAGEMENT

A.   Purchaser shall not permit the filming, recording, reproduction or broadcast, either visibly or audibly of any portion of the Artist's performance without the prior written consent of Vendor.

B.   Artist shall have the right without the payment of any consideration to Purchaser, to tape, film and/or otherwise record Artist's performance and to use any such recording as Artist sees fit.

C.   NO CAMERAS, AND TAPE RECORDERS NOT PERMITTED. Artist shall have the right to abstain from performance upon notice of such equipment even if such person is Authorized press unless such person has obtained prior written consent from Artist or Vendor. Vendor security will to the best of its ability screen all patrons to prevent filming and recording. It is understood that CELL PHONE CAMERAS ARE EXEMPT.

7. SECURITY

A.   Purchaser shall be responsible and liable for any and all of Vendor's and Artist's equipment from the time of load-in to load-out. Purchaser shall provide a minimum of two (2) personnel commencing at sound check for the stage door and dressing room areas.

B.   No person will be allowed on stage, backstage or in the dressing room areas at all prior to performance, during performance or after performance without Vendor's approval. Any of Vendor's personnel shall have the right to enforce said restriction.

C.   Purchaser shall be responsible for the safety of all of Vendor's personnel commencing at sound check and accompanying said personnel as long as needed. Security staff shall be discussed with Vendor upon arrival at venue.

D.   NO CANS, BOTTLES, HARD OBJECTS are to be allowed in venue.

8. DRESSING ROOM

Artist requires one (1) private dressing room and a private bathroom. These rooms must be clean, well heated or cooled and lockable with a key for the Tour Manager. Space heaters required if below 60° F. Dressing room must have direct access to stage. NO WALK THROUGH HALLS.

9. <u>FOOD AND DRINK</u>

Artist requires the Venue provide the following items:

A. LOAD-IN: Purchaser to provide coffee, tea, milk, sugar, honey, pastries, doughnuts, a variety of juices and fruit for four (4) in Artist's crew and Union personnel and local stagehands. This shall be ready for load-in time. Sandwiches, soda, milk, and coffee shall be available in the case of an afternoon load in.

B. HOT MEAL for ten (10) shall be available after sound check (menu to be provided by Artist's Tour Manager).

C. Coffee, tea, 2 Gallons of Milk, sugar, lemons, honey, limes, etc.

   1 case of assorted sodas

   3 Quarts of Juice (apple, orange, grapefruit)

   4 cases Heineken

   12 large plastic bottles of non-carbonated Spring Water

   Assorted fruits

   Accompanying paper napkins, cutlery, cups, ice, etc.

   25 Hot and Cold cups

   16 Large Towels

   2 coolers and 2 bags of ice

   Salt, pepper, toothpicks, ashtrays

   1 Liter of Vodka

Timing and placement of these items shall be coordinated with Artist's Tour Manager.

10. <u>SOUND, LIGHTS AND PRODUCTION</u>

It is agreed, all sound and lighting expenses, as well as any additional production expenses, shall be paid for in full by Purchaser in advance of performance. Vendor shall have the right (but not the obligation) to provide sound and lighting companies of its own choice and the right to approve all outside companies hired by Purchaser. Artist has full hands-on control of all consoles (sound and lights). Artist requires a multi-channel communication system between house and monitors.

A. Purchaser shall provide two (2) Full trusses (front and rear stage) and four (4) super troopers with operators. Four (4) Genie towers can replace trusses.

B. Purchaser shall provide access to the venue not later than twelve (12) hours prior to doors opening to the public. Artist shall set up all equipment and instruments, road cases, etc. at its own discretion and allow whatever space available to support acts. BACKLINE DOES NOT MOVE.

C. Purchaser shall furnish parking facilities for a twenty-four-foot (24') truck and van or bus within fifty feet (50) of Stage/Load-in door.

D. Purchaser shall provide a minimum of four (4) loaders to be available from load-in until Artist and Artist's personnel depart.

E. A minimum of two (2) twenty (20) Amp circuits are required on stage, both with four (4) receptacles—one stage right, one stage left—for Artist's instruments plus one hundred (100) amp single phase for PA and lights. In all cases, adequate power shall be Purchaser's responsibility. Purchaser shall be solely liable for any personal injury due to improper grounding or power problems.

F. B-EFX (Bass Effects) for PA sound reinforcement in the sub-bass area which consist of separate X-over 2 DBX 160 compressors; One (1) Stereo or two (2) mono Total Parametric Equalizers and sub-woofer speaker cabinets needed per say determined by size of venue (negotiated with Artist's Sound Engineer). Support act will be able to set up their equipment and sound check only after Artist Production Manager gives approval.

G. C-EFX (Lighting Effects) Sixteen (16) Aircraft lights to be hung on trusses as crowd lights. Twelve (12) to be hung on rear truss, four (4) on floor stands for floor effects.

H. Two (2) Fender Reverbs with separate master volume control; Two (2) SVT Ampeg Bass Amps (tops and bottoms); One (1) sixteen inch (16") and one (1) eighteen inch (18") Floor toms with stands.

I. Spectrum Analyzer with calibrated mic (such as Klarc Technic 1/3 Octave Spectrum Analyzer and calibrated mic).

J. Always, Purchaser agrees to take out audience seats if physically possible. Stage shall be no less than four feet (4') high, thirty feet (30') deep and twenty-five feet (25') wide by set up. Proper snow removal equipment and rain covers must be available in inclement weather.

K. Artist shall be allowed two (2) hours for sound check. During sound check, no one shall be allowed in venue, no doors shall be opened, no distracting noises shall be tolerated and should be quieted by Purchaser. Security shall guard all backstage entries and dressing rooms while Artist is sound checking. No one permitted without Backstage Pass.

L. Support bands will be allowed to set up their equipment only after Artist has finished sound checking and their Production Manager approves space allocation for the support act.

M. If sound and lights are provided by Purchaser, all systems schematics and details must be provided to Artist's Sound and Lighting Engineers 14 days prior to show and must be approved in writing via fax or email no later than 7 days prior to show date.

N. It is Purchaser's obligation to inform Artist's Production Manager of any mandatory Union breaks, curfews, fire regulations or peculiarities at least seven (7) days prior to tickets being placed on sale, as subsequent evaluation thereof may place the performance in jeopardy.

O. Purchaser shall provide one (1) Drum riser twenty-four inches (24") high by eight feet (8') wide by eight feet (8') minimum.

P. Monitors - as per discussion with Artist's Sound Engineer.

11. BACKSTAGE PASSES AND COMPS

Tour Manager shall provide All Access and House Only passes to Venue staff and Security Personnel as required. No house/venue issued passes will be honored. No one other than bona-fide working personnel, police or fire department are permitted back stage unless approved by Tour Manager or accompanying an Artist staff member with a tour laminate.

12. TRANSPORTATION, PERMITS, VISAS, CLEARANCES

A. At Vendor's request, Purchaser shall provide Vendor with all local transport for ten (10) people to and from airport, Artist's hotel and concert venue. One fifteen (15) seater van or two (2) limousines.

B. Purchaser shall provide at their sole cost all necessary permits, licenses, immigration clearances and authorizations as may be necessary if concert is performed outside of the United States.

C. Purchaser shall provide one (1) first class hotel suite within three (3) blocks of venue for use by Artist on the day of the show.

13. <u>TICKETS</u>

With respect to performances where the act is being paid based on a percentage, the following provisions shall apply:

A. Purchaser shall furnish _____ not later than ten (10) days before the scheduled performance with a ticket manifest signed and certified by a bonded ticket provider/ printer, setting forth the number of tickets to be sold in each category, and all tickets shall be sold in accordance with the price stated.

B. Purchaser shall be responsible to pay Vendor its percentage for every seat occupied within place of Performance, except for twenty-six (26) complimentary tickets, which may be distributed to the Press by Vendor; and twenty-four (24) complimentary tickets per show for use by Artist. Any unused portions of Artist's complimentary tickets may, with permission of the Artist, be placed on sale on the day of performance. There will be NO GUEST LIST and NO PRESS LIST.

C. Representatives of Vendor shall have the right to enter the box office at any time prior to, during and after the Performance to examine and make extracts from the Box Office records of Purchaser relating to the gross receipts from the engagement.

D. Percentage payments provided for herein shall be accompanied by an itemized written signed statement from the Purchaser setting forth accurately the computation of said percentage payments.

E. All pricing for tickets, the scaling of the house and any discounting of tickets must be approved by Vendor. Such approval will not unreasonably be withheld.

F. Purchaser further agrees to have on hand at the place of engagement on the night of the show, for counting and verification by a representative of the Artist, all unsold tickets. Artist shall be compensated for the difference between tickets manifested and the number of unsold tickets verified by Artist's representative. If purchaser violates any of the preceding provisions of this paragraph, it shall be deemed that the

Purchaser has sold a ticket for each seat in the house at the highest price.

G. It is fully understood and agreed that no deductions whatsoever are to be made from the contract price contained herein or from any percentages.

14. INSURANCE

A. Purchaser shall keep in full force and effect, at its sole expense, for a period commencing forty-eight (48) hours prior to the performance(s) and terminating forty-eight (48) hours after the performance(s), public liability insurance, including contractual liability, with respect to the place of performance in companies and in form acceptable to the Vendor to afford protection to the limit, per occurrence, of not less than Two Million Dollars ($2,000,000) with respect to personal injury and Two Million Dollars ($2,000,000) with respect to property damage.

B. Purchaser hereby indemnifies Vendor and Artist and saves them harmless from and against any and all claims, actions, damages, liability and expenses (including attorneys' fees) in connection with the loss of life, personal injury and/or occasioned wholly or in part by any act or omission of Purchaser, its employees, agents, concessionaires, licensees, contractors or employees.

15. MISCELLANEOUS

A. Vendor may terminate this agreement if:

a. Artist or any member of Artist's group shall die, become ill or incapacitated for any reason;

b. In Vendor's judgment, performance of the engagement may directly or indirectly expose Artist, any employee of Vendor or Purchaser or any portion of the audience to danger of death, of injury by any outbreak of violence or civil strife of any kind;

c. Performance of any of Vendor's obligations shall be rendered impossible or impractical by any reason of strikes, civil unrest, unforeseeable act or order of any public authority, epidemic, dangerous weather conditions, national or local state of emergency, fire or other event or condition of any kind or character;

d. Performance of any of Vendor's obligations shall expose Artist or any member of Artist's group, Vendor or Vendor's employees, agents or independent contractors to civil or criminal proceedings of any kind;

e. If this agreement shall be terminated for any of the reasons referred to in this paragraph, Vendor shall promptly refund to Purchaser any amount theretofore paid by Purchaser to Vendor pursuant to this agreement, and Vendor shall not be liable to Purchaser for any other loss, damage or expense claimed to have been suffered by Purchaser as a result of such termination;

f. Vendor reserves the right to cancel this engagement not later than thirty (30) days prior to play date by notice in writing to Purchaser at address given on contract;

g. No provision contained in any concert hall lease, which is inconsistent with any provision of the contract or this rider shall be binding on Vendor unless Vendor shall consent in writing thereto;

h. If, on or before the date of any scheduled performance hereunder, the financial standing or credit of Purchaser has been impaired or is unsatisfactory, Vendor shall have the right to demand payment forthwith of the guaranteed compensation specified in the contract, and if the Purchaser fails or refuses to make such payment forthwith, Vendor shall then have the right to cancel the contract. In the event of cancellation, neither Vendor nor Artist shall have any further obligation to Purchaser hereunder and Vendor shall retain any monies theretofore paid Vendor by Purchaser; and Vendor and Artist shall be entitled to pursue any and all remedies available to them by law;

i. If Purchaser breaches any of the provisions contained herein, refuses or neglects to provide any of the items required of Purchaser hereunder, or fails to or refuses to proceed with the presentation of the engagements which are the subject of this agreement and/or make any of the payments referred to herein, or fails to furnish the type, size and quality of technical equipment requested by Vendor and Artist, or if at any time prior to or during the actual Performance of Artist, should said technical equipment be otherwise than in perfect working condition, then in any of such events, (1) Vendor or Vendor's representative, in Vendor's sole discretion, may thereupon terminate this agreement without liability of any kind to Purchaser; (2) Vendor and Artist shall have no further obligation to perform hereunder; (3) Vendor shall retain all amounts theretofore paid to Vendor by Purchaser; (4) Purchaser shall remain liable to Vendor for all additional compensation herein provided;

and (5) Vendor shall also be entitled to exercise all remedies then available to Vendor by law;

j. Except where specified, all performances hereunder shall be held indoors and shall not be subject to cancellation due to inclement weather conditions;

k. Purchaser warrants and represents that it has the legal capacity to enter into this contract. Purchaser further warrants that it has or will secure (at its sole cost and expense) any and all applicable permits, licenses, etc., regarding the presentation of the concert as may be required by any applicable state, local or federal law, rule, regulation or statute, having jurisdiction over the concert.

l. The contract (1) cannot be assigned or transferred without the written consent of Vendor; (2) contains the complete understanding of the parties, and (3) cannot be amended or varied except by instrument in writing signed by the parties. The validity, construction and effect of the contract shall be construed under the laws of the State of _____ applicable to contracts made wholly to be performed therein.

_____ _____

AGREED TO AND ACCEPTED

PURCHASER

DATE

AGREED TO AND ACCEPTED

VENDOR ON BEHALF OF ARTIST

DATE

Helpful Stage Guides

DIY Stage plot

drums + 2ft high 8×8 riser

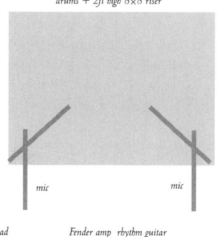

monitor   *monitor*

mic   *mic*

Marshall amp   lead   *Fender amp   rhythm guitar*   *bass amp*

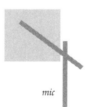   

mic   *mic*   *mic*

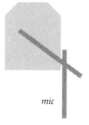

mic   *mic*   *mic*

Lead Guitar   *Lead Vocal + Rhythm Guitar*   *Bass + Vocals*

effects box

monitor   *monitors*   *monitors*

Microphone Input Chart

For Live Production or Studio

Date _____

Show_____

Input	Instrument	Microphone	Notes

XYZ Band Lighting Plot

Par 56 Lights with Gels
4 Channel Dimmers
8 Channel Board
(this is as simple as it gets)

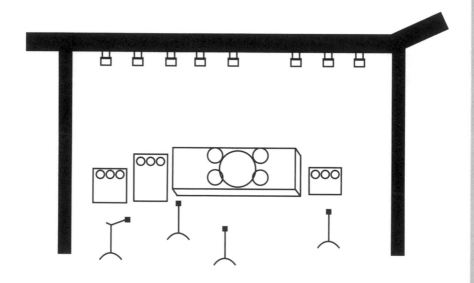

Sample Artist- Management Agreement

Misha Baker ("Artist")
352 E. 9th St.
#4C
New York, NY 10003
Dated as of July 1, 2010

Starmaker Management Associates, LLC.
1700 Broadway, 19th Floor
New York, NY 10019

Dear Misha,

The following, when signed by you and by an authorized representative of Starmaker Management Associates, LLC. ("Manager"), will constitute a complete and binding agreement (the "Agreement") with respect to your engagement of Manager as your exclusive personal manager:

1. Territory:
   The world.

2. Scope of Manager's Activities:

   (a) Manager shall be your exclusive personal manager, during the Term, and throughout the Territory, solely in connection with your activities in the entertainment industry, and shall confer with, counsel, guide, advise and assist you in all matters pertaining to such activities, including, without limitation, in connection with phonograph records, music publishing, personal appearances, modeling, acting and the use of your name and likeness for commercial purposes.

(b) Manager's services hereunder shall include, without limitation, the following:

    (i) assisting you in the selection and procurement of literary and artistic material for your exploitation as an artist;

    (ii) assisting you in the selection and engagement of producers, engineers, mixers, writers, musical directors, choreographers, vocal coaches, video directors and producers, and other creative and technical personnel;

    (iii) counseling and assisting you in the development of a professional act;

    (iv) acting as your liaison to record and publishing companies, merchandisers, booking agents and other actual and potential users of your talents and services; and

    (v) assisting you in the selection of, and preliminary negotiation with, the following: theatrical, booking and similar agencies; other third parties that seek and/or procure employment and engagement for artists; and other potential users of your talents and services; and

    (vi) regularly reviewing with you all actual and potential venues and engagements of your services in the entertainment industry and all other matters relating to your professional career therein.

3. <u>Term:</u>

The term of this Agreement (the "Term") shall consist of one contract period commencing as of the date hereof and continuing until June 30, 2012.

4. <u>Manager's Commission:</u>

(a) During the Term, and provided Manager performs its services in accordance with the terms and conditions of this agreement, you shall pay a commission ("Manager's Commission") to Manager of twenty (20%) percent of your Gross Income (as hereinafter defined) derived from any and all areas of the entertainment industry, including the music industry, to include, but not be limited to, music, TV, film, acting, writing, commercials, songwriting, publishing, Broadway and live theatre, merchandise, electronic games and any new and developed areas by Manager and Misha Baker, during the term and which relate to Misha Baker's work in the entertainment business, except as specifically provided for hereunder.

(b) Intentionally Deleted.

(c) As used in this Agreement, "Gross Income" shall mean all income received by you in connection with your activities during the Term in the entertainment industries, as a recording artist, songwriter, producer, actor, model, writer, publisher and all other fields of endeavor and commercial uses of your name and likeness approved by you, except as specifically provided for hereunder. Income derived from agreements which were substantially negotiated prior to the expiration of the Term and entered into within three (3) months after the expiration or termination of the Term ("Post Term Agreements"), shall be deemed to have been entered into during the Term.

(d) Notwithstanding the foregoing, Gross Income shall not include, and there shall be deducted therefrom, the following:

(i) all music publishing income retained by or payable to third parties including, without limitation, songwriter royalties payable to co-writers and publishing company administration fees;

(ii) bona-fide third party costs and fees incurred in connection with motion picture, television and other types of synchronization or general licenses;

(iii) actual recording, production and other recoupable or non-recoupable costs of master recordings and audiovisual works (other than payments [e.g., musician's fees and producer's fees] to you as a portion of those recording costs);

(iv) fees, advances, royalties and other payments paid to third parties including, without limitation, record producers,

producers and directors of audiovisual works, and band members;

(v) income derived by any entity in which Manager has a proprietary or income interest;

(vi) that portion of your income from any "package" which is payable in commissions to a talent agent or is otherwise payable to third parties as part of the cost of production;

(vii) (A) reasonable tour expenses (e.g., monies paid to technical and creative personnel, monies payable for transportation and accommodations), (B) monies paid to opening or other support acts, and (C) monies paid for hiring and transporting "sound and light" facilities and other similar or related production costs (e.g., video projection and special effects equipment);

(viii) any income derived by you from any business investments, or entrepreneurial or other non-entertainment-related activities. Notwithstanding the foregoing, in the event that you request Manager to render any services in connection with any such activity, you and Manager agree to negotiate in good faith Manager's compensation therefor;

(ix) costs incurred to collect Gross Income, including, without limitation, reasonable attorneys' fees and other legal costs, and auditors' costs (regardless of whether any audit recovery results);

(x) any judicial or arbitrators' award which you receive in the nature of punitive or reputational damages; and

(xi) Intentionally deleted.

(xii) income derived from MTV, VEVO (or related entities) in connection with voiceovers performed by Artist, as well as producing and/or writing relating thereto, unless otherwise agreed to by Artist, in writing, pursuant to an opportunity procured by Manager.

(xiii) income derived from any other voiceovers performed by Artist, pursuant opportunities not procured by Manager, or are not branded as the performances of Artist.

(xiv) the amount representing the production costs of the audiovisual work titled "On the Prowl Live from Miami" (the "DVD"), but only from the gross revenues generated from the exploitation of the DVD.

(xv) the amount representing the production costs of the audio work titled "On the Prowl Live From Miami" (the "Live CD"), as well as the amount representing the photo shoot and artwork therefor, but only from the gross revenues generated from the exploitation of the Live CD.

(xvi) 50% of the amount of publicist and bio fees and expenses paid by Artist during the Term, but only from the gross revenues generated from the exploitation of musical and audiovisual products.

(xvii) amounts representing the costs of any new studio recordings paid for by Artist during the Term, which such costs are mutually agreed to by Artist and Manager. Such amounts spent by Artist which would be considered reasonable, taking into consideration all reasonable facts and circumstances, shall hereby be deemed to be agreed to by Manager.

(e) Notwithstanding anything contained herein, provided Manager is not in material breach of this Agreement, Manager's entitlement to Manager's Commission after the Term ("Post Term Commission") shall be as follows:

(i) The Manager's Commission derived from agreements entered into during the Term (including agreements relating to Term Product [as defined below]) shall be as follows: (A) twenty percent (20%) of gross income in perpetuity on any and all Term Product (e.g., records, videos, films, books, movies, synch licenses, publishing, songwriting, etc.); (B) twenty percent (20%) of live dates that were booked during the Term, but were performed after the Term is over.

(ii) "Term Product" shall mean all (A) master recordings and other products embodying your performances or using your name, image, voice or likeness which are recorded, produced, manufactured during the Term, and released during the Term or within one year after the end of the Term, and (B) compositions written by you embodied in master recordings which are recorded by you during the Term, and released during the Term or within one year after the end of the Term. For clarification, the following items shall not be considered Term Product hereunder:

A. "On the Prowl Live From Miami" (DVD)

B. "On the Prowl Live From Miami" (CD)

C. "Alley Cat" (CD)

D. "Unplugged Sessions" (CD)

E. "Hissy Fit" (CD)

(f) All Gross Income derived from your activities which are subject to this Agreement, shall be paid to and collected by your independent accountant ("Business Manager"), and such Business Manager will render monthly accountings and payment hereunder (if any) to Manager. Said Business Manager is hereby authorized and directed by you to pay the Commission (and all reimbursable expenses pursuant to paragraph 6 hereof) directly to Manager. Any and all Gross Income received directly by Manager shall be delivered by Manager, to Business Manager (or to you as set forth in this paragraph below) within five (5) days following your or Manager's receipt thereof. Notwithstanding the foregoing, until such Business Manager is engaged by you, you shall have the right to collect all Gross Income hereunder, and to pay the Commission to Manager in accordance with the terms hereof.

(g) Notwithstanding anything contained herein to the contrary, Manager agrees to reduce Manager's Commission, in connection with gross revenues generated hereunder, from any non-music industry related services rendered by Artist if such services would customarily be subject to a commission by a third-party agent, manager, etc., in an amount equal to such third-party's reasonable and customary commission amount, but, in any event, by no more than 50% of Manager's Commission hereunder.

5. <u>Manager's Power of Attorney:</u>

Manager's power of attorney shall be expressly limited to executing agreements with respect to live appearance "one-nighters" or a series of live appearance "one-nighters," not to exceed more than three (3) consecutive appearances, with your prior written approval of such activities where reasonably feasible.

6. <u>Management Expenses:</u>

(a) You (or Business Manager) will reimburse Manager for any and all reasonable expenses incurred by Manager with your knowledge, on your behalf, directly in connection with the activities referred to in paragraph 2 hereof, provided that: (i) you will not be responsible for any portion of Manager's overhead expenses; (ii) subject to subparagraph 6(a)(iii) hereof, if Manager incurs travel expenses on behalf of both you and other of Manager's clients, you shall be responsible only for your pro rata share of such expenses and (iii) Manager shall not incur without your prior written consent (A) any single expense in excess of One Hundred

Dollars ($100) or (B) aggregate monthly expenses in excess of One Thousand Dollars ($1,000).

(b) Manager shall furnish you or the Business Manager with appropriate documentation of Manager's expenses within thirty (30) days after the date such expense is incurred, and reimbursement of such expenses, as appropriate, shall be made in connection with the monthly accountings referred to in subparagraph 4(e) hereof.

7. <u>Accountings and Audit Rights:</u>

Upon written notice by either party to the other, the party to whom such notice is addressed shall furnish an accounting to the other party of all transactions between the parties since the last such accounting, within thirty (30) days of such request; provided, however, that neither party shall be obligated to account to the other more than four (4) times in any one (1) calendar year period. Each party shall have the right to reasonable inspection of the other's books and records at any time within one (1) year after an accounting statement is rendered hereunder to the inspecting party in order to verify the accuracy of such accountings; provided, that such inspection may take place not more frequently than once with respect to each such statement and only once per any calendar year. Such inspection may be made only upon the inspecting party giving the other party written notice at least thirty (30) days prior to making any such inspection. Each party shall be deemed to have consented to all accountings rendered by the other hereunder and said accountings shall be binding upon each party and not subject to objection for any reason unless specific written objection, stating the basis thereof, is given to the other party within two (2) years after the date rendered.

8. <u>Warranties and Representations:</u>

Each of the parties hereto respectively warrants, represents and agrees that it is not under any disability, restriction or prohibition, either contractual or otherwise, with respect to its right to execute this agreement or to perform fully the terms and conditions hereof.

9. Indemnification:

Each of the parties hereto agrees to indemnify, and hereby do indemnify, save and hold the other harmless from all loss, damage and expenses (including legal costs and reasonable attorney's fees) arising out of or connected with any claim by any third party which shall be inconsistent with any agreement, warranty or representation made by the indemnifying party in this agreement; provided same is reduced to final adverse judgment or settled with the prior written consent of the indemnifying party. You and Manager each agree to reimburse the other, on demand, for any payment made at any time after the date hereof with respect to any liability to which the foregoing indemnity applies.

10. Cure:

In order to make specific and definite and/or to eliminate, if possible, any controversy which may arise between the parties hereunder, you and Manager agree that if at any time you or Manager, as applicable, believe that the terms of this Agreement are not being fully and faithfully performed hereunder, you or Manager, as applicable, will so advise the other in writing by registered or certified mail, return receipt requested, of the specific nature of any such claim, non-performance or misfeasance, and the party receiving such notice shall have a period of Thirty (30) days after receipt thereof within which to cure such claimed breach.

11. Independent Counsel:

(a) Each of the parties hereto warrants and represents that in executing this agreement, they have relied solely upon their own judgment, belief and knowledge and the advice and recommendations of their own independently selected and retained counsel, if any, concerning the nature, extent and duration of their rights and claims hereunder, and that they have not been influenced to any extent whatsoever in executing this agreement by any representations or statements with respect to any matters made, if any, by any party or representative of any party hereto.

12. Key Man:

During the Term, Topper Katz ("Katz") shall be actively involved in, and primarily responsible for, the activities and services to be provided by Manager hereunder. In the event that Katz is not actively involved in, or primarily responsible for, the activities and services to be provided by Manager, your sole remedy shall be to terminate the Term, upon written notice to Manager, effective upon the date on which Katz is no longer actively involved in, or primarily responsible for, the activities and services to be furnished by Manager hereunder, and you shall be relieved of any obligation to pay Manager's Commission with regard to Gross Income received after the effective date of such termination, specifically including any income payable pursuant to paragraph 4(e).

13. <u>Notices:</u>

All notices pursuant to this agreement shall be in writing and shall be given by registered or certified mail, return receipt requested or telegraph (prepaid) at the respective addresses hereinabove set forth or such other address or addresses as may be designated by either party. Such notices shall be deemed given when mailed or delivered to a telegraph office, except that a notice of change of address shall be effective only from the date of its receipt.

14. <u>Additional Provisions:</u>

(a) This agreement contains the entire understanding of the parties hereto relating to the subject matter hereof and cannot be changed or terminated, except by an instrument signed by the parties hereto. A waiver by either party of any term or condition of this agreement in any instance shall not be deemed or construed as a waiver of such term or condition for the future, or of any subsequent breach thereof. All remedies, rights, undertakings, obligations, and agreements contained in this agreement shall be cumulative and none of them shall be in limitation of any other remedy, right, undertaking, obligation or agreement of either party.

(b) This agreement has been entered into in the State of New York, and the validity, interpretation and legal affect of this agreement shall be governed by the laws of the State of New York applicable to contracts entered into and performed entirely within the State of New York.

Very truly yours,

Starmaker Management Associates, LLC.

By:_____

CONSENTED AND AGREED TO:

_____

Misha Baker

Helpful Websites and Telephone Numbers

Online Help

AOL access numbers . . . . access.web.aol.com

Earthlink access numbers . . . . earthlink.net/dialup/

Embassies . . . . embassyworld.com

Fedex tracking . . . . fedex.com/us/pckgenvlp/track/index.html

Golf courses . . . . golf.com/golf/courses_travel

Guitar Centers . . . . gc.guitarcenter.com/locations/

Health clubs . . . . healthclubs.com

Home Depot . . . . homedepot.com

Immigration and visas
(Traffic Control Group) . . . . tcgworld.com

Local directions . . . . mapquest.com

Local time and date . . . . timeanddate.com

National Weather Service . . . . weather.gov

Product comparison/ratings . . . . epinions.com

Product comparison/
lowest price . . . . mysimon.com

Radio Shack locator . . . . radioshack.com

Sam Ash . . . . samashmusic.com

Starbucks locator . . . . starbucks.com/store-locator

Sunset times . . . . www.usno.navy.mil/USNO/astronomical-
applications/data-services/rs-one-year-us

UPS tracking . . . . ups.com/tracking/tracking.html

Vegetarian restaurants . . . . vegetarianusa.com

Webzen Global Games Portal . . . webzen.com

Health food stores . . . . happycow.net

YMCAs . . . . ymca.net

Zip code finder zip4.usps.com/zip4/welcome.jsp

Helpful Numbers

Technical Support

Airborne Express Tracking 800-247-2676
AOL technical support 800-827-6364
Apple technical support 888-275-2273
Earthlink technical support. 800-729-8099
eFax technical support. 800-958-2983
FedEx tracking. 800-463-3339
Geek Squad 800-423-5778
Mac Warehouse 800-925-6227
UPS tracking 800-742-5877

Airlines

Alaska. 800-426-0333
American 800-223-5436
Continental 800-784-4444
Delta. 800-221-1212
JetBlue 800-538-2583
Northwest 800-441-1818
Reno Air. 800-736-6247
Southwest. 800-435-9792
United 800-241-6522
U.S. Airways. 800-943-5436

Car Rental

Alamo. 800-327-9633
Avis. 800-331-2112
Budget 800-527-0700
Dollar. 800-800-4000
Enterprise. 800-261-7331
Hertz 800-654-3131
National. 800-227-7368
Payless 800-237-2804
Thrifty 800-367-2277
Value. 800-428-2583

Lost or stolen credit cards

American Express 800-327-1267
Discover 800-347-2683
MasterCard 800-307-7309
Visa 800-847-2911

INDEX